No Haven for the Oppressed

NO HAVEN
for the Oppressed

United States Policy Toward Jewish Refugees,
1938-1945

by Saul S. Friedman
YOUNGSTOWN STATE UNIVERSITY

Wayne State University Press   Detroit   1973

Published simultaneously in Canada
by the Copp Clark Publishing Company
517 Wellington Street, West
Toronto 2B, Canada.

Library of Congress Cataloging in Publication Data

Friedman, Saul S   1937–
    No haven for the oppressed.

    Originally presented as the author's thesis, Ohio State University.
    Includes bibliographical references.
    1. Refugees, Jewish.   2. Holocaust, Jewish (1939–1945)   3. United
States—Emigration and immigration.   4. Jews in the United States—Political
and social conditions.   I. Title.
D810.J4F75   1973   940.53'159   72–2271
ISBN 0–8143–1474–0

Publication of this book was assisted by the
American Council of Learned Societies under a grant
from the Andrew W. Mellon Foundation.

Contents

Preface

This manuscript represents the product of twelve years of research into the complicity of the Western democracies in what has popularly been termed the Holocaust, the slaughter of European Jewry in World War II. Several readings of Malcolm Hay's *Europe and the Jews* generated intense discussions on this subject with an elder brother, Norman, while we were both students at Kent State University. Norman's death in 1964 served as the motivation for a short research paper for Foster Rhea Dulles of Ohio State University on the wartime Anglo-American Conference on Refugees at Bermuda. The anguish of that research was the germinal of this paper.

My investigations of the Jewish refugee question have since been guided and expanded by Professors Robert Chazan, John Burnham, Harry Coles and Robert Bremner of Ohio State University. I am, however, especially indebted to Professor Marvin Zahniser, who took on an unknown student several years ago and guided him through the difficult days of general examinations, research grants, and the final editorial winnowing. Because of the excellent advice and direction given me by these scholars, I hope that this book constitutes a synthesis of American social, diplomatic, and minority history for the period 1938–1945.

In approaching such a difficult subject I have also been generously aided by a number of government historians and private archivists, including Miriam Leikind of Rabbi Silver's Temple in Cleveland, Ezekiel Lipshutz and Mrs. D. Abramowicz of YIVO, Hester Groves of the American Friends Service Committee, Robert Shosteck of the National B'nai B'rith Headquarters in Washington, Richard Ploch, curator of rare books and special collections at Brandeis University, Dorothy Brown, professor at Georgetown University, Arthur G. Kogan, chief of the research guidance and review division of the Historical Office of the Department of State, Dean Allerd of the Office of Naval History, Thomas Hohmann of the Modern Military Records Division, and numerous unnamed persons in the National Archives, the Library of Congress, the Roosevelt Library at Hyde Park, the American Jewish Archives at Hebrew Union College, the Cleveland Public Library, and the Ohio State University who made my travels and studies less trying.

I am, moreover, indebted to those persons, at one time intimately involved in the decision-making processes of refugee questions, who have given freely of their time to answer questions related to this dissertation. Among them I wish to thank Harold Willis Dodds of Princeton University, who added valuable insight into the Bermuda conference; Lillie Shultz, Leona Duckler, and Richard Cohn of the American Jewish Congress, who broadened my understanding of Rabbi Stephen Wise; former presidential adviser Benjamin Cohen, I. S. Kenen of the American Israel Public Affairs Committee, and Helen Eckerson, chief of the statistical section of the Department of Immigration and Naturalization.

But most of all, I wish to express my gratitude to my wife, Nancy, who tolerated the painful seizures of creativity and revision and encouraged me to continue with this project, which is dedicated to the oppressed children of all races and of all time.

S. S. F.

Introduction

In the spring of 1941, when the United States was not yet formally embroiled in World War II and when it was still possible to rescue Europe's persecuted Jews from Vichy France, Isaac Chomski, a doctor representing the OSE (Jewish Health Protection Society), the American Joint Distribution Committee, Secours Suisse (Swiss Aid), and HIAS (Hebrew Immigrant Aid Society) was placed in charge of 111 child refugees at the local Quaker relief office in Marseilles.* All but five of the children, whose ages ranged from eight to fifteen, were Jewish. Each carried a small, untidy bundle or a battered valise which held belongings remaining after wanderings in two or three different lands. Each child also wore a white numbered card about his neck, a card which read "Father died in concentration camp at Buchenwald," "Mother died in French internment camp at Gurs," "Parents sent to Lublin," or simply "Parents unknown."

Throughout the 500-mile train ride which carried the group on its way to the Spanish border and its ultimate destination, the S.S. *Mouzinho*, docked in Lisbon harbor, Chomski was struck by the solemnity of the children, their stoic acceptance of the meager food provisions, and their unlaughing silence as they watched a host of French university towns—Nîmes, Montpellier, Toulouse, Tarbes—pass by. Only rarely did a child volunteer to speak with the doctor, and this conversation was generally followed by a tearful breakdown as the young refugee confided his fears of going to America, where he had "no one."

* A list of organizations cited in the text, with abbreviations, appears on pages 236–40.

9

On Sunday morning as the train neared the small provincial town of Oloron, thirty miles from the Spanish border in the department of Basses-Pyrenees, Chomski noted a transformation in the children. Awake even before dawn, they were in a festive mood, for many hoped to glimpse their parents for one last time this day. The children knew that close to Oloron was Gurs, the notorious French concentration camp where 10,000 Jewish refugees were living under the most primitive conditions. Originally constructed to house 3,000 Spanish Loyalist refugees, Gurs had been converted into a detention camp for German nationals (including Jewish refugees) by the French government in 1939. By 1941 it was serving as a deportation center to the East. Thirty persons died of hunger, exposure, or disease in Gurs each day, but this did not dampen the enthusiasm of Chomski's charges, who hoped that the prisoners would be released for a few moments to meet the train. Klaus, a boy from Germany, showed Chomski a photograph of his father. Tall, stately, his World War I German officer's uniform bedecked with medals, the father was one of many still detained in Gurs.

The train pulled into the Oloron station amid shouts of the excited children and the anxious parents lining the platform. Scenes of unbelievable tragedy were enacted in the ten minutes that sympathetic gendarmes permitted the train to sit at the depot. The children, having saved the bread which had been their last evening's meal, forced it on the adults. Children who had no parents gave their ration to strangers. Chomski records that even the French guards wept before such human misery.

A man, bearded, unkempt, and wearing rags, walked hesitatingly up to the son he had not seen in two years, and, with some embarrassment, spoke: "Klaus, my son, don't you recognize me?"

The boy recoiled for a moment. Suddenly, he lunged forward, burying his head in his father's tattered coat. Then he reached up to kiss the grimy forehead and sobbed, "Papa, Papa, Papa."

Later, in the corridor of the moving train, Klaus stood holding a letter from his father. With German deliberateness,

10

the doomed man, fearful that three minutes might not be sufficient to bid his son farewell, had written: "My dear son, my beloved Klaus, do not forget your father." [1]

Klaus and the other children under Chomski's supervision arrived in the United States in June 1941. They were the fortunate ones. According to figures compiled by the World Jewish Congress and the American Jewish Congress, more than 1,000,000 of the 6,000,000 Jews exterminated by the Nazis in World War II were children under age fifteen.[2] Twenty-five years ago the villains in this drama were relatively easy to denote—Hitler, the Nazis, the German people. They were the ones who pulled the triggers or dropped the cyanide pellets. They were the ones who were insensitive to the screams from passing cattle cars and the stench of burning flesh. Others watched with curious fascination, however, and did little or nothing to stay the crucifixion of European Jewry.

To many people the death of six million Jews is merely a statistic, about as meaningful as the population of Upper Volta or the average annual precipitation in the Hadhramaut. For some, though, the specter of genocide is still quite real. The animal carcasses which were once human beings, starved, beaten or tortured in the reconcentrado camps of Cuba, by bashi-bazouks in Armenia, or *Nachtigall* battalions in the Ukraine, are not easily forgotten in a world which has recently witnessed the reenactment of such terrors in Biafra and Pakistan. The memory of these terrors, the hope that they would not be recreated, is what prompted the late journalist Arthur D. Morse to write *While Six Million Died: A Chronicle of American Apathy.*[3]

Morse's work belongs to a new school of revisionist history which has prompted much critical comment about the extermination of the Jews in World War II. In recent years historians, dramatists, and novelists have imputed partial responsibility for the massacre of the Jews to the Pope, the Western democracies, and the Jews themselves. The first and most celebrated of these works was Rolf Hochhuth's play, *The Deputy.*[4] Published in Germany in 1964, the play aroused the anger of Catholics around the world because it portrayed Pius

XII as a latter-day Pontius Pilate who washed his hands of the fate of the Jews. According to Hochhuth, the papacy could have done more to halt the flow of cattle cars to extermination camps in Poland. Its failure to intervene amounted to the Vatican's acquiescence in Hitler's scheme of genocide.

Two years after *The Deputy* appeared, Hans Habe published *The Mission*, a quasi-historical novel which explored the failure of the Western democracies to rescue the Jews of Germany-Austria on the eve of World War II.[5] Habe argued that the thirty-two nations meeting at Evian, France, in July 1938 in a special refugee conference called by President Franklin D. Roosevelt turned a deaf ear to the plans and entreaties of international Jewish organizations and representatives of the German-Jewish community to ransom the 600,000 Jews yet under Nazi control. By so doing, Habe contended, the democracies made it clear that they did not want Hitler's Jews, either.

Jean-François Steiner's novel, *Treblinka*, created another wave of excitement.[6] This time a Jewish survivor of what has been popularly termed "the Holocaust" attempted an analysis of the many aspects of the genocide of World War II. Steiner's parents died in Nazi concentration camps and through his book runs a strain of bitterness, directed not merely at the murderers, but at their victims as well. Steiner's contention was that the relative success of the Nazis could not have been achieved without the passive submissiveness of the Jews and that some Jews openly collaborated in the extermination scheme to save or prolong their own lives. Because *Treblinka* so condemned the Jews in some passages in the original French, Steiner was asked to rewrite certain segments before the book appeared in English.

Morse's volume was the first work to delve into the role of the American government in the fate of the Jews. The author claimed that America did not do all it could have done to aid the Jews. At a time when Jews desperately sought haven from Hitlerism before the war, the U.S. rigidly adhered to its discriminatory quota system of immigration, repulsed from its shores shiploads of refugees, declined to participate in League of Nations' refugee conferences, and refused to advance Jewish claims in Palestine. With the outbreak of worldwide hostilities American leaders actually tightened up admission procedures. They did so by fabricating a host of excuses about an inability to trust Hitler in any negotiations over human life, a lack of shipping, a lack of funds to purchase or maintain "refugees" (the favorite euphemism of government officials in referring to Jews), and a lack of available ports or refuges. Morse also charges that the U.S. Department of State repeatedly frustrated British efforts to rescue more refugees and that on several occasions the department suppressed information concerning the plight of the Jews so that it did not reach American Jewish leaders who might then have mobilized public opinion favorable to action. Morse believes the reason for this was clear— anti-Semitism at the highest levels of the State Department, and he names Assistant Secretary of State Breckinridge Long and his special assistant for refugee affairs R. Borden Reams, Cordell Hull's top advisers on refugee questions, as the principle culprits.

Despite its prepublication syndication in *Look* magazine and despite its obvious appeal to Jewish book buyers, Morse's book has not done well financially and has never come close to making a bestseller list. Perhaps its very lack of commercial appeal best explains why the work was until recently unique in its field of scholarship. The classical studies of American immigration policy either cover a period too early to be of much help in an analysis of the refugee Jew in the Holocaust, or else they refer only tangentially to the problem.[7] The many works which have attempted an analysis of the refugee question between 1933 and 1945 similarly have been deficient in that, limited in time by the availability of source materials (State Department records on this period and many files at the Roosevelt Library at Hyde Park have been open to researchers only since 1965), they have not adequately probed the government machinations on both sides of the Atlantic which created and intensified the refugee problem.[8]

Thus, Morse attempted to fill a void by his examination of materials in Washington, London, New York, and Stockholm. That he did not succeed completely is evident from the ambivalent evaluations of his efforts by qualified Jewish historians. Selig Adler gave Morse a favorable review, but has privately indicated that Morse's research methodology left much to be desired.[9] In like manner, Zosa Szajkowski, archivist of YIVO (the Yiddish Institute for Scientific Research in New York), recently commented that while Morse's work was important ("the story must be told"), he regretted that Morse had not even touched the impressive library at YIVO.[10] Henry L. Feingold offered the harshest critique of all. Feingold attacked Morse for his failure to explore many collections related to refugee matters available at Brandeis University, his failure to comment on the critical divisions in the Jewish community during this period and on Roosevelt's exploitation of that division, his failure to do more than intimate that Jews in high government positions in the New Deal were reluctant to champion the cause of the refugees for fear that this would provoke talk of "double loyalties," and his failure to appreciate the anti-alien spirit of the 76th and 77th congresses, which were preoccupied with America's economic distress.[11]

While Morse does paint a tragic picture of perfidy at the top ranks of government, he rarely probes beneath the surface of an action to discern motives. Instead, the reader is left with the simplistic impression that rampant anti-Semitism among Washington officials always explained inaction. Such an explanation, however, leaves numerous questions unanswered. What were the internal stresses, the domestic pressure groups arguing for and against immigration reform, with which the government had to contend during this period? What was the impact of the Great Depression in molding public opinion on the immigration question? What were Americans' general attitudes toward all Jews before and during the war, and what factors influenced these attitudes to stiffen against increased immigration during the war? How did the disorganization of the American Jewish community throughout this period deprive it of effective bargaining power in achieving its multiple goals? What were the realistic possibilities of large-scale settlement of emigrant Jews in Latin America or anywhere else in the world at the time of the Evian conference in 1938? The Bermuda conference in 1943? What was the nature of Anglo-American relations on immigration questions in this seven-year period? How did the Palestine controversy contribute to America's own immigration problems? How did the U.S. government balance military priorities and pleas from refugees during wartime? What were the realities of shipping facilities, and did the "empty bottoms" which Morse maintains could have been used to transport refugee Jews back to the United States during the war actually exist? How practical would proposed negotiations with the Nazis for the release of Jews have been at any time in this period? What resources did the Allies have by way of money, manpower, and refuge to accommodate the refugees? And, finally, what was the record of UNRRA and the Allies toward these same refugees when the war ended? This book will explore these questions.

1. Haven of the Oppressed?

*D*ecades *before Assistant* Secretary of State Breckinridge Long or North Carolina Senator Robert R. Reynolds came to Washington, the United States had ceased to be what Thomas Paine had envisioned in 1776—"an asylum for mankind." Perhaps it had never been such an ideal sanctuary. Despite the platitudes of presidential addresses, Sunday sermons, editorials, and political platforms, the immigrant to the United States had often encountered hostility from those persons already here.[1]

As early as 1797, Representative Harrison G. Otis of Massachusetts, a firm Federalist who feared a French-type revolution, expressed the dread of American nativists when he said, "When the country was new, it might have been good policy to admit foreigners, but it is so no longer."[2] Otis's sentiment expressed convictions popular throughout much of the nineteenth century as well. This sentiment, however, had evolved over the years. By the late nineteenth century new fears had supplanted the old—fear on the part of the farmer that he would lose his land to coolie labor, fear on the part of the privileged commercial interests that anarchistic Slavs or Italians might destroy the structure of America's free enterprise society, fear on the part of the modernist German Jew that he might be embarrassed by his kaftaned brethren who fled Russia, fear on the part of the racial eugenicist that the flood of East European immigrants, numbering more than 400,000 a year by 1880, might mongrelize American civilization.

On August 3, 1882, after its efforts had been frustrated for nearly a decade by presidents reluctant to disturb sensitive

17

relations with China and Japan, Congress passed the first restrictive immigration law in American history. Directed principally at the Chinese, who were totally excluded, the law also barred lunatics, idiots, and "persons likely to become a public charge" from admission to the United States.[3] In the next twenty years the forces of the supra-nationalist American Protective Association, Samuel Gompers's American Federation of Labor, and congressional restrictionists coalesced to force the exclusion of contract laborers, criminals, persons with loathesome diseases, polygamists, and anarchists. The restrictionists in Congress, led by Henry Cabot Lodge, Sr., were frustrated in only one venture—their demand for a literacy test for all new immigrants.[4]

At the turn of the century, the restrictionists were further buoyed by the overwhelming support of their efforts by leaders of the American scientific community. Madison Grant of the American Museum of Natural History, Lothrop Stoddard of Columbia University, Burton Hendrick of Yale, Charles Conant Josey of Dartmouth, David Starr Jordan of Stanford, William Ripley of M.I.T., and Harry Laughlin of the Eugenics Office in Washington all expressed the commonly held view that there were superior and inferior races of mankind, that "new" immigrants, particularly the Jews, possessed inherently inferior personal qualities, and that continued unlimited immigration would be injurious to the economic, social, and political life of the United States.[5] Edward A. Ross of Wisconsin summed it up:

> Ten to twenty percent are hirsute, lowbrowed, big-faced persons of obviously low mentality. I have seen gatherings of foreigners in which narrowed sloping foreheads were the rule. The shortness and smallness of the crania were noticeable. In every face there was something wrong. One might imagine a malicious jinn had amused himself by casting human beings in a set of skew molds discarded by the creator.[6]

Over the outraged cries of restrictionists, the United States remained open to more than 900,000 immigrants a year in the decade before World War I. In this new wave of immigration Jews, who constituted more than 10 percent of the arrivals, were especially visible because they tended to cluster in the urban centers of the East, 70 percent of them in New York City alone.[7] As a result, much sympathy for the victims of pogroms at faroff Kishinev or Balta was predictably transmuted into overt anti-Semitism when these same people were nearer at hand. The *American Jewish Yearbooks* of 1910–1916, published by the American Jewish Committee, take note of this intensification of Judeophobia in the United States, and it is no coincidence that the Anti-Defamation League of B'nai B'rith was founded in 1913 to combat increased discrimination and libels against the Jews.

World War I convinced American idealists, Woodrow Wilson among them, that the notion of unrestricted immigration should be laid to rest. The 1910 census data showed that more than 11,000,000 Americans were either natives of, or offspring of natives of, European states adhering to the Central Power Alliance. Even before America's entry into the war in April 1917 fear of German-American disloyalty, accentuated by the inept espionage of Heinrich Albert, Franz von Papen, Constantin Duma, and Captain Karl Boy-Ed, had resulted in the passage of a comprehensive immigration act on February 5, 1917. Anti-anarchist provisions in the 1903 law were expanded to exclude or deport any person who at any time had belonged to an organization which preached violence or sabotage. Proponents of a literacy test, foiled in their efforts since 1894, rejoiced at the inclusion of such a clause in the 1917 law. Hindu and East Indian laborers were barred, along with "persons of constitutional psychopathic inferiority," "vagrants," and "chronic alcoholics." One liberal feature of the law was a special provision exempting persons fleeing persecution because of race or religious faith (understood to refer to Jews) from the literacy test.[8]

As Higham noted, "The war virtually swept from American consciousness the old belief in unrestricted immigration."[9] Bigotries born in anti-German, anti-pacifist, anti-radical patriotic societies like the Knights of Liberty, the American Defense Society, and the ever-vigilant American Protective League did not die with the armistice. Labor strife in the postwar recession coupled with a new influx of immigrants from lands contaminated with Bolshevism—141,132 in 1919, 430,001 in 1920, 805,000 in 1921—convinced the self-proclaimed patriots, organized labor, and Congress that something had to be done to preserve the national character of the United States. Nathan Glazer wrote, "In 1921, America had decided to stop the kaleidoscope and find out what it had become." [10]

The resulting legislation, passed on May 19, 1921, also proved inadequate. This first Johnson Act, named for Congressman Albert Johnson of Washington, a wealthy timber magnate, permitted immigration at the rate of 3 percent of the number of foreign born from each European nationality in the United States in 1910 and set an annual limit of 357,803 immigrants. Despite this provision, immigration totals continued to rise— 522,919 in 1923 and 706,896 in 1924.[11] The desire to accommodate persons who had contracted for passage to America before the law was enacted, the humanitarianism of consular officials, and the need for stoop labor all contributed to lax enforcement of the first Johnson Act.

In 1924, Congress responded once more to a wide range of restrictionist pressures. Samuel Gompers, speaking for the American workingman who then enjoyed an unprecedented level of prosperity, championed restriction. His views were echoed by John B. Trevor, an ubiquitous New York attorney representing several elitist American groups, Kenneth Roberts in a series of articles in *Saturday Evening Post,* and eugenicists Madison Grant and Harry Laughlin, whose long discourses before congressional committees about the dilution of the American bloodstream had even frightened segments of the business community into reversing their traditional stand in support of unlimited immigration. Even the normally taciturn President Coolidge in his first State of the Union address advocated further reduction of immigration.[12]

Over the strenuous opposition of Catholic and Jewish lay groups, and despite the eloquent remonstrances of Congressmen Emanuel Celler (D.-N.Y.), Adolph Sabath (D.-Ill.), Samuel Dickstein (D.-N.Y.), and Fiorello LaGuardia (Soc.-Prog.-N.Y.), Congress passed a second law bearing Johnson's name. The purposes of this act, according to the House Committee on

Immigration and Naturalization, were manifold: to maintain our standard of living, to sustain our institutions for the care of the socially inadequate, to preserve our basic political institutions, and "to preserve the basic stream of our population." [13] More succinctly, the bill which Coolidge signed into law on May 26, 1924 was designed to keep out what Kansas Congressman J. M. Tincher termed "Bolshevik Wops, Dagoes, Kikes and Hunkies." [14]

The Johnson-Reed Bill, or National Origins Act as it was subsequently named, provided for an annual immigration of 164,667 persons, 2 percent of each Caucasian nationality represented in the United States population in 1890.[15] The new quota, effective July 1, 1929, would be 153,714, based on proportional representation in the United States population in 1920. Of these, more than 120,000 visas were to be awarded to Great Britain, Germany, Ireland, and Scandinavia, those North and West European stocks which had presumably created the American republic.

The cutback from 1921 quotas was most severe among the "undesirable" nationalities of Southern and Eastern Europe. Poland, for example, was cut from 30,977 permits in 1921 to 6,524 in 1924. Italy was restricted to 5,802; Russia to 2,712; Hungary to 869; Yugoslavia to 845. Senator David Reed from Pennsylvania, coauthor of the measure, commented: "I think most of us are reconciled to the idea of discrimination. I think the American people want us to discriminate; and I don't think discrimination itself is unfair. We have got to discriminate." [16]

What the new law meant in terms of human suffering can never be calculated, but it is not difficult to imagine hopeful individuals waiting anxiously for years for precious visas to the United States. By 1939 this meant a wait of four to six years for potential emigrants from Hungary.[17] Also, although 2,616,000 immigrants were permitted under the quota system between 1930 and 1946, only 560,000 persons were ultimately admitted to the United States in this period. One obvious reason for this is that the system was heavily slanted in favor of those North-western Europeans with little inclination to come to the United States. Another was that Hitler's domination of Eastern Europe

21

made it difficult for persons to flee during wartime.[18] But also true was the fact that the American government made itself inhospitable toward immigration during this period.

Institution of the strictest provisions of the National Origins Law coincided with the collapse of America's financial system. Plunged into the Great Depression, the country found itself with as many as fifteen million persons unemployed, upwards of 30 percent in some industrial areas.[19] To make matters worse, immigrants were still coming into the United States at a rate of more than 300,000 a year in the years after the Johnson-Reed bill had been signed into law. To prevent an escalation of America's domestic woes, Hoover issued a White House directive on September 8, 1930, instructing consular officers "before issuing a visa . . . to pass judgment with particular care on whether the applicant may become a public charge and if the applicant cannot convince the officer that it is not probable, the visa will be refused." [20]

Hoover's strict interpretation of a clause originally designed in 1882 to protect the nation against international vagrants (and which was rarely enforced in the previous half century) created a tragic irony because immigrants were simultaneously denied the right to secure jobs in advance of their arrival in the United States under the Alien Contract Labor Law of 1885. Thus, only the independently wealthy might attempt to emigrate to America during the last years of the Republican administration. Immigration totals, which dropped from 241,700 in 1930 to 97,139 in 1931 and to 35,576 in 1932, reflected this legalistic snare.

In October 1932 Hoover attributed the decline to the end of persecutions in Europe. He said: "With the growth of democracy in foreign countries, political persecution has largely ceased. There is no longer a necessity for the United States to provide an asylum for those persecuted because of conscience." [21] Several months later the annual convention of the American Federation of Labor challenged the president's statement when it reaffirmed its stand against change in existing immigration laws because "there is not a country in the world where there is not religious or political persecution." [22] And on January 30, 1933, Adolf Hitler was appointed chancellor of Germany by Field Marshal von Hindenburg.

The legacy of the Hoover administration continued to haunt consular officials and potential immigrants through the Hitler epoch. Although Breckinridge Long could say that "the historic attitude of the United States as a haven for the oppressed has not stopped," that "literally, the reports of the consular offices to Department of State form one of the most thrilling and one of the most saddening and awful pages of our human history," [23] others passionately disagreed.

"Surely the American consular officials are today the world's most skilled experts in misery," Martin Gumpert noted.[24] Much of the problem could be attributed to bureaucratic red tape. The potential immigrant had to present an unexpired passport, a police certificate attesting to his good conduct in the past, a certificate from the Public Health Surgeon attached to the consul stating that the applicant was not suffering from "any loathsome or contagious disease or from an illness or physical handicap which might make him a public charge," duplicate records of all pertinent personal data (for instance, birth, marriage, divorce certificates), and a thorough financial statement indicative of his assets (certified through employers' statements or bank records), as well as an affidavit filed by some relative in this country affording the complete assets of the immigrant's guarantor and the specific percentage of support that he might expect to receive from this guarantor. One improper entry among the volume of fifty or sixty pages could result in a rejection of the application and could necessitate refiling.[25]

When it became obvious in 1934 that Nazi Germany would not cooperate in supplying all the documents needed by emigrants, Secretary of State Cordell Hull instructed American consuls to waive the police certificate requirement where efforts to secure these might involve "personal risk" for the emigrant.[26] Still, American consular offices in Germany throughout the 1930s were timorous about interpreting the law and their instructions liberally. An individual might be rejected because of a stiff knee, a missing finger, or even after a two-year wait in refugee camps, because he was underweight.[27]

The most confusion, however, existed in the application of Hoover's LPC directive, which remained in force until January 1937, under which the probability and not the possibility of an immigrant's becoming a public charge was made the basis of rejection. Some consuls would only accept financial guarantees sworn by immediate relatives (parents, children), while for others the testament of a virtual stranger was sufficient.[28] An affidavit filed by someone with a fixed income might be sufficient in one case and not in another. One consul might require a sponsor to deposit $2,000 in a blocked bank account. Another might reject the affidavit of a wealthy physician who attempted to serve as a guarantor of an individual simply because the physician had not been a source of support for the immigrant in the past.[29]

All of this was ludicrous, because a spokesman for the Department of Labor, charged with the responsibility of enforcing this nation's immigration laws in the Roosevelt administration, had indicated that the guaranty bond was "legally worthless," "cannot be enforced," and "the Department makes no effort to enforce it." [30]

The interpretation given to the LPC clause after 1937 was equally unrealistic in the face of the economic policies of the German government *vis-à-vis* emigrants. Since the potential immigrant to the U.S. was forbidden to contract in advance for a job in this country and since it was technically forbidden for some charitable organization to underwrite his travel expenses or serve as guarantor, the person himself had to show sufficiently impressive assets to remove any doubts that he might become impoverished in America. This was nearly impossible. In 1933 emigrants from Germany could only take 75 percent of their assets after taxes. By the spring of 1938 this figure had shrunk to 10 percent, as the Nazi Property Registration Act of April 26, 1938 declared all "private fortunes" over 5,000 DM subject to confiscation.[31] By the end of the summer of 1939, an individual with 10,000 DM in a German bank (roughly $4,000) deemed himself fortunate if the Reichsbank gave him 600 DM ($240) to take out of the country.[32] A financial analysis of emigrants in such a position was not only impossible, but unfair.[33]

Strict enforcement of the LPC clause was all the more unfair because more people were leaving the United States than were entering it in the heart of the depression. Between 1933 and 1937, 174,067 persons entered this country, while 221,239 departed—a net loss of 47,172.[34] The immigration total for 1933 (23,068) was the lowest in history since 1831. But even that was insufficient to placate the vast numbers of restrictionists in this country who called for additional cuts in quotas, a suspension of all immigration until America's domestic problems were resolved, or an absolute halt of all immigration.

The cyclical nativism, which Higham assessed as near-dormant in 1925 because of America's prosperity and general indifference to world affairs,[35] surged again in the 1930s for various reasons. Economic dislocation, the consolidation of power of the communist regime in the Soviet Union, the fear that this regime, expressly committed to furthering world revolution, might attempt the corruption of America's institutions all gave rise to a new wave of anti-alien sentiment in that decade.[36] Simultaneously, the word "communist" was made synonymous with "Jew" in the lexicon of super-nationalists around the world.

Adolf Hitler, rising to power on the basis of a stridently anticommunist platform which equated Bolshevism with "international Jewry," popularized the fear that "Red Jews," "alien Jews," "Jewish-Bolshevists," "Jewish radicals," and "non-Aryans" were plotting to destroy the foundations of Anglo-Saxon civilization.[37] The United States, which had not yet shed the medieval regard of the Jew as the unassimilable alien,[38] where the Jews of New York's lower East End provided a substantial portion of American Communist party leadership, and where a once-impoverished Jewish minority was achieving enviable economic, social, and political successes, was not immune to such fears. Moreover, the oldtime "100 percent" patriotic organizations, panicked businessmen who regarded the New Deal as the vanguard of American Bolshevism, and the newly-founded neo-fascist cliques of the 1930s were not immune to the Nazis' use of the Jews as scapegoats.

Restrictionist sentiment flowed from many sources in this period. On the far right, neo-Nazi organizations gained in appeal by assaulting Jews, Bolsheviks, and aliens. According to a report of the House Committee on Un-American Activities, dated January 3, 1939, there were 135 organizations in the United States which the committee then regarded as fascist. Of these perhaps only 25 percent were bona fide organizations, that is, something more than mere rackets operated by individuals through the mails or out of almost empty offices.[39] And even among this group there were some, like George Deatherage's Knights of the White Camellia, Gerald Winrod's Defenders, Parker Sage's National Workers League, Joseph Kamp's Constitutional Education League, Gerald L. K. Smith's Committee of One Million, and Harry Jung's American Vigilant Intelligence Federation, which consisted more of inflated membership rolls than actual adherents.[40]

This is not to say that the neo-Nazi groups were inconsequential to membership, public sympathy, financial support, or influence. The Dies committee reported that the German-American Bund, constructed on the foundations of the Chicago Teutonia Society and the Friends of the New Germany, received its inspiration, program, and direction from the Nazi Ministry of Propaganda, which was spending $300 million annually to foment worldwide fascist revolution.[41] Although somewhat clumsy in its efforts to enlist the active support of the 20,000,000 Americans of German descent that it desired to enroll in the fight against "Jewocracy," the Bund claimed a dedicated membership of 25,000, operated twenty-four retreat camps across the country, distributed thousands of pamphlets, sponsored a daily national radio program, and packed Madison Square Garden for patriotic rallies in 1939 and 1940.[42] Moreover, through its control of the German-American press, estimated at better than 90 percent pro-Nazi by 1940,[43] the Bund attempted to frustrate administration policies which they construed as prejudicial to the Fatherland, including any proposals for the harboring of refugees from Germany.[44]

Actively collaborating with the Bund in its execration of Bolsheviks, aliens, and Jews was William Dudley Pelley's Silver Shirt Legion of America.[45] The Silver Shirts claimed a membership of 100,000 in twenty-two states before Pelley's arrests, first for embezzlement, then for violation of the Espionage Act in 1942. These figures were undoubtedly inflated, but there is no question that the group's program of "Christian Democracy" had great appeal for readers throughout America. Pelley advocated an alien registration day for persons of "Hebrew blood," imprisonment of Jews who attempted to use gentile names, prosecution of Jews who supported a Zionist state (on grounds of sedition), disenfranchisement of Jews, abrogation of all civil rights for Hebrews (including the right to hold property), and the establishment of an urban ghetto in one city in every state to pen up all Jews.[46] With such concepts for his grist, Pelley was able to operate an $80,000 publishing plant in Asheville, North Carolina, which flooded the nation with three and one-half million tons of his brand of journalism (*Pelley's Weekly, The Liberation Magazine,* and books of the Skyland Press) in the nineteen months prior to August 1938. The Dies committee concluded that the Silver Shirt Legion was the largest, best financed, and best publicized fascist movement in the country.[47]

Even more influential than Pelley, however, was Father Charles E. Coughlin of Royal Oak, Michigan. He began his famous radio broadcasts in 1926 after a cross was burned in front of his parish church and evolved from an advocate of the New Deal in 1932 into the principal backer of William Lemke for the presidency in 1936, and finally by 1938 into a mouthpiece of the German World Service News Agency, the propaganda wing of the Deutsches Ausland Institut.[48] In 1936, Coughlin founded *Social Justice,* a tabloid with a reported weekly circulation of one million. In his Sunday radio broadcasts, which drew upon the resources of a $1,500,000 nonprofit corporation, Coughlin fulminated against aliens who were depriving native Americans of jobs and especially against "Jewish communists" who had engineered the Bolshevik takeover of Russia in 1917. He even revived the century-old canard of the "Protocols of the Elders of Zion" until his superior, Cardinal

G. W. Mundelein, belatedly moved to muzzle him in December 1938.[49]

An American Institute of Public Opinion poll conducted in January 1939 showed that Coughlin's weekly broadcasts were heard by a regular audience of 3,500,000. Fifteen million Americans listened to him occasionally, and more than half of these apparently were in substantial agreement with Coughlin. Much of this agreement could be attributed to his dated economic theories rather than to prejudice, as fully one-half of the Negroes and one-tenth of the Jews polled indicated agreement with some of his ideas.[50] The Dies committee concluded, however, that not more than one million Americans "can be said to have been seriously affected" by Coughlin's philosophy.[51] Even that nucleus of racist strength was apparently spent among dissident factions of the social justice movement, cells of the leaderless Christian Front, and the several thousand follower of Joe McWilliams's Christian Mobilizers.[52]

This dissipation of energies among neo-Nazi groups reduced their potential for revolution in the United States in the depression. Many hopeful American Führers refused to subordinate themselves or their incomes to any other leader, and the residual anti-Catholic feeling of earlier decades precluded any real union with the principal supporters of Coughlin.[53] Still, such groups could coordinate their efforts for specific purposes, including immigration restriction.[54] They did enjoy important pipelines to restrictionist Congressmen. Their waves of anti-Semitic literature did leave an indelible impression upon the consciousness of America. As Myers wrote (p. 350): "Organizations of the character described may and do have a transient existence, but their published matter sinks into many a receptive mind, there to abide long after the perpetrators responsible have disappeared and their malodorous methods have been forgotten."

A shade to the political left of the blatantly Nazi pressure groups were the self-proclaimed patriotic organizations, hastily constructed by the archons of American business to protect the republic during the 1930s. Foremost among these were the Crusaders, a one-million member group originally conceived as a bulwark of prohibition. However, it shifted its focus from temperance to Americanism in 1933. Closely associated with George Christians's neo-Nazi White Shirts, the Crusaders were heavily underwritten by J. Howard Pew of Sun Oil, Irenee, Pierre, and Lammot DuPont, Sewell Avery of Montgomery Ward, and the directors of Weirton Steel.[55] These same persons, along with Alfred Sloan of General Motors and E. T. Stotesbury of the House of Morgan, were major contributors to the Sentinels of the Republic, a nationwide organization dedicated to the creation of an American corporativist state. The Sentinel president, Alexander Lincoln, scored "the Jewish brigade Roosevelt took to Washington" and once wrote that the fight for Western civilization could only be won "if we recognize that the enemy is worldwide and that it is Jewish in origin." [56]

Successful businessmen and Americans of substantial pedigree were counted as friends and backers of a host of such corporativist bodies. While these men themselves did not disseminate anti-Semitic propaganda, it was unlikely that they were ignorant of the policies of the groups they subsidized. James Rand, president of Remington Rand, J. H. Alstyne, president of Otis Elevator, Sloan, and the DuPonts contributed to Merwin K. Hart's long-lived New York State Economic Council, which Supreme Court Justice Robert Jackson regarded as fascist.[57] Mrs. A. Cressy Morrison of the Daughters of the American Revolution and Colonel Robert R. McCormick of the *Chicago Tribune* endorsed Elizabeth Dilling's Paul Reveres, "We Mothers March on Washington" (which opposed Lend Lease), and Dilling's pamphlet *The Red Network* (which accused the YMCA, John Dewey, the American Civil Liberties Union, and Sinclair Lewis all of being Bolsheviks).[58] John Snow's League for Constitutional Government had the warm support of H. W. Prestis, chairman of the National Association of Manufacturers. Ralph Easley's National Civic Federation maintained simultaneous connections with Nazi agents Boris Brasol and George Sylvester Viereck and the presidents of A.T. & T., New York Life, Firestone Tire, Aetna Life, Anaconda Copper, Republic Steel, and Packard Auto.[59]

All of these groups, like the more respectable American

Liberty League (organized in 1934 ostensibly "to preserve the principles of the Declaration of Independence for succeeding generations of Americans")[60] championed 100 percent Americanism. In general, this meant the equating of atheism, socialism, liberalism, pacifism, and New Dealism with Bolshevism. It meant opposition to trade unions, child labor laws, immigration reform, and even pure food and drug measures like the Tugwell Bill. It meant slanting the news in what Congressman Elmer Holland (D-Pa.) termed "the Vermin Press" to distort what was the program and ideology of fascism.[61] It meant arousing nationwide fear, suspicion, and race hatred to promote encroachments upon the Constitution and civil liberties.[62] And on several occasions, apparently, it meant an actual effort to overthrow the government.[63]

The neo-fascist cliques and their minions could rely upon the active assistance of longer-lived elitist organizations in their efforts to curb alien inroads into American society. The one-million-member American Legion and its night-riding cousin, the Black Legion,[64] John Trevor's 2,500,000-member American Coalition (which had done so much to promote the Johnson Acts in the 1920s and which counted the DAR and Sons of the American Revolution among its 115 affiliates),[65] Francis Kinnicutt's frenetic Allied Patriotic Societies, the 150,000-man Junior Order of American Mechanics, the American Medical Association, the BPOE (Elks' clubs) and Chambers of Commerce[66] all spoke out in sympathy for the nation's 12,000,000 unemployed, the 443,000 World War I veterans without jobs, the 660,000 children on Social Security rolls.

None of these groups had ever championed the cause of America's poor during times of prosperity, and none had ever befriended organized labor. But now they bombarded Congress with resolutions and recommendations favoring the halting of all immigration. More aliens, they argued, could only harm the common laborer because jobs would be even more scarce. Admission of Jews as a special refugee class could only set a precedent for later arrivals of persecuted Spaniards or "Mongolians." Admission of Germans or Russians might lead to the creation of a Nazi or Bolshevik underground. Admission of children without their parents would only result in pressure to reunite families, with the attendant weakening of immigration laws. In addition, the patriots recalled the century-old cliche that "the frontier has vanished." Only by halting all immigration until America's domestic woes were solved could these dangers be averted.[67]

Even the 5,000,000-man American Federation of Labor subscribed to some of these views during the Hitler era. Traditionally hostile to the introduction of any new foreign population and to the menace of cheap labor, the AFL wavered on the immigration question, first in March 1939 advocating complete restriction "till our house is in order," then favoring the Wagner Bill to admit 200,000 non-Aryan German children as special nonquota immigrants in the summer of 1939, then reaffirming its traditional stand on exclusion at its annual convention in October 1943.[68]

The AFL's position reflected not the lunatic fringe of American society but the prevailing sentiment of the man on the street. Ninety-five percent of Americans polled by Elmo Roper in 1938–1939 expressed disapproval of the existing regime in Germany. At the same time, however, only 8.7 percent answered in the affirmative when queried: "If you were a member of Congress, would you vote yes or no on a bill to open the doors of the U.S. to a larger number of European refugees than now are admitted under our immigration quotas?" Fully 83 percent of those surveyed expressed total opposition to admission of more refugees, up 16 percent since the summer of 1938, despite the public's increased knowledge of persecutions against German Jews that winter.[69]

Such results could not be attributed to an inadequate sampling. In November 1938, right after the massive pogrom of *Kristallnacht*, which left synagogues and Jewish business establishments in rubble in the final effort of the Nazis to impoverish Jews before World War II, 77 percent of those polled by George Gallup's American Institute of Public Opinion (AIPO) opposed the idea of admitting a larger number of Jewish refugees. Also, in January 1939 two of three persons polled by the AIPO opposed any scheme to admit 10,000 non-

Aryan refugees to the United States on a nonquota basis.[70] The editors of *Fortune* asked, "Would Herr Hitler and his German-American Bunds be safe in the joyful conclusion from this that Americans don't like the Jews much better than do the Nazis?" [71]

With anti-alienism so widespread, it is not remarkable that more than seventy bills directly touching on immigration or registration of aliens were introduced in the Seventy-sixth Congress (1939–1940). Members of this Congress which included in the House Jacob Thorkelson, a Republican from Montana, a man who contributed numerous articles to the journals of Winrod and Pelley and who was a close adviser to General Moseley; Republican Representative Clare Hoffman of Michigan, who warmly received Elizabeth Dilling in his office during the Lend Lease struggle and who was designated by Klansman Edward Smythe as Secretary of Public Health and Morals in the coming fascist cabinet; Democrat John Rankin of Mississippi, whose virulent diatribes against the Jews precipitated a heated debate on the House floor which resulted in a fatal stroke to Michael Edelstein in June, 1941; and Hamilton Fish (R.-N.Y.), whose secretary George Hill was indicted as a paid liaison between congressmen and Nazi fronts operated by George Viereck and Prescott Dennett. Viereck's Flanders Hall publishing firm circulated the defeatist works of Gerald Nye (R.-N.D.) and Rush D. Holt (D.-W.Va.). Through Dennett, Senators Ernest Lundeen of Minnesota, Burton Wheeler of Montana, Rufus Holman of Oregon, D. Worth Clark of Idaho and Henry Dworshak of Idaho were unknowingly supplied with fascist propaganda, which was then inserted in the *Congressional Record* and subsequently reprinted at government expense.[72]

Although these politicians were unable to undermine the democratic system, they did succeed in creating an atmosphere of fear and doubt on Capitol Hill, an atmosphere in which anti-alienism thrived. Martin Dies, whose experience at the head of the House Un-American Affairs Committee should have merited him special attention as an expert on anti-American threats, tried in March 1939 to introduce legislation which would have excluded or expelled alien communists, required the registration of all alien organizations, and forbidden the employment of fascists or communists by the federal government.[73] About the same time Representatives Joseph Starnes (D.-Ala.), John Dempsey (D.-N.M.), Stephen Pace (D.-Ga.), Frank Welchel (D.-Ga.), and Howard Smith (D.-Va.) introduced bills to register and fingerprint all aliens; to deport "dangerous" aliens, aliens "inimical to the public interest," or aliens "engaged in espionage"; to exclude aliens who advocated "essential changes" in the form of the American government; or even to cut off immigration completely for five, ten, or an indefinite number of years.[74]

The man in Congress who syncretized all of the alien phobias, fascist sympathies, and Jew-hatred in the country at the time was Democratic Senator Robert Reynolds of North Carolina. Some people had a tendency to underrate Reynolds as a country eccentric who endorsed Lucky Strike cigarets, chewed plugs of tobacco in the Senate chamber, and knew little about foreign affairs. (Late in 1938 he returned from "Hungria" and announced that it was wrong for Hitler to have taken "the Sudan.")[75] But Reynolds was an astute politician who could not be dismissed lightly. Elected to the Senate in 1932 over the incumbent Cameron Morrison, whom he had blasted as a "fish-aig" (Bolshevik) tool, Reynolds knew well the effectiveness of red-baiting. He was a party regular on votes relating to the Roosevelt administration's programs when such fealty was becoming a rarity among his fellow Democrats, and he hoped to trade off support for the president's court reorganization bill, WPA, TVA, and devaluation in exchange for the administration's silence on immigration and alien questions.[76] Reynolds, a friend of Trevor, Deatherage, Winrod, and Coughlin, was moreover able to use the prestige of his position as chairman of the Senate Committee on Military Affairs to further the goals of the multifarious racist and patriotic organizations in the United States.

Reynolds repeatedly fulminated against aliens, "foreigners who are now here, who have never made application for American citizenship, and who never intend to make application for American citizenship." [77] Using no verifiable data, he maintained that there were six million aliens living in the U.S., four million of whom were employed. This last group not only was confounding the employment situation for native Americans, but was also drawing off millions of dollars to spend abroad rather than in the United States.[78] He stated in 1939: "I say we ought not to permit a single person from foreign shores to set foot upon the shores of America for ten years or longer, until such time as every unemployed American has been provided with remunerative employment." [79]

Reynolds's critics noted that his mathematics were less than precise. In a manner much like that of Senator Joseph McCarthy, he continually juggled new figures (all admittedly "unofficial") to thoroughly becloud the immigration issue. The six million aliens referred to on January 13, 1939, became seven million three days later—"seven million potential enemy spies within our midst, boring from within like termites." At the same time, ten million unemployed Americans became thirteen, fifteen, or twenty, by the simple stroke of Reynolds's pen. Ultimately, by the end of March, Reynolds settled upon the figure of twenty-six million unemployed Americans (hastening to add that this figure included the partially employed as well).[80]

As far as Reynolds was concerned, there was a sinister conspiracy afoot, engineered by the Jews, the same people who were "trying to deprive the Arabs of their rightful possessions in Palestine." Since Europe was wresting itself free of "the Jewish yoke," the Jews were trying to propagandize the American public, make it more amenable to a flood of immigrants. Instead of offering special immigration dispensations to Jews ("who don't become integral parts of American life except after generations and under pressure," Reynolds contended), he argued that the government should address itself first to the "30,000 WPA workers losing their jobs daily," or the "600,000 young people who reach working age every year in the U.S. and who face a jobless future," or the "3,000,000 Americans" working for WPA, or the "8,000,000 sons and daughters of American sharecroppers" who lived in hovels, wore tattered and

torn clothes, lacked proper medical attention and basic education, and subsisted on thick gravy and biscuits.[81]

To correct this situation, Reynolds in 1939 established the
Vindicators, another super-patriotic organization, whose em-
blem was a coiled snake on a field of red, white, and blue, and
whose motto was "Crush the Enemies of America." He intended
to create a united force of 5,000,000 vocal, loyal Americans, all
lobbying for an end to conscription, the resumption of friendly
relations with Germany and Italy, and the passage of numerous
bills which Reynolds had introduced in the Senate with the
familiar restrictionist stamps of alien registration, exclusion of
aliens whose entry would be inimical to American interests,
employment of American citizens on "American jobs," deportation of aliens subsisting on relief, and the prohibition of
separation of families by barring the entry of aliens who left
dependents abroad.

None of Reynolds's programs ever reached fruition, and
few of the proposals advanced by the ever-changing melange of
worried capitalists, 100 percenters, communist-hunters, and
profascists that constituted the restrictionist pressure blocs before World War II were ever enacted into law. But if Reynolds
and the thousands of American restrictionists who regarded him
as their spokesman in Washington were unable to move Congress to further tighten immigration quotas, they were nonetheless effective in preventing the friends of the stateless from
gaining any successes either. The Johnson-Reed Act remained
on the books throughout the Nazi epoch, and the American
government remained committed to its strict enforcement long
after the expansionist policies of Adolf Hitler had convinced
many Americans that their government should offer humanitarian relief to the victims of German persecution.

Once more the United States had witnessed the triumph
of nativism. The restrictionism or anti-alienism of the 1930s
and early 1940s was not, however, the creation of contemporary
cranks or smooth-working propaganda mills. Rather, it was the
revival of a primitive human emotion, a distrust and fear of
the other, which, Higham argues, has surfaced periodically in

35

response to America's national anxieties and the limits of her tolerance.[82] But while the nativist fears of Harrison Gray Otis, Henry Bowers, Denis Kearney, and Madison Grant may have taken their small toll in human suffering, the twentieth-century exclusivism, based on self-interest, joblessness, insecurity, anti-Bolshevik hysteria, and hardcore anti-Semitism, was to share partial responsibility for genocide. William Leuchtenberg wrote (p. 286), "For every refugee who came to this country, many more who could have been saved died in Hitler's extermination chambers."

2. From Anschluss to Evian

Shortly before dawn on Saturday, March 12, 1938, advance patrols of the German Eighth Army filtered unopposed across the Austrian border to secure abandoned fortifications at Passau, Salzburg, and Kiefersfelden. By four o'clock that warm spring afternoon Adolf Hitler crossed the border in an open-air Mercedes at his birthplace, Braunau-am-Inn, ostensibly as a visitor on the way to his mother's grave, but actually as a conqueror filled with vengeance for the humiliations he had sustained in his native land two decades before. Hitler would be received in Vienna by cheers of 200,000 persons singing the "Horst Wessel Lied" to the ringing of church bells in steeples draped with the swastika.

This bloodless coup was the culmination of four years of concerted intrigue and assassination directed by the Hitler regime against the Austrian republic. Just twenty-four hours before the Anschluss, Austrian Chancellor Kurt von Schuschnigg had been proceeding with plans for a national referendum which would defiantly proclaim the nation's independence of Nazi influence. Schuschnigg had stationed 5,000 men, constituting Austria's standing army, in positions along the German border. They were pledged to die for their nation's honor and freedom. Hopelessly outmanned and outgunned by the German Wehrmacht, lacking the support of any adherent of the so-called Stresa Front, and facing Nazi revolutionary activity in Graz and Styria, Schuschnigg yielded before the threats of Adolf Hitler.[1]

A world which had seen Hitler flaunt the Treaty of Versailles by repudiating its war guilt clause and by rearming

Germany with tanks, planes, and a powerful navy, which had permitted Hitler to propagandize the inhabitants of the Saar and Rhineland back into the Reich, which had looked askance as Hitler refortified Germany's frontiers, should not have been particularly horrified when the Nazi tyrant scrapped his mutual security pact with Schuschnigg and stormed into Austria.

Seventy-six thousand Austrian patriots, Catholics, Jews, and government officials in Vienna were trundled off to jails by the Nazis within hours after the invasion. Six thousand persons were dismissed from the ministries of public safety and education. General Otto Zehner, the last Austrian defense minister, was murdered, and the rest of the general staff was pensioned off. To ensure its loyalty the tiny Austrian army was sent on parade in Germany, there to be integrated into the Wehrmacht.[2]

Britain and France reacted passively to the Anschluss and treated it as an accomplished fact even before the Germans had reached the outskirts of Vienna. London and Paris accepted Goering's vouchsafe that German troops would be withdrawn as soon as the Austrian situation stabilized. No protest was raised by the Soviet Union. In the United States, German Ambassador Hans Heinrich Dieckhoff cabled his superiors that he had discussed the matter with Secretary of State Cordell Hull on March 12 and "from a few questions, it was apparent that Mr. Hull thoroughly understands our actions."[3] Only the Czechs, who had volunteered to assist the Austrians in precisely such a crisis, stood ready to fight Germany, and they were unable to act alone.

The democracies could ill afford to be so blasé. Suddenly what had always been regarded as a domestic problem, Germany's persecution of its Jews, now loomed before the world in more dramatic proportions. Somehow mankind had become inured to the harshness of the Nuremberg Laws as they slowly but methodically declassed and dehumanized Germany's 700,-000 "non-Aryans." Now that malevolence was being transmitted beyond the original confines of the Reich. Now the 1,600-year-old Austrian-Jewish community, never as wealthy nor as secure as German Jewry, was to be subjected to an instantaneous terror.

In the first few days of the Anschluss, 500 Jewish leaders, including Otto Loewi (1936 Nobel Prize winner in medicine), Heinrich Neumann (a noted ear specialist who had treated both King George of England and the Duke of Windsor), Baron Louis de Rothschild, eighty-two-year-old Sigmund Freud, and Felix Salten (author of *Bambi*), were arrested.[4] Anti-Jewish caricatures showing large hook-nosed figures wearing a hammer and sickle, with palms outstretched, were plastered on public buildings in Vienna. Graveyards were desecrated with jeering invitations for Jews to come to the one place where they would be welcomed. Jewish stores, newspapers, and offices were plundered. Reichsmarshal Goering announced that all Jews with more than $2,000 in savings or property had to register such personal wealth with the state, which reserved the right to confiscate said property "wherever necessary."[5] Jews were disfranchised, thereby preventing their interference in the special plebiscite on April 10, which the Nazis had arranged to sanction the Anschluss.[6] Jews were evicted from apartments and dismissed from medical schools and college faculties. Austrian literature and music were purged of the works of Stefan and Arnold Zweig, Franz Werfel, Vicki Baum, Mahler, Bizet, Mendelssohn, Toch, and Korngold.[7] According to a dispatch from the Jewish Telegraphic Agency on March 18, Vienna was becoming a city of whispers.

The expressed purpose of this persecution, according to the Nazi official organ, *Voelkischer Beobachter*, was to rid Austria of its Jews. By all gauges, the Nazis were succeeding. Before the Anschluss the daily mortality figure among Jews in Vienna was six. Within a fortnight, the figure was fifty, with many deaths attributable to starvation, beatings, or suicide. In the same period more than 30,000 persons queued up before the American consulate, and another 10,000 before the Australian consulate, in Vienna to seek visas. Officials estimated that 95 percent of these persons were Jewish.[8]

Because legal emigration did not proceed with the speed

and precision that the Germans desired, they devised new techniques of expulsion. Early in April a group of fifty-one Jews, many of them children, were rousted from their homes in the Burgenland, forced at gunpoint to board an old, vermin-infested barge, and then abandoned in the Danube near the Hungarian shore. They stayed there, in no man's land, without food, money, or warm clothing, while Austria, Czechoslovakia, and Hungary all denied them entrance.[9]

What began here as an experiment in terror developed into an institutional part of the Nazi program through the remainder of 1938. After the Munich partition of Czechoslovakia in September, 20,000 more Jews were expelled from the Sudetenland. Late in October another 18,000 Jews of Polish origin residing in Germany were rounded up in the middle of the night and driven to the swampy borders of Poland, where guards told them to run for their lives and then shot over their heads.[10] Any convenient ditch or open field between Germany and its neighbors now could serve as a dumping ground for unwanted Jews. They came to rest in stables or along the roads of Nitra, Tarpolcany, Zilina, Michalovce, Prestany, Zbonszyn, and Zbaszyn, to sit in silence beside huge vats of steaming soup contributed by the Joint Distribution Committee, to sleep on straw supplied by local peasants, to freeze in Europe's most severe winter in a century, to die of typhus and typhoid which were rampant among those who had not gone mad.[11]

The concept of "no man's land" was not limited to Nazi Germany. The Anschluss merely unleashed latent hostilities toward the Jews in virtually every state which had signed League of Nations' minority treaties.[12] The Ronyos Garda (Guards in Rags) in Hungary, the Iron Guard in Rumania, the Hlinka Guard in Slovakia, and the Sic in the Western Ukraine all actively barred Jewish refugees from their homelands and turned on their own fellow nationals. Shortly after the Anschluss, Mussolini announced that the 15,000 Jews who had come to Italy after 1919 would have to leave within six months and that the remaining Jews would be barred from participating in the economic life of Italy. For four days in October, anti-Semites in Slovakia and Hungary shunted 10,000 Jews back and forth across their common borders, until they came to rest in miserable camps operated by the Joint Distribution Committee near Kosice, Poland.[13] One of those expelled expressed the grief of what he called "these human tennis balls" when he said, "I can't survive like a criminal. I can't gate-crash in this world. If this goes on, I'll kill myself." [14]

From a practical standpoint, then, the Anschluss warned every one of Europe's seven million Jews that he was in immediate jeopardy of becoming a stateless refugee.[15] On July 21, 1938, Estonian Minister of Welfare Otto Kask stated that his country (with 5,000 Jews constituting 0.5 percent of the population) could accept no more refugees because of a rising tide of anti-Semitism. Like statements were issued by government spokesmen in Lithuania and Latvia.[16] And in a communiqué to Cordell Hull, dated August 30, 1938, American Ambassador to Poland Anthony Biddle underscored the growing anxieties of the Slawoj-Skladkowski government over the Jewish question. Poland, according to Foreign Minister Colonel Josef Beck, with three million Jews, resented being treated as the dumping ground of Europe's undersirables. For Beck and other officials in the anti-Semitic Camp of National Unity, which dominated Poland's government, there was no difference between the Jewish refugee problem and Poland's Jewish problem. The international community had to treat these questions as one and the same and had to provide some outlets of emigration for Polish as well as Austrian or German Jews.[17]

The fear that Poland might indeed emulate Germany by expelling masses of Jews across its boundaries was supported by an intensified anti-Semitic press and radio campaign conducted by the government in the summer of 1938. This was followed by hints that "if other means fail," Poland might adopt "German methods" of calling attention to her Jewish problems.[18] Equally distressing to Washington were reports coming from Ambassador Hugh Wilson in Berlin that the Anschluss was merely a prelude to future German assaults on the Balkans for control on Hungarian wheat, Rumanian oil, and Czech munitions. Wilson predicted that Hitler would not be satisfied until he had absorbed the Sudetenland, as well as Austria, and he worried that the peace of the world rested with the state of mind of "this nervous man." [19] Despite Wilson's sagacity, the State Department's only official comment on the Anschluss, apart from a few bitter words which Undersecretary Sumner Welles addressed to Ambassador Dieckhoff on March 15,[20] was that it was studying the situation.

Much of the American public, however, was less reserved. The major New York daily newspapers, like most papers across the country, editorialized against Nazi brutality in Austria and the snowballing effect of expulsions into no man's lands. The Catholic monthly *Wisdom*, the *Messenger*, national organ of the Evangelical and Reform Churches in the United States, the National Methodist Student Conference, the YMCA, the World Conference of the Society of Friends, Bishop William Manning of the Cathedral of St. John the Divine in New York, Harry Emerson Fosdick, Al Smith, Representative Samuel Dickstein of New York, Vito Marcantonio, a New York Republican, were among those who spoke out against the Nazi coup.[21] Donald O'Toole, a Democrat from Brooklyn, even introduced a bill in Congress calling for severance of diplomatic relations with Germany "until that nation relinquishes coercive, forced control of Austria, and further abates persecution of minorities because of race or creed." [22]

Roosevelt shared this popular revulsion at the course of events in Europe and was subsequently blamed by Dieckhoff for the sudden frost in American policy vis-à-vis Austria. Roosevelt was well aware of how this country had already been culturally and scientifically enriched by refugees from Hitlerian persecution, including people like Albert Einstein, Enrico Fermi, Niels Bohr, Max Reinhardt, Kurt Weill, Thomas Mann, George Grosz, Otto Klemperer, Julius Ehrlich, Nahum Glatzer, Richard Goldschmidt, Karl Lange, Rudolph Schoenheimer, and countless others, most of them Jews.[23] He was also well aware that the Jews in America constituted his most loyal and most vocal base of support.[24] Thus, at a cabinet meeting on March 18, 1938, Roosevelt, in what Treasury Secretary Henry Morgenthau described as an unusually serious mood, expressed his concern over the fate of the German Jews. "America was a place of refuge for so many fine Germans in the period of 1848. Why couldn't we offer them again a place of refuge at this time?" [25]

The answer should have been obvious. Figures compiled by the American Federation of Labor showed unemployment in 1938 stood at 11,000,000, nearly 20 percent of the work force.[26] The hopes for emergence from the depression had been smashed in the recession of 1937, which had expanded the welfare rolls, shaken public confidence, and left FDR despondent. Roosevelt hardly needed to add the sensitive question of immigration to the series of domestic squabbles that he already had on his hands in the spring of 1938. The nation had not yet forgiven his badly handled "court-packing" scheme of 1937 and would presently express disapproval of an equally bungled purge of conservative Democrats in Congress.[27] Roosevelt's popularity had reached a new low, and a nationwide survey indicated that barely one-half of the people would have voted for him if the presidential election had been held that November. Immigration reform should have been the farthest thing from the president's mind that spring, especially after he had received a telephone call from one of his whips on Capitol Hill who informed him, "For God's sake, don't send us any more controversial legislation." [28] Restrictionists had taken no chances, however, and once more William Green of the AFL, John Rankin of Mississippi, Reynolds, and John Trevor went on record as opposing any legislation which might flood the country with communist agitators and competing workmen.[29]

The president could hardly have bucked popular sentiment, which, while sympathetic to the plight of the "non-Aryans" in Germany, was nevertheless firmly opposed to the admission of additional refugees in the spring of 1938. Only 4.9 percent of those persons polled by Roper felt that the United States should welcome the victims of Nazi persecution if this meant suspending immigration quotas. And 18.2 percent felt that such refugees should be permitted to enter the United States within existing restrictions. But 67.4 percent of the Americans polled argued that conditions here being what they were, the government should "keep them out." Ironically, although the position of the Jews under Nazism was critical, 20 percent of the American Jews polled also favored an absolute exclusionist policy.[30]

If there was a foreign policy question which truly interested Americans (after the all-encompassing domestic crisis), it was not what was going on in Austria, but Japan's mutilation of our long-fancied protégé, China.[31] Most Americans felt that the Jews in Europe were at least partially to blame for their present sufferings.[32] Better than 60 percent of those polled by the Opinion Research Corporation (ORC) in the spring of 1938 objected to the Jews who were already in this country.[33] A substantial portion of the followers of demagogs like Coughlin and Gerald L. K. Smith believed there were too many Jews in the country already.[34] The influential Jesuit weekly *America* washed its hands of the situation in Europe, despite the fact that 15 percent of the potential refugees in Germany and Austria were Christians, because "it remains mainly a Jewish problem." [35] And a consistently sizable block of Americans, one in eight, indicated through 1938 and 1939 that they would support an organized anti-Semitic campaign against the Jews on a par with that being waged by the Nazis.[36] The nation did not particularly appreciate its own Jews, let alone seek any more that might complicate the employment situation. It is significant that in virtually every poll conducted by Gallup, Roper, ORC, and NORC through February 1946 the group singled out by most Americans as posing the greatest menace to the country was the Jews.[37]

Roosevelt had learned the previous fall that he could ill afford to antagonize public opinion. By his own admission a novice in the field of foreign affairs (shortly after the Anschluss, he wrote a friend, "I am in the midst of a long process of education—and the process seems to be working slowly but surely"),[38] FDR had been miserably unsuccessful in his attempts to secure international peace late in 1937. The American-sponsored international disarmament conference at Brussels had foundered because of quarrels among the democracies and because Germany, Italy, and Japan did not send delegates.[39] Then on October 5, 1937, Roosevelt stated that it might become necessary to quarantine aggressor nations which were "creating a state of international anarchy and instability from which there is no escape through mere isolation or neutrality." [40]

The president was not prepared for the response to his quarantine speech. Cheered abroad as a harbinger of American entry into a system of collective security, the speech was lacerated by isolationist newspapers and spokesmen in Congress as an unwarranted departure from America's traditional stance of neutrality.[41] Welles wrote presidential aide Samuel Rosenman of the surprise and dismay the president had felt about the attacks on his speech in this country. Rosenman later noted, "It was a mistake he seldom made—the mistake of trying to lead the people of the United States too quickly and before they had been adequately informed of the facts or spiritually prepared for the event." [42]

Once singed by such abuse, and thoroughly aware that Congress was "in a nasty mood" and eager for a chance "to clip the President's wings," [43] Roosevelt stepped warily to avoid provoking further outcries against his programs. Rosenman noted that henceforth FDR was careful not to recommend any drastic action without first giving the people the facts to the extent that military security allowed (p. 168).

At the same time, however, FDR was under great pressure from powerful Jewish groups in the country like the B'nai B'rith, the American Jewish Committee, the Zionist Organization of America, the Jewish Labor Committee and the American Jewish Congress, as well as the nonsectarian National Coordinating Committee, to do something to succor the Jews of Europe. Roosevelt, surrounded by Jewish intimates like Treasury Secretary Henry Morgenthau, Commerce Secretary David Niles, personal advisers Samuel Rosenman and Benjamin Cohen, economic advisers Bernard Baruch and Mordecai Ezekiel, Supreme Court Justices Louis Brandeis and Felix Frankfurter, and maintaining close lines of communication with Rabbis Stephen Wise and Abba Silver, Governor Herbert Lehman, and the NCC's Gentile chairman, Joseph P. Chamberlain, must have felt the tremendous impact of such pressure.

In actuality, however, the Jewish community in this country was as riven as the fascist bloc, but with the added complication of having no common, ultimate goal. Wise, an indomitable soul who had been instrumental in founding the Zionist Organization of America, the American Jewish Congress, and the World Jewish Congress, complained in 1937 that he had Roosevelt all but convinced to issue a presidential decree in March 1933 which would have admitted victims of political and religious persecution to the U.S. Only through the intervention of Eric and James Warburg, wealthy New York Jews who convinced Roosevelt that tales of persecution under Hitler were greatly exaggerated—"atrocity and rumor mongering"— was the plan rejected.[44]

Wise continued to have difficulties with the more reserved American Jewish Committee and B'nai B'rith when he proposed a full-scale boycott of German goods and mass demonstrations against Nazi persecution early in 1933.[45] Similarly, when Baruch Vladeck of the Jewish Labor Committee promised cooperation in such matters in 1937, Wise noted sourly, "He may cooperate in the boycott where the cooperation is altogether to their advantage, we doing all the work and they appropriating the major credit, but that's all." [46]

Even when Pittsburgh philanthropist Edgar Kaufmann convinced the American Jewish Congress, the American Jewish Committee, B'nai B'rith, and the Jewish Labor Committee to merge their efforts in the summer of 1938 under one General Jewish Council, the groups failed to cooperate. Throughout 1938 and 1939, Wise and his executive secretary, Lillie Shultz, scored the separate fund-raising tactics of the American Jewish Committee, which merely duplicated the work of the United Jewish Appeal and deprived the other three organizations of a greater share of American support.[47] By April 1941 the leaders of the Congress were paranoid about every action taken by the other groups. An example was Congress Vice-President Lipsky's warning to Wise that "the Congress will soon be facing a planned underground attack, which will come from the American Jewish Committee, the Jewish Labor Committee, and possibly the B'nai B'rith." Lipsky suggested avoiding the initiation of any attack, in favor of building up the structure and influence of the Congress.[48] By the end of the month the Congress had withdrawn from the General Jewish Council, a move which ended any thought of Jewish unity.

What happened in the General Jewish Council was not unique. Disorder and disagreement permeated every aspect of the Jewish Community's plans to help the victims of Nazism. Not until July 1940 did HIAS, the Joint, the National Council of Jewish Women, and the National Refugee Service (the creation of the National Coordinating Committee in 1939), which collectively spent upwards of $30,000,000 on relief in Europe between 1933 and 1941,[49] decide among them what role each should play in the transporting and receiving of immigrants. Some Jewish organizations championed emigration to the United States, while others opposed this, fearful that increased Jewish immigration might result in violent anti-Semitic eruptions.[50] The Zionists labored to help thousands of persons leave Austria and Germany and go to Palestine. They were frustrated in this aim by the Central Conference of American Rabbis, which as late as 1935 was on record as opposed to such a concept, and by dissidents in the American Jewish Committee like Lessing Rosenwald, who held that Jewish nationalism only promoted the idea that there was a Jewish race as well.[51]

At the same time organizations like the American Jewish Congress and the National Coordinating Committee, which favored admission to the U.S. of larger numbers of Jewish refugees on a nonquota basis, could argue strongly in support of their views. First, they rejected the restrictionists' contention that immigration was contributing to the depression. They cited data to show that immigration was self-regulating in times of economic distress, that far from competing with unskilled native labor, those persons who had fled to the U.S. from Nazi Germany were mainly professionals who were badly needed in this country, that many of these persons had actually expanded job opportunities for Americans, rather than constricted them.[52]

The experience of Western Europe with German-Jewish refugees should have demonstrated the beneficial influences on employment of such immigration. In 1934 a special Dutch commission reported that the number of persons employed as a direct result of new economic activity introduced by the refugees was approximately equal to the number of immigrants taken in by the Netherlands since the rise of Hitler.[53] Sir Samuel Hoar, British Home Secretary, later noted in the House of Commons that 15,000 British workers were directly employed by 11,000 refugees.[54] And R. F. Harrod, president of the Economic Section of the British Association, in 1938 rejected the notion that existing unemployment was a good reason for discouraging immigration, concluding that the expansion of numbers is often good for employment and the contraction bad.[55]

The irony of this situation was that American immigration laws were allegedly designed to keep out the inferior elements of Europe. The persons now knocking at the door were refined, literate, professional Germans, whose average worth was once estimated at $25,000.[56] But even if the refugees were not all capitalists, scientists, or shopkeepers who transferred complete enterprises to the U.S., they still offered another potential tonic to the U.S. economy. Many of the immigrants were children, aged persons, or wives, people not seeking jobs and posing virtually no threat to those who did hold jobs. In fiscal 1938, for example, fewer than 20,000 of America's 68,000 immigrants fell in the employable male category.[57] Between 1931 and 1940 not more than 49,000 new job competitors were introduced in this country by immigration.[58] These people did not oust native Americans from jobs which the latter already held. They were not radicals or criminals. They did not subsist on welfare, and they did not lower the American standard of living.[59] In fact, every new immigrant with a family meant more mouths to feed, bodies to clothe, shelters to build, minds to educate, services to render, and products to sell.[60] That they by no means constituted a menace to the economic life of the country was clear to Labor Secretary Frances Perkins who testified in February 1939:

> The number of immigrants admitted into the U.S. in the last five years has averaged less than 50,000 per annum. It is unlikely that this number has greatly affected the conditions of the unemployed in this country, especially when consideration is given to the fact that a large part of the number admitted were dependents of citizens or aliens legally here, or were otherwise not of the employee class.[61]

While some persons in the U.S. labored in the Herculean task of convincing the government that the admission of Jews to this country would aid the economy, they also realized that many Jews in Europe did not want to leave their homelands, no matter how miserable their lot. Until the Anschluss the Hilfsverein der Juden in Deutschland, founded in 1901 to help less fortunate East European Jews, was committed to the idea of holding on rather than emigrating.[62] Until the Anschluss the German immigration quota of 27,370 was never filled. This desire to remain with the familiar, even in times of evil, was best summarized by Marie Ginsberg, who wrote:

> Many thought that the Nazi regime was but a passing phenomenon and, though prohibited from practicing their professions, still did not see that they ought to leave the country, but tried to make a living in trade or existed on their savings, hoping that a change of government would reinstate them in their former positions. Even those who did detach themselves from Germany clung to Europe, because they wanted to be ready to return as soon as circumstances permitted.[63]

Even if planned emigration had been possible in 1933, the Anschluss had changed that. In the summer of 1938 the European office of the Joint Distribution Committee in Paris warned that mass emigration was impossible because of situations in the immigrant countries, which had little capacity for absorption and which had unemployment problems of their own. Noting the ominous prospect of three million more potential Jewish refugees in Poland (something which had perturbed World Zionist Organization President Chaim Weizmann as early as 1936), the Joint bravely resolved to treat the problem in the host countries through relief, rehabilitation, and training.[64]

There is a tribal myth among Jews that anytime two Jews congregate, three opinions are present. This adage approximates the dissension which existed in the American Jewish community on the eve of World War II. Presidential aide Benjamin Cohen noted that Roosevelt was well aware of this division. While Roosevelt was sympathetic to the German refugees ("knocked pillar to post"), he also recognized that the Jews were unable to present any united plan of action to save their brethren.[65]

49

Moreover, none of Roosevelt's Jewish advisers spoke out strongly for special action on behalf of the Jews in Europe. In the face of criticisms of Roosevelt's "Jew Deal" and "Jewocracy," such leaders as Baruch, Rosenman, Frankfurter, Niles, and Morgenthau, "leaders of the periphery" according to Kurt Lewin's terminology, opted for mendicancy rather than leadership.[66] Insecure themselves, constantly wary of raising the specter of double-loyalty which was the grist of anti-Semites, these persons ever-exerted themselves to display their Americanism, their concern for this nation's welfare to the exclusion of all others, even when doing so meant the deaths of loved ones in Europe.[67]

Because of the explosiveness of the Jewish refugee question, and because no one could offer him a satisfactory suggestion as to how to resolve the problem, Roosevelt tempered his humanitarian impulses with the harsh realities of the times. It simply was not politically expedient for him to suggest any breaking down of U.S. immigration walls. A fight over refugees might be just the opening his enemies were seeking to jeopardize his entire legislative program, including relief and public works projects, rearmament, and revision of neutrality legislation. FDR made it clear to Mrs. Roosevelt, who had taken a keen interest in refugee affairs, that he was not willing to run that risk. "First things come first," he said, "and I can't alienate certain votes I need for measures that are more important at the moment by pushing any measure that would entail a fight." [68]

Still, Roosevelt recognized the moral necessity of doing something to aid the Jews in Europe. Legitimately the problem should have been within the province of the League of Nations, but the League had been incapable of handling refugee questions in the past. After World War I the league had been instrumental in underwriting international loans to cover the cost of transporting and integrating 2,000,000 Greeks and Turks and 220,000 Bulgarians in new lands.[69] Faced with the discomforting prospect of 1,000,000 White Russian, 300,000 Armenian, 50,000 Saar German, and countless other political and religious refugees, the League had established the Nansen Organization for Help to Refugees in 1921. The Nansen Office, directed by

Norwegian polar-explorer Fridtjof Nansen, attempted to regularize the emigration of persecuted peoples by issuing an international passport, which at one point was honored by fifty-two nations.[70]

The Nansen Office was aided after October 1933 by the Autonomous Office of High Commissioner for Refugees from Germany. This organization, formed in a reaction to the wave of anti-Jewish persecution in Germany, received at least the tacit endorsement of the United States. Joseph Chamberlain participated in organizational deliberations, and James G. McDonald, an Ohioan who had written at length against German barbarities in World War I and who was then chairman of the Foreign Policy Association of the United States, was named High Commissioner.[71]

Neither the Nansen Office nor the High Commissioner was able to handle the flow of German-Jewish refugees, to say nothing of the potential wave of persons in Eastern Europe. The Nansen Certificate, that quasi-passport which accorded emigrants social and economic rights equal with those enjoyed by nationals in any host country, was valid only for one year and only if the emigrant's original country would certify that he could return to his homeland. Quite obviously, then, the Nansen Office could be only mildly successful. From the time it entered the League of Nations in 1934 the Soviet Union agitated to abolish the office, which it charged was giving protection to counter-revolutionaries living abroad. After the rise of Hitler no German-Jewish refugee could qualify for one of those protective certificates, because none could obtain the necessary guarantee of the right to return to his homeland. By the summer of 1938 the Nansen Office, which had issued only 4,782 passports during the previous fiscal year, admitted its inability to cope with more than several thousand refugees at best.[72]

The High Commissioner's Office proved to be of little help. For one thing it was set up as a totally autonomous organization, divorced from the League of Nations. It was established mostly to appease the U.S. which, while interested in its success, did not want to become a party to any official League organization. But another reason for such autonomy was to spare the League's treasury a constant drain on its resources. Although it had been initially funded with 25,000 francs from that treasury, the commission was dependent upon voluntary contributions to support its programs. Before he resigned in fury and frustration in December 1935, McDonald did succeed in raising several million dollars to aid approximately 100,000 persons.[73] But McDonald's 3,000-word letter of resignation was as much an indictment of unwise reliance upon philanthropy to solve the refugee problem as it was of the Nazism that had created the problem.[74] Lacking a firm financial base, without a secretariat until 1936, duplicating instead of supplementing the work of the Nansen Office, the High Commissioner was virtually powerless and by 1938 was placing no more than fifty to 100 refugees a week in countries surrounding Germany.[75] It was powerless to touch refugees from Hitler's persecution in Austria (technically beyond the territorial limits of Germany and hence outside the jurisdiction of the commissioner's office). The office had been the subject of many proposals, all negative, most suggesting its abolition or, at best, its merger with the Nansen Office.[76]

With the Anschluss, Roosevelt also was compelled to conclude that the League and its operatives were incapable of dealing with the Jewish refugee problem. The president wrote later in 1941 that an orderly plan for intergovernmental cooperation was needed to deal with mass emigrations because the abilities of private organizations to find places of refuge had been overtaxed.[77] On March 23, 1938, Roosevelt directed Hull to invite the representatives of more than thirty nations to another international conference on refugees. For the first time the U.S. government pledged its fullest, official support.

On March 24, 1938, Hull issued the following statement to the press:

> This government has become so impressed with the urgency of the problem of political refugees that it has inquired of a number of Governments in Europe and in this hemisphere whether they would be willing to cooperate in setting up a special committee for the purpose of facilitating the emigration from Austria and presumably from Germany

of political refugees. Our idea is that whereas such representatives would be designated by the Governments concerned, any financing of the emergency emigration referred to would be undertaken by private organizations within the respective countries. Furthermore, it should be understood that no country would be expected or asked to receive a greater number of immigrants than is permitted by its existing legislation. In making this proposal the Government of the United States has emphasized that it in no sense intends to discourage or interfere with such work as is already being done on the refugee problem by any existing international agency. It has been prompted to make its proposal because of the urgency of the problem with which the world is faced and the necessity of speedy cooperative effort under governmental supervision if widespread human suffering is to be averted.[78]

This communiqué aroused much interest at the League of Nations, and it also established hard principles from which government officials, including Hull and Roosevelt, were bound not to stray.[79] Noteworthy among them were: (1) that no particular ethnic, political, or religious group should be identified with the refugee problem or the calling of the conference; (2) that nothing should be done to interfere with the operations of existing relief organizations, no matter how ineffectual those organizations might be; (3) that all assistance for refugee work should be drawn from purely voluntary sources; and (4) that no nation should be required to amend its current immigration laws to accommodate the refugees.

Roosevelt and Hull could defend the use of the euphemism "refugee" instead of "Jewish refugees." The League of Nations had estimated that there were still some 300,000 White Russians, 120,000 Armenians, 20,000 Nestorian Iraqis, and 30,000 Italians in need of assistance in 1938, as well as some 400,000 Spanish Republicans subsisting in French detention camps, another 3,000,000 of their countrymen who were labeled "internal refugees," and the millions of Chinese who had been uprooted by the Japanese invasion.[80]

Although this was true, the fact remains that in 1938 the Jewish question *was* the refugee question. The persecution and expulsion of the Jews were especially vicious, the potential number of persons affected was the greatest, the willingness of

European nations to welcome the victims of persecution was the lowest. The intergovernment meeting was called not in response to the Spanish Civil War nor Bolshevik purges, but as a direct consequence of the persecution of the Jews of Austria and Germany. This question would dominate the entire conference. The number of "refugees" discussed at Evian—600,000—was identical with the Jewish population of greater Germany. Walter Adams, secretary to Sir John Hope Simpson's Survey of Refugee Problems, conducted under the joint auspices of the Royal Institute of International Affairs, claimed the word refugee was a mere euphemism for Jew. U.S. Immigration Commissioner James Houghteling would later concede that the term "refugee" was useless as far as official definition went. Harold Willis Dodds, principal U.S. delegate to the Anglo-American Conference on Refugees at Bermuda in 1943, indicated some years later, "Everyone knew that when you talked about refugees in those days, you were talking about the Jews." [81]

Roosevelt knew it, too, for he wrote of the proposed conference that "the policy of the German Government toward Jewish minorities was the prime cause of the entire problem." [82] Nevertheless, the government, partially for defensive purposes at home, where anti-Semitism was strong, partially for the sake of the Jews abroad whom it was feared would suffer additional persecution if their case was singled out for mention, held to the official fiction in 1938 and throughout the war years that there was nothing unique about the Jewish refugee problem. The wording of Hull's call for an intergovernment conference obscured the true problem and prematurely burdened the conference with the same restrictions which had severely limited the League's refugee bodies.

Roosevelt and Hull could hardly have been encouraged by official responses to their announcement. Within four hours after receiving Hull's cable Italian Foreign Minister Galeazzo Ciano notified the American Ambassador William Phillips that although he recognized the humanitarian character of the proposal, "Italy could not participate in any move to care for the enemies of Fascism or Nazism." [83] Rumania and Poland, in offering to attend the conference, conditioned their participation upon some discussion of their Jewish problems as well. Russia hedged, fearing that the United States planned to revive the White Russian question. And Canada expressed concern over duplication of the work of existing League offices.[84]

In America, the response to Hull's call was anything but positive. AFL President Green gave his support on the condition that nothing be done in juggling quotas, which might prejudice labor's position. Representative Richard Jenkins of Ohio again warned against becoming embroiled in Europe's problems, and John Rankin of Mississippi, a strong anti-Semite, warned that "almost every disgruntled element that ever got into trouble in its own country has pleaded for admission into the United States on the ground that they were oppressed at home." [85] Roosevelt even received several pieces of hate literature from persons calling themselves "most ardent supporters." "Please spare us," these few letters ran. "Why open the door for more Jews? Don't we have enough of that scum here already?" [86]

On the whole, however, Roosevelt and Hull were cheered by the editorial opinions in British, American, and French periodicals, which applauded the idea of an international conference on refugees.[87] By the end of spring, acceptances had been received from Great Britain, the Dominions, Denmark, France, Belgium, Norway, Luxembourg, Sweden, Switzerland, the Netherlands, Panama, Mexico, Costa Rica, Honduras, Nicaragua, Cuba, Haiti, the Dominican Republic, Colombia, Venezuela, Peru, Ecuador, Chile, Brazil, Paraguay, Argentina, Bolivia, and Ireland. France had generously offered to host the conference at Evian-les-Bains, a small town in the Alps.

Nazi Germany, which had precipitated the call to Evian with its seizure of Austria and subsequent brutalization of that nation's Jewish community, would not attend the conference on the shores of Lake Geneva. Nor were the interested East European nations accorded delegate status at Evian. Even before the conference began the Western democracies decided upon a distinction between "sender" and "receiver" states. The East Europeans, who were permitted to send unofficial observers, were designated as "senders" of refugees.

3. The Intergovernmental Committee

There was a tragic element of truth in the statement circulated among Europe's Jews in 1938 that the world was made up of two types of countries: the kind where Jews could not live and the kind where Jews could not enter. This aptly described the situation as representatives of more than thirty nations and thirty-nine private organizations gathered at Evian on July 6, 1938.

Persecution of the Jews in Germany and Austria had inspired the conference. A somewhat more subdued persecution in the Baltic and Balkan states was being viewed warily by diplomats and humanitarians. Potential receiver nations like Switzerland, Holland, Belgium, Czechoslovakia, and France were saturated with refugees, and France had even instituted a series of regulatory decrees on aliens which one observer called *super-scélérat*.[1] Refoulement, the subject of League discussions in every year since 1932, was even more pronounced in 1938 when some nations required transit visas of Germans fleeing their country, others permitted only non-Aryans to cross the border, and still others which had welcomed refugees in 1933 stationed armed guards along barbed-wire fences to repulse any new immigrants.[2] Every English-speaking nation was committed to severe restriction of immigration. Palestine was off limits to Jews as a result of demonstrations staged by Haj Amin al-Husseini, Grand Mufti of Jerusalem. And Latin American nations were also not eager to import Europe's problems.

For its own reasons the United States, once having called for the conference, soon abdicated all responsibility for preliminary preparations in favor of the French. On May 7, Hull named Myron C. Taylor, onetime chairman of U.S. Steel, as ambassador extraordinary and plenipotentiary to head the American delegation to Evian. Taylor's single qualification in the field of negotiation was his successful resolution of contract differences with John L. Lewis in 1936. An Episcopalian of Quaker stock, the sixty-four-year-old Taylor had resigned from the U.S. Steel Corporation to take a sabbatical for what he termed "philosophic meditation on the problems of modern civilizations." He was called from this sabbatical to head a delegation which also included George Warren, a well known authority on refugee questions in his capacity as director of the National Coordinating Committee's International Migration Office, Robert Pell, an attorney from the State Department's European Division, and George Brandt, a senior officer in the Immigration Division. Taylor left for Rome in the second week of May and fretted away two months, awaiting instructions from Washington.

At the same time Ambassador Joseph Kennedy in London noted a growing concern in the British Foreign Office about the conference. What organizational steps were being taken by the United States? What definite proposals would the Americans make? How did the U.S. envision the scope of the work: Would conference resolutions be binding or would they be merely recommendations to the respective governments? Hull's evasive reply to Kennedy indicated that the French were assuming responsibility for all arrangements and that the secretary would apprise the British of the American position as to scope and procedure "in the near future." [3] No such memorandum was forthcoming before the meeting, and on the eve of the conference the British were still totally in the dark as to the nature of U.S. refugee policy.

Great Britain was not the only party to be unaware of what policies other participants might advance once the conference began. Twenty-one of the thirty-nine private organizations represented at Evian were Jewish.[4] Each of these submitted conflicting memorandums that were heavily inscribed with innocence. (Punsters capitalized on the fact that *Evian* spelled backward was *naïve*.) The Jewish Agency for Palestine, unaware that the British had already informed Taylor that Palestine was absolutely out of the question as a haven, extolled the virtues of sending Jews to the Middle East, where they would be needed and welcomed by their brethren.[5] Sixty-five-year-old Heinrich Neumann, released from a concentration camp to propose international sponsorship of Jewish emigration from Germany at a ransom price of $250 a head,[6] was unaware that Stephen Wise had rejected a similar scheme in January 1936 as "Blackmail! Blackmail!"[7] Wise's World Jewish Congress itself was talking of the feasibility of floating a $60,000,000 international loan to assist in the resettlement of German Jews,[8] while Agudas Israel, the Board of Deputies of British Jews, the Council of German Jewry, and the Jewish Colonization Association were rejecting potential shifts of millions of people.[9] And as if to compound the confusion among the various Jewish bodies in the U.S., the abortive Jewish People's Committee for United Action against Fascism and Anti-Semitism was calling for the redistribution of unused immigrations visas and the immediate admission of German Jewish refugees to this country.[10]

Certainly Wise should not have anticipated serious consideration of any of these proposals. He was a member of the President's Advisory Committee on Political Refugees, organized immediately after the call for an international conference, and he and other members had been fully briefed by Assistant Secretary of State George Messersmith on what to expect of Evian at the first meeting of the Advisory Committee at the State Department on May 16, 1938.[11]

According to Messersmith, the government hoped to create some permanent apparatus, based in a European capital, to cope with the long-range problem of refugees. This proposed intergovernment committee was to complement the work of the High Commission and Nansen Office. Initially it would be restricted to Austria and Germany, to avoid encouraging other governments to persecute their own minorities. Because of current economic conditions, no nation would be compelled to expand existing immigration quotas. The U.S., which had accepted more than its share of refugees since 1933, envisioned no plan of official assistance to refugees, because this also might encourage the Nazis to apply greater pressure on Jews and other non-Aryans. Neither should the committee expect results on Palestine. "Any attempts to interject in an active form the Palestine and Zionist problems should be rejected, as there are so many passions involved and so many major problems that any endeavor to consider these problems would probably lead to the early disruption of the committee," Messersmith told the group.[12]

Messersmith conceded that the replies to Hull's invitation had been reserved in tone and that all nations tended merely to render lip service to humanitarianism. Because of the complexities of the problem, because the work could only proceed at a slow rate, and because the expectancies of "certain groups" were totally out of proportion with potential results, Messersmith recommended that the work of the international committee not be overpublicized.[13]

Ambassador Taylor enunciated that same position in his opening remarks on July 6. The world was faced with a peculiar migration problem, he said, one that was not the outgrowth of government colonization or economic motives. Six hundred thousand persons, "men and women of every race, creed and economic condition," were in immediate need of sanctuary because of government-sponsored persecution. And the number was increasing daily. The United States favored a long-range, comprehensive program for the orderly departure of refugees with their property from their native lands, but Taylor stressed that this country would do nothing to impair existing immigration laws. The U.S. would accept 27,000 refugees a year, the quotas for Austria and Germany. Not once in his address did Taylor, who was selected by the delegates to chair the conference, use the word "Jew." [14]

Having established a precedent for inaction, the American delegation listened as one national representative after another disavowed the initiative in resolving the refugee problem. Canada's Hume Wrong ignored the vast stretches of uninhabited territory in Manitoba and Saskatchewan and begged off because of serious unemployment problems which limited his nation's capacity to absorb additional immigrants. The representatives of Belgium, the Netherlands, New Zealand, Ireland, and Switzerland did the same. France's Henry Bérenger, onetime representative to the League of Nations' High Commission for German Refugees and also former president of the Foreign Relations Committee of the French Senate, said that his country had already accepted more than 25,000 German refugees in 1938 and that henceforth it would accept no more without transit visas. He made a pointed reference to the fact that Australia and the United States owed their greatness to the influx of European immigrants.[15] The intimation that now would be a good time for these vast nations to accept more refugees was not lost on Australian Minister of Commerce Lt. Col. T. W. White, who snapped that his young country preferred to build up its manpower from the source from which it had sprung. "It will no doubt be appreciated," White added, "that as we have no real racial problem, we are not desirous of importing one by encouraging any scheme of large-scale foreign migration." [16]

The U.S. could not look to Great Britain for any startling rescue proposals, either. Taking his cue from Taylor, the chief British delegate Lord Earl Winterton said that although his government "had no intention of abandoning their policy of granting asylum to refugees," England could not accept more immigrants because of its own economic crisis.[17] Several days later Winterton dismissed the idea of Palestine as a potential refuge as totally untenable. As the mandatory power, Great Britain had been obligated to facilitate Jewish immigration to Palestine, but nothing more. "The record that has been achieved in this respect is one that calls for no apology," he added. Winterton claimed that 300,000 Jews had entered Palestine since 1920, 40,000 from Germany alone over the past several years. He said that further mass immigration was impossible because of the size of the state, "special considerations on the local scene," and the fact that Palestine was "in a period of transition." [18]

Having suffered these self-abnegations and homilies in

plenary session, the conferees then appointed two subcommittees, a general committee to hear in executive session the various testimonies of private relief organizations and a technical committee chaired by the Nansen Office's president, Michael Hansson of Norway, to review the immigration laws and practices of participating countries. For several days, in and out of the conference rooms and amidst the lovely gardens and terraces of the Royal Hotel, unofficial relief delegations waylaid the diplomats as they strolled or dined to suggest a plethora of refugee settlements in West Australia, French North Africa, Shanghai, Angola, Alaska, Madagascar, Tanganyika, Rhodesia, or Mindanao.[19]

The region which most occupied the attention of the delegates, however, was Latin America. In their eagerness to come up with some proposal for public consumption, the American and European delegates fantasized that Latin America would be ideal for the German refugees. That region was underpopulated, its climate was suitable for European settlement, and colonization would result in the exploitation of the vast agricultural and mineral wealth of South and Central America. The Anglo delegates read into the past generosity toward the refugees on the part of Brazil, Argentina, Colombia, Chile, Mexico, and Peru a present willingness to accept more.[20]

It was evident even from the most cursory reading of the opening remarks of the delegates from these countries, however, that the opposite was true. Without fail, virtually every Latin state expressed hostility at the thought of accepting more "non-Aryan" immigrants.[21] M. A. LeBreton of Argentina pointed out that his country had taken thirty-two Jewish immigrants for every forty-eight who had entered the U.S. since 1935, yet Argentina was only one-tenth the size of the United States.[22] Chile's García Oldino noted that since 1933 his nation had accepted 14,000 refugees. Before the days of Hitler, Chile had only 2,200 Jews, which meant its Jewish population had increased 672 percent.[23] Bolivia also could point to a 600 percent increase, and Paraguay to 58.3 percent rise. M. J. M. Yepes of Colombia expressed the Latin nations' fear of a refugee inundation when he warned the delegates that successful resettlement of thousands of Jews could well result in Evian's becoming the "Wailing Wall" of all who claimed to be persecuted.[24]

Far from responding with generosity to the Jewish crisis engendered by the Anschluss, the Latin states tightened up their immigration laws. Vociferous pro-Nazi German minorities in Argentina, Brazil, and Chile exaggerated the evils of refugee relief and destroyed every such plan put forward.[25] Now every Latin state required show or landing money to be held by the government for a period of years against the possibility that an individual might become a public charge. Such rules were coupled with further discrimination against Jews. Colombia's entry fee of $290, to be held in escrow for two years, was hiked to $500 and five years for Jews from Eastern Europe. Brazil and Argentina restricted visa applications to persons with "close relatives" already residing in those countries. Argentina, with 225,000 Jews, passed a series of laws establishing quotas in the professions. Trinidad prohibited immigration from nations south of Belgium or east of France. Mexico, Paraguay, and Bolivia demanded that all future immigrants be legitimate agriculturists. And Venezuela's spokesmen bluntly stated that Jews were not wanted and permission to immigrate would not be granted.[26]

Only the tiny Dominican Republic held out any prospect of serving as an actual haven. On July 9, 1938, Virgilio Trujillo-Molina delighted the weary delegates by announcing his government's willingness to accept 100,000 refugees. Trujillo said:

> The Dominican Government, which for many years has been encouraging and promoting the development of agriculture by appropriate measures and which gives ample immigration facilities to agriculturists who wish to settle in the country as colonists, would be prepared to make its contribution by granting specially advantageous concessions to Austrian and German exiles, agriculturists with an unimpeachable record, who satisfy the conditions laid down by the Dominican legislature on immigration.[27]

Hailed as a major breakthrough in the refugee question by Roosevelt, the Dominican offer was little more than an empty gesture by a self-seeking despot.[28] The Trujillo regime received a good deal of favorable publicity as a result of its announcement, but it never intended to really succor the desperate Jews of Germany. It is doubtful whether more than a handful of the 600,000 highly urbanized Jews of Austria-Germany could have satisfied the entry requirement of "agriculturists with an unimpeachable record." Moreover, experts from the U.S. Department of Agriculture doubted that the Dominican Republic, with its limited land supply, could absorb 100,000 more persons.[29] In fact, by the end of 1941 the Dominican Republic Settlement Corporation, chartered in October 1939 with Washington's approval, placed a mere 500 Jewish families in what was formerly Santo Domingo.[30]

Despite this obvious antipathy of the Latin republics toward nonfarming Jewish immigrants, the Evian conference recommended a host of research projects to probe the possibility of settlement in the Western Hemisphere. Through 1939 the British were especially keen about Guiana, which had been suggested as a haven for the Nestorians in 1935. Rejected then as unfit for Caucasian habitation because of its poor soil, lack of transportation, tropical diseases, floods, and drought, Guiana had hardly improved in four years. In 1939, Karl Pelzer, geographical consultant for the Johns Hopkins Institute of Pacific Relations, believed the prospects for settlement of even 30,000 persons along the thin coastal belt of Guiana to be "negligible."[31] Similar criticisms were made of most of the Central and Latin American regions in studies by some of the foremost geographical and agricultural experts in the Western world, including George and Merle McBride of the University of California, Leo Waibel, formerly of the Universities of Kiel and Bonn, George Roberts, onetime president of the National City Bank of New York, Robert Strausz-Hupe of the University of Pennsylvania, Raye Platt, Alec Golodetz, and Cyril Henriques of the American Geographical Society, and Frederick Nutter Cox, an experienced civil engineer who had labored for more than fifteen years as chief of the Public Works Department in the Punjab.[32]

These studies agreed on certain essential points: (1) Latin America needed agricultural workers, and the Jewish refugees most assuredly did not belong to this class; (2) each Latin state faced serious irrigation and water purification problems, which would only be intensified by new colonies; (3) the climates of most Latin states were intemperate, and tropical diseases likely would take a high death toll among European settlers; (4) in each state there was a residual anti-Semitism, manifested principally among German hyphenates, but found among long-resident Spanish descendants as well; (5) German Jewish refugees would face a religious as well as linguistic barrier in settling in the Latin South; (6) the ultimate cost of such settlement would be tremendous because of the need for road construction, improved health and sanitation facilities, and the expense involved in setting up homesteads. Latin America, therefore, would not make the most inviting refuge.

After a week of fruitless haggling the Evian conference adjourned on July 15, 1938. Taylor, who had won the admiration of those present as a first-rate negotiator, delivered the valedictory. This final communiqué called attention to the involuntary emigration from Germany which threatened "the processes of appeasement in international relations" and recommended:

(1) That the life of the conference called by Roosevelt be prolonged and that the body be formalized under the title Intergovernmental Committee on Refugees (IGCR), consisting of whatever members of the world community who wished to participate.

(2) That the IGCR maintain an executive council, based in London, with a chairman, four vice-chairmen, and a director, whose function would be to negotiate "to improve present conditions of exodus and to replace them with conditions of orderly emigration" from Germany.

(3) That the scope of the committee's concern be limited to persons forced to leave Germany and Austria who had not established themselves permanently elsewhere, or those who might yet have to flee these countries because of their political opinions, religious beliefs, or racial origin.[33]

The final communiqué did not discuss the problem of additional refugees in Eastern Europe should Hitler's proposed expansion in this direction occur on schedule.[34] Nor did it clearly distinguish among the functions of the League High Commission, the Nansen Office, and the IGCR, a problem which was to plague the IGCR's first director, George Rublee, for the next six months. Nor did it clear up the problems of statelessness and the need for some improvement on Nansen passport procedures. And finally, the communiqué did nothing to obligate any government financially to the IGCR. Instead, it read, "The governments of the countries of refuge and settlement should not assume any obligations for the financing of involuntary emigration."[35] The IGCR was to be a voluntary organization, like the League Commission on Refugees, and totally dependent on private donations.

Reacting to what it termed the "niggardly" positions of the democracies, *The New Republic* editorialized:

> What a demonstration these nations might have provided for the world if they could have gone on wholeheartedly to act in the spirit of the cause that brought them together! If they had proclaimed at once that the unfortunate victims of persecution would be welcomed elsewhere, promptly and with as few obstacles as possible. The humane superiority of democracy over its enemies would have been strikingly demonstrated. Unfortunately, however, many of the delegates protested that their countries had no room for the victims, and even the more liberal offers were scanty enough.[36]

The article generally summed up the reaction of the American press to the conference, which was immediately called a failure. Some newspapers, like the St. Paul *Dispatch*, the Louisville *Journal*, and the Houston *Chronicle* looked for bright spots and concurred with Jonah Wise, representative of the Joint Distribution Committee, who said that while "no miracles could be expected," the conference nonetheless marked "a twilight of hope." Others, like the Boston *Post* and San Francisco *Chronicle*, scored the "selfishness of nationalism and floundering methods of the conferees." The Richmond *News Leader* added, "Some of us are a bit ashamed of our country."[37]

Roosevelt could not conceal his disappointment over the

outcome of the meeting. He had been hopeful of some dramatic proposal from another country and was ever mindful of the pathetic letters from refugees at home and abroad showering him with blessings, but he conceded in 1941: "Unfortunately, most of the governments seemed overly cautious in their attitude about receiving these refugees; and while they were generally sympathetic, no constructive plans were submitted." [38]

FDR might have included the U.S. among those hesitant governments which he criticized. Shortly after the conference ended, Taylor cabled Hull requesting that the U.S. demonstrate its willingness to accept a substantial number of the 600,000 German refugees in the next five years. The ambassador believed that because of health, age, and other such factors only 300,000 of these would ever be able to emigrate. If the United States, the moving force behind the IGCR, did not act, "other countries of settlement will claim that they are not obligated to commit themselves, and we shall have no plan to present to the German Government," Taylor said. [39]

Hull's reply was akin to that of a schoolteacher upbraiding an errant schoolboy. The secretary reminded Taylor of America's rigid immigration laws and pointed to the rising restrictionist tide in Congress which would oppose any juggling of quotas. Taylor was to explain to the other representatives of the IGCR that America, merely by taking its legally allotted number of German refugees, 27,300 a year, would in five years have accepted more than one-third of the total which Taylor said should be evacuated. [40]

Hull preferred to pin his hopes for resolution of the refugee problem on the efforts of George Rublee, the seventy-year-old attorney named to direct the IGCR. A Wilsonian Democrat, Rublee had acquired extensive administrative experience during World War I as a member of the Federal Trades Commission, the Treasury Department's Legal Section, and the U.S. Shipping Board. He also had represented the United States at the Allied Maritime Transport Council in London in 1919, as legal adviser to the American Embassy in Mexico City between 1928 and 1930, as a member of the American delegation to the London Naval Conference in 1930, and as special consultant to the government of Colombia between 1930 and 1933. It is doubtful, however, whether in all his administrative and diplomatic experiences Rublee had ever been as hamstrung by such balky instructions as he received from the second meeting of the IGCR in London on August 3, 1938.

No one yet had inquired whether the German government would even talk with him, but the IGCR now gave Rublee authority to arrange "the normal emigration" of Germany's 600,000 refugees. To avoid confusion only the American ambassador in Berlin, Hugh Wilson, was to approach the German Foreign Ministry to secure an invitation for Rublee. Rublee was then to enter into "exploratory discussions" with Nazi officials, preparatory to working out some sensible scheme of emigration aimed at siphoning off refugees to South America.[41] Such was the plan as approved at London and later endorsed by Hull, to whom Rublee reported scrupulously, although he was under no official obligation to do so.

Wilson soon complained to Hull that it was practically impossible to see any official of consequence in Berlin at the end of the summer. Germany was preoccupied with the Sudetenland controversy during August and September. Foreign Minister Joachim von Ribbentrop had been away from the capital since July, and when he did return, he disdained to meet with "an official person" representing a committee which Germany did not recognize "on matters affecting German internal affairs." Not until October 18 did Wilson finally obtain a hearing with German Secretary of State Ernst von Weizsaecker. At that time Weizsaecker contemptuously rejected the ambassador's entreaties on behalf of Rublee and the IGCR, noting that Germany had followed developments in the committee and "had not been able to see that any particular headway had been made for the absorption of Jewish emigrants." [42]

Weizsaecker could not have been more astute had he been reading Rublee's confidential reports to Hull. Rublee waited in vain for an invitation from Berlin, for months busying himself in London with studies of relief possibilities around the world, seeking additional funds to supplement his meager $50,000 operational budget, and growing ever more enraged by the lack of cooperation of so-called receiver nations. Late in August he lamented, "The Allies are not terribly concerned over the fate of refugees still in Germany." [43] France, Belgium, and Holland enacted new restrictions barring immigration from Germany. On September 1, Brazil, which along with the U.S., Great Britain, and France held a vice-chairmanship in the IGCR, resigned its seat. The next day Argentina barred all further immigration, arguing that it had a higher percentage of Jews than any other nation. On September 13, Chile, never sympathetic to the Jews, formally withdrew from the IGCR. Within two weeks, the three most industrialized Latin American nations had thus renounced all interest in refugee matters. In view of the interest that had been expressed in South America by other nations at Evian and London, this trend could only be termed disastrous, as other Latin states were certain to follow the lead of Argentina, Brazil, and Chile. From London, Rublee wrote Hull that fall: "With the exception of the United States and the United Kingdom, doors have been systematically closed everywhere to involuntary emigrants since the meeting at Evian." [44]

If anything, Rublee was being generous to the British, who seemed inclined to minimize his mission. At first tolerant of what seemed to be legitimate procedural delays at the time of the Munich crisis, Rublee grew increasingly exasperated with the British in October and November. Five days after Roosevelt sent a message to British Prime Minister Neville Chamberlain expressing the hope that the direct contacts established at Munich might be helpful in expediting deliberations over "religious persecution," [45] Rublee telephoned Acting Secretary of State Sumner Welles to complain that the British "must be persuaded to take the matter more seriously." Two days later he was more blunt. He charged that the British had made "no real effort to open up their colonies or use their influence with the Dominions," that far from the Germans being reluctant to speak with him, "it is apparent that the British are reluctant to have me talk with Germany," that British attitudes were "wholly unsatisfactory." A week later he charged that the

British were "sullen" over the prospect that he might indeed get to Berlin.[46]

On October 25, Rublee relayed the distressing news to Washington that the British were actively discriminating between "Aryan" and "non-Aryan" refugees. Independent of the IGCR, the British were attempting to bring Sudetenland Aryans, who, it was alleged, were more assimilable than non-Aryans, to the dominions.[47] At the same time IGCR Chairman Lord Winterton introduced a resolution to expand the committee's authority to encompass Czech refugees, as well as Austrians and Germans. Rublee pointed out that for the first time in the committee's history the draft memorandum distinguished between Jews and non-Jews. After noting for Hull that the overwhelming majority of the persons with whom the committee was obligated to deal were Jews, Rublee added,

> If we were to begin to differentiate, even to the extent of indicating in a formal document that there are different categories based on religious and racial origins, encouragement would be given to the deplorable and growing tendency in many countries to discriminate against persons of Jewish faith, with the result that any problem of finding places of settlement for the great mass of involuntary emigrants would become insoluble and I should not be in a position to convince the governments participating in the IGCR to receive involuntary emigrants in greater numbers than are received by them at the present time.[48]

Hull agreed that this country could not countenance any discrimination, and the U.S., while agreeing to the expanded scope of the IGCR, succeeded in quashing Winterton's suggested distinctions among German refugees.

Still, the British continued to be troublesome through the rest of 1938. Their ambassador in Washington, Ronald Campbell, presented Welles with a démarche on November 17 stating that Great Britain was willing to give up a portion of its immigration quota for use by German refugees. This reallocating of unused quotas had been considered in the U.S. on numerous occasions. Just two days before, however, Roosevelt had stated publicly that there would be no increase in the German quota. Welles, highly critical of the British position on refugees anyhow, was convinced that the British offer had been made solely to discomfort the U.S. He reminded Campbell that quotas were granted by Congress under existing laws and were not the free property of nations to which they were assigned. When Welles informed Campbell that the offer would have to be communicated to the president and perhaps even made public, the insincerity of the gesture was revealed. In Welles's words, the ambassador "became very disturbed," and backed down, suggesting that the matter not go beyond Hull and Welles since the offer was "unofficial" (i.e., not sanctioned by the British cabinet).[49]

British diplomatic flu and a sequence of more pressing engagements derailed Myron Taylor's efforts through November to prod the IGCR to some kind of action. Then during the first two weeks of December rumors were circulated by the British Embassy in Berlin and the Foreign Office in London that the Nazis were about to send a "high ranking" diplomat to open negotiations with Rublee's assistant director, Robert Pell, in Brussels. When this trip never materialized, the British, who seemed to have more knowledge of what was going on in Berlin than anyone else (American Ambassador Wilson was recalled to the United States in November), attributed the failure to an illness which had bedridden the mysterious visitor.

Finally on the morning of December 15, 1938, the American Chargé d'Affairs in England notified Washington that Hjalmar Horace Greeley Schacht, president of the Reichsbank and minister without portfolio in the Nazi Cabinet, was to visit London, not Brussels, that day to discuss the Jewish problem with several British experts attached to the League Commission on Refugees. Almost as an afterthought, Rublee was invited to join with Montagu Norman of the Bank of England and Sir Frederick Leith-Ross, chief economic adviser to the British government. While American diplomats had abided by the procedures set out in August to open a single line of communication with the Nazis, the British had worked through Lord Edward Halifax to open separate contacts. Disgruntled by this breach of diplomatic etiquette, America's chargé in

Berlin, Paul Gilbert, also noted, "It will be recalled that my knowledge of the proposed Brussels meeting derives solely from the Foreign Office." [50]

Why should the British have deliberately engaged in such duplicity? The answer was obvious to Taylor, Hull, and Rublee. At Evian, Taylor had wrestled with the British to prevent the IGCR from becoming merely an adjunct of the League High Commission.[51] He thought he had won, but while the U.S. strove to avoid any connection with a League-instituted operation, the British tried just as hard to steer it toward a full-scale international commitment. Hull acknowledged as much when he informed Rublee on November 16, "We realize that the British are constantly pressing to have the Committee made an auxiliary of the League High Commission." British complaints about duplication of work and conflict over places of transit or refuge or finances were regarded as façades by the State Department, for there was never any doubt that the British considered the IGCR one more lure by which to embroil the U.S. in the affairs of the League of Nations.[52]

The British were also concerned that nothing, not even the IGCR, top-heavy as it was with bungling Americans, should be permitted to jeopardize the delicate policy of appeasement which had been established in dealing with Hitler in 1938. On November 14 from his offices in London, Rublee thought he detected a hopeful change in the British attitudes. Writing to Hull, he noted, "For the first time since my arrival in London, I feel that recognition is finding its way in high political quarters that the mistreatment by Germany of a half-million oppressed people is a definite obstacle to general appeasement in Europe." [53]

What had finally jarred the British from their lethargy, what had forced the recall of Ambassador Wilson, and what had spurred the Germans to such serious action as sending a man of Schacht's esteem to negotiate with representatives of the international committees was Kristallnacht, the systematic devastation of Jewish residences, businesses, and houses of worship in Germany on "Black Thursday," November 10, 1938.

Until that date the Nazi regime seemed committed only to a policy of humiliation and degradation of the Jews in Germany. The Nuremberg Laws of September 1935 had reduced Jews and *Mischlings* to the status of stateless subhumans. In March 1938 another law abolished the legal entity of Jewish community organizations dating back centuries and incorporated all such bodies under the state-supervised Reichsvertretung der Juden in Deutschland. Between July and September, Jews were barred from holding positions as physicians, lawyers, financial advisers, salesmen, realtors, and tourist guides. In the same period, 200 Jewish-owned banks were closed. All Jewish publishing firms were ordered to liquidate. All Jews were ordered to add the name "Israel" or "Sarah" to their given "Aryan" names. In such a context, the *Voelkischer Beobachter*, the official Nazi organ, could rightfully boast, "German citizens of the Jewish race existed once—they will never reappear!" [54]

It was at this time that the Polish government tried to outwit the Nazis by revoking the citizenship of its nationals who were living abroad. The Germans reacted swiftly by rounding up 18,000 Polish Jews before the deadline of October 29 and dumping them across the border into no man's land. Among these unfortunates were the parents of Herschel Grynszpan, a seventeen-year-old student in Paris. The boy received a letter from his parents, who had lived in Hanover for thirty years and who were now attempting to exist in a boxcar near Zbaszyn. Half-crazed with grief ("I could bear it no longer," he wrote, "I am not a dog"), Grynszpan purchased a cheap revolver, entered the German Embassy on Monday morning, November 7, and shot the legation's Third Secretary, Ernst vom Rath. Vom Rath died the next day.[55]

This assassination was the provocation the Nazis required to plunge Germany into a final bloodbath that would purge it of all its Jews. Beginning with coordinated assaults against the Jewish communities at 2 a.m. on November 10, the terror raged unchecked in Germany for several days. In a single night twelve synagogues in Berlin, five in Frankfurt, and eighteen in

Vienna were gutted by men working in the *Raeuberzivil* coats fancied by the Nazis. At Worms a synagogue dating back to 1034 was leveled. Many priceless objects, including a Torah scroll from the thirteenth century, a table and chair reputedly belonging to the Jewish sage Rashi, and imperial documents concerning the Jews and dating from the sixteenth century, were lost.[56] Nearly 600 synagogues were bombed, burned, or confiscated by the Nazis in "the Night of Breaking Glass." Police stood by or joined the looters. Some of the buildings later became dormitories for *Hitlerjugend*, sporting clubs, or itinerant house painters. Others became stables. Cemeteries throughout Germany were desecrated. The remaining business premises of Jews were demolished. Some 50,000 Jews were rounded up and thrown into concentration camps at Dachau and Buchenwald. In some places Jews were lynched. Suicides among Jews now increased to 1,000 a month.[57]

According to Joseph Goebbels's Propaganda Ministry, all of this was really the "spontaneous" reaction of the German people to the killing of vom Rath.[58] The actual responsibility for Kristallnacht, the Nazis argued with questionable logic, rested with the Jews themselves. On November 12, with the embers of destruction not yet cool, the German government issued a new set of decrees calling for the elimination of Jews from the economic life of Germany. Under these laws all Jewish businesses, industries, and real estate were to be liquidated and Aryanized by January 1, 1939. Jews whose business premises had been damaged were forced to make repairs at their own expense before the property was transferred. The Jewish community as a whole was required to pay an "atonement fine" of one billion marks ($400,000,000) to compensate the government for inconveniences sustained during Kristallnacht. Jews were barred from all trades and ordered to divest themselves of all stocks, bonds, securities, gold, platinum, and silver within the week. They were to be reimbursed in German marks for only 10 percent of their valuables. Through such measures as the institution of a new flight tax the Nazi regime was enriched by an additional $37,000,000 during November and December of 1938.[59]

Morse claims that Kristallnacht virtually shattered Rublee's hopes to initiate fruitful negotiations with the Germans, but Rublee expressed the opposite view in his final report to the President's Advisory Committee in February 1939.[60] Then Rublee reasoned that adverse German reaction to the excesses of Nazi terrorism during Kristallnacht, coupled with hostile world opinion, had forced Hitler's government to seek a diplomatic solution to its Jewish problem.[61]

Rublee's analysis, based on direct conversations with Hermann Goering, was supported in reports reaching Cordell Hull from the German underground by the end of 1938. However, it was not concern for the feelings of the international community which had prompted the Nazis to welcome negotiations with the previously ignored IGCR. Rather, it was simple economics. The German state, in the midst of a highly touted industrial Four Year Plan, was facing bankruptcy because international boycotts threatened to strangle production.[62] As an example, just that fall Goering had informed a group of gauleiters that I. G. Farben's foreign orders had been curtailed by 40 percent since the middle of 1938, and the outlook for 1939 was not much better.[63]

With Goering's concept of *Grossraumwirtschaft* or autarky jeopardized, the Germans needed cash, international exchange, to rectify their economic imbalances. One logical means to obtain it was by blackmailing the world community for the safety of German Jews. The extremely delicate work of officials in the *Reichswanderungsamt* (Office of Migration), described by Joachim Prinz as "benevolent till Kristallnacht," was made impossible by new demands for forced emigration.[64] *Das Schwarze Korps*, a semi-official military journal, preached "extermination with fire and sword" of all Jews who did not leave the Fatherland.[65] Even the generally mild-mannered von Ribbentrop thundered against "800,000 bad Jews" in Germany in an interview with France's Foreign Minister Georges Bonnet. Von Ribbentrop expressed the official policy of the government when he told Bonnet that these "Eastern," "poverty-stricken," "diseased" Jews, who had wormed their way into the heart of German life and become rich at the expense of indigenous Aryans had to go—now.[66]

There was another reason why the Nazis moved so swiftly against the Jews. This became evident when Schacht presented the German proposal to the Western diplomats assembled in London on December 15. The Reichsbank president noted that Jewish property yet outstanding in Germany amounted to six billion marks (roughly two and one-half billion dollars). The Nazis envisioned confiscation of this sum, but in a manner which was draped with an humanitarian façade.

Schacht claimed that Germany (including the Austrian and Sudeten regions) contained 600,000 persons who under the Nuremberg Laws could be considered to be Jews. Of these, 200,000 were aged people with no likelihood of leaving the country. Another 250,000 were women and children, and 150,-000 were employable males. Schacht's scheme called for the departure of 50,000 of these males each year for three years. Far from leaving penniless (Goering had said the week before that it was "absurd" to expect the Jews to leave without any assets), they would be assisted by a trust fund to be established from one-quarter of all Jewish property in Germany, roughly a billion and one-half marks. This fund, to be administered by one Jewish and two Aryan trustees, was to be raised by the Jewish community within a year in foreign exchange. From the proposed interest of 4 percent and annual amortization of 2 percent, the Jews would be permitted to buy German goods in Germany, which they could then take with them when leaving the country. As a condition to the plan, all persecution of the Jews would stop.[67]

Such a scheme was not really remarkable. Practically the same idea had been broached by the Reich Ministry of Economics to the Jewish Agency in Palestine three years earlier. The so-called Haavara (Transfer) System which was roundly condemned as "blackmail" by Wise, was actually implemented to permit 20,000 German-Jewish refugees desiring to go to Palestine to contract for the purchase of German goods valued at 130,000,000 marks and their eventual transport to Palestine.

Payment for this property came from blocked accounts in Germany. And although individuals lost as much as 50 percent of their assets, they at least, it was rationalized, came out of Germany with something.[68]

Myron Taylor had suggested to Hull on August 15, 1938 that the German government might be receptive to a broader application of the Haavara System. Hull's reply absolutely rejected any such scheme, stating that the Haavara plan had been limited to a small number of emigrants and that a broader application of the scheme would provide Germany with an artificial trade lever in international affairs. Hull said, "We cannot consider extension of that system to this country or look with favor on its extension to other countries." [69]

Hull disapproved in October of a Rublee-sponsored measure that would have financed emigration from Germany with proceeds derived from an increase of German exports, if international boycotts against German products were lifted. It was so similar to Schachts's proposal of December 15 that FDR referred to both as the Rublee Plan.[70] Rublee's suggestion differed from that of the German in several ways. Rublee envisioned a complete restoration of German trade with countries which formerly absorbed that nation's export specialties. Half of the proceeds derived from this increase, over the present "base level" of exports, would be applied to assisting refugees. As a start toward facilitating the immediate departure of 50,000 non-Aryans, the German government was to cease all persecution and was to be asked to contribute fifty million pounds sterling from its foreign exchange to bonds payable in dollars. The Germans would receive an average annual dividend of five reichsmarks for each dollar in bonds thus issued, although the interest rate would fluctuate depending upon the wealth of the emigrant. Rublee emphasized that the German government could readily turn a 100 percent profit on these bonds within a few years.[71]

Hull replied that such a plan would place the entire obligation for the refugees on the world's commercial markets, that it could create a new competition by German products, and that it could even rebound against the Jews in the form of overt anti-Semitism if the Jews were then blamed for creating unfair trade advantages for the Germans.[72] He repeatedly affirmed his preference for some plan which would enable emigrants to take free exchange out of Germany (an idea which he conceded was impractical because of the critical situation of German finances at the end of 1938), or which would permit the refugee to take out convertible marks (*sperrmarks*), which could then be used to purchase non-German goods through free foreign exchange. As a last resort Hull even contemplated the funding of a Bank of International Settlement, which might grant loans to emigrants. But even this would depend upon the willingness of the Germans to contribute to the assets of such an institution.[73]

The Americans, having considered and rejected the above possibilities, should not have been stunned by Schacht's proposal, and yet the official reaction was one of indignation. Ambassador Taylor called the offer blackmail, "asking the world to pay a ransom for the release of hostages in Germany and barter human misery for increased exports." [74] Sumner Welles blasted this unsubtle return to medieval diplomacy: "No one who has been consulted believes that it would be possible to raise the sum mentioned or even an appreciable part of it under the terms outlined. The plan is generally considered as asking the world to pay a ransom for the release of hostages in Germany." [75]

Apart from such visceral reactions to the thought of blackmail or ransom, Americans had other basic objections to the German plan. In an effort to convince the democracies that the problem would not be too taxing, Schacht had spoken of the necessity of finding refuges for 150,000 German males. He had said nothing about their 300,000 dependents. Moreover, in promising that persecution of the remaining Jews would cease, he offered no guarantees, nor did he concede that expulsion of the Jews, together with confiscation of their property, constituted one form of persecution.

Nevertheless, at the insistence of the British, the Schacht Plan was not dismissed outright. Rather than viewing it as the Nazis' final bid, the British contended that it should be considered a basis for future negotiations. Indeed, Schacht left this impression when he finally accorded Rublee his long-awaited invitation to visit Berlin in January 1939, a month before the third scheduled plenary session of the IGCR in London.

To expedite Rublee's mission, the British, who had procrastinated for so long, startled the Americans on December 16, 1938 by proposing the establishment of two additional committees. The first, to be headed by Rublee, was to include financial experts from the governments of the United States, Great Britain, France, the Netherlands, and Sweden. The other was to consist of prominent Jews from these and other major receiving nations, as well as "churchmen interested in non-Aryans." [76]

Both committees died aborning: the first when Welles (acting for Hull who had gone off to Lima for the hemispheric conference) protested that there was no qualified banker in the employ of the government and that a qualified banker would not be aware of the intricacies of government policy; the second when Jewish leaders in London and Paris categorically opposed the creation of any committee which might lend an air of credulity to the canard that there was such a thing as an international Jewish Sanhedrin or conspiracy.[77]

The best counter-proposal that Rublee could take when he and Pell journeyed to Berlin was a plan which had originated with Welles on December 21. In this scheme a central financial organization was to be established in London with an initial funding of $50,000,000, some of which the Nazi government would contribute voluntarily. The function of this agency, subordinated to the IGCR, was to sponsor specific settlement projects for German refugees. Welles believed that as many as 100,000 persons could be assisted through loans totaling as much as $2,500 a family. The plan possessed several advantages over any previously discussed. The officers of the bank would be international financiers instead of Nazi "trustees." The bank would be self-sustaining because all expenditures would be in the form of loans rather than outright grants like those which had depleted the resources of voluntary relief organizations. The Germans would gain no economic advantage through a rise in exports. Yet Germany would inevitably profit through the departure of what it considered a racially undesirable element.[78]

Rublee finally arrived in Berlin on January 10, 1939, more than four months after his mission had been chartered. He may well have wished that he had never left London. After two days of unproductive talks the Germans broke off negotiations to study the "modifications" made in the Schacht Plan by Welles. When discussions resumed on January 21, Rublee was dumbfounded by the Germans' absolute rejection of Welles's loan plan. The next day, discussions were postponed once more, and Rublee learned only later that Schacht, who was considered unreliable and defeatist by the Nazi elite, had been removed from his position as Reichsbank president.

Rublee continued to press the negotiations with Goering and Schacht's successor, Helmut Wohlthat of the Economics Ministry. In February he wrested several concessions from the Germans: (1) that Jews would reenter the various trades until they could emigrate from Germany; (2) that Jews would obtain a moderate form of relief from the all-encompassing *Fluchsteuer* or flight tax (the Germans were deliberately vague about this pledge and continued to confiscate jewelry, precious metals, and works of art); (3) that the Germans would ease up on the issuance of bogus visas to Jews for South American countries, a practice which had resulted in the suspension of all immigration in some Latin states; (4) that the Germans would expect no compensation or aid for their exports once the orderly emigration of Jews began; and (5) that an international organization like the one proposed by Welles would be established, but without any German assistance.[79]

From a current standpoint it is impossible to assess the reasons for this policy change by the German government. Perhaps the Nazis felt that by cooperating with the democracies they might puncture the economic boycotts imposed upon them. Perhaps they thought that they would be well off in getting rid of the Jews at any cost. Or perhaps the Nazis merely derived childish delight in tantalizing the West, for German actions toward refugees through the spring and summer months of 1939 gave no indication of easing the persecution, nor of the ending of the confiscation policy.

On February 12, Rublee delivered his final report to the IGCR plenary body in London. In his eyes the refugee outlook was now "encouraging." He noted all that had been done by the committee in the past six months and recommended that the IGCR continue to explore all possible settlements for involuntary emigrants and that it establish the international corporation so necessary to the financing of this emigration. Both ideas were accepted. Rublee then resigned, feeling that his task had thus been completed after six months in office.[80] His place as director was taken by Herbert Emerson, League Commissioner on Refugees from Germany since September 1938 and League Commissioner on all refugee questions since the abolition of the Nansen Office in December. Finally the various relief committees had come under the direction of one man.

Until Hitler's march on Poland in September 1939 the IGCR seemed unable to achieve any of its stated purposes. While Executive Director Robert Pell tried to convince Wohlthat that extensive surveys were being undertaken and that new settlements might shortly be opened in Australia, Canada, Alaska, Finland, Sweden, Tanganyika, the Guianas, the Philippines, or the Dominican Republic, the British Foreign and Colonial offices continued to negate the committee's efforts.[81] Ignoring the fact that any unilateral action taken by His Majesty's Government would affect the entire refugee problem, the British jealously regarded any discussion of the colonies as an invasion of a purely imperial question.[82] Then on May 17, 1939 the British government dealt a deathblow to Zionist hopes for Palestine by issuing a White Paper which restricted total Jewish immigration over the next five years to 75,000 persons, dependent upon "the economic absorptive capacity" of Palestine.[83]

Leaders in the World Zionist Organization and the Zionist

Organization of America had worked desperately through the last months of 1938 and into 1939 to prevent the enactment of just such a policy.[84] Not only had they failed, but their efforts had antagonized the British. Disgusted with the Jews, Emerson told Pell, "The trouble in this whole refugee affair was the trouble of the Jews and most European people. There was always some other scheme in the background for which they were prepared to sacrifice schemes which were already in hand." [85] Thus Emerson and Winterton refused to be prodded by another Jewish delegation from Germany which begged the committee for a scrap of paper or anything to show the Nazis as proof of the democracies' intention to provide refuge for the Jews. Not even the threat of a second and more disastrous Kristallnacht could move the IGCR leaders.[86]

This diplomatic paralysis also partially accounts for the delay in funding the international corporation to assist refugees. Neither the British nor the American governments felt any direct responsibility to contribute to the corporation.[87] As a result, when the Co-Ordinating Foundation was chartered on July 20 at the fourth plenary meeting of the IGCR in London, its total assets came to £200,000. This sum was a mere 2 percent of the $50,000,000 fund which Welles had recommended in December. More significantly, the operating funds were drawn almost exclusively from a voluntary pledge of $1,000,000 given by Paul Baerwald, chairman of the Joint Distribution Committee, who was also a member of the board of directors of the foundation. In short, American Jews contributed the entire budget to what had been established as an international agency.[88]

By this time, however, it hardly mattered what the IGCR stood for. On June 8, 1939, Roosevelt, the man without whose active support the committee could not hope to succeed, expressed dismay over the apparently insoluble problem of refugee placement. In a communiqué to Taylor he said:

> It must reluctantly be admitted that this Government's efforts to stimulate concrete action by other Governments to meet the problem have been met at best by a lukewarm attitude. In view of the attitude of other Governments, and the

reluctance which may have been shown to contribute toward the Committee's expenses during its first year, it is apparent that few Governments are willing to contribute on the present basis to the Committee's support for another year.[89]

Roosevelt's solution, coming one month before the Co-Ordinating Foundation was chartered and two months before the outbreak of World War II, was the virtual abolition of the IGCR. Such functions as the committee deemed crucial, for instance, the surveys then being conducted by Isaiah Bowman and Owen Lattimore of the Johns Hopkins Institute for Pacific Relations, should be transferred to the League of Nations' Office on Refugees. The IGCR should maintain only a skeletal staff in London, paid from voluntary contributions "as member governments might consider appropriate." It would be most appropriate, Roosevelt felt, if the IGCR was to continue in existence, "though in an inactive form." [90]

Roosevelt was to reverse himself again in October when in a special conference at the White House he called for "redoubled vigor" on the part of Emerson, Winterton, and the IGCR to assist innocent victims of the European war.[91] By that time, however, it was too late. British delegates pleaded an insufficiency of funds because of war expenditures.[92] Paul van Zeeland, the former Belgian premier who had assumed the post of executive president of the Co-Ordinating Foundation, conceded that the activities of the organization had been "reduced to almost nothing" and that any program of refugee relief would have to wait until "the peace conference." [93] Even Herbert Emerson had given up hope by this time. He told Ambassador John Winant that the war had forced the suspension of both the committee's and league's activities on behalf of refugees. His position as IGCR director henceforth was "purely honorary," and the committee maintained an office in London with the skeletal force and limited budget Roosevelt had recommended earlier.[94]

A frustrated Roosevelt called for the deactivization of the IGCR during the last summer of peace in Europe precisely at the moment when Emerson was telling the committee that more than 500,000 persons needed immediate assistance for emigration. Of these, 167,000 were confessional Jews drawn from pre-Hitler Germany, 42,000 were confessional Jews from Austria, 127,000 were non-Aryan Christians (labeled Jews by the Nuremberg Laws) from Greater Germany, 140,000 were Jews in European countries of temporary refuge, and 16,000 (mostly Jews) were persons in non-European countries of temporary refuge.[95]

The overwhelming preponderance of refugees in need of immediate aid on the eve of World War II, then, were Jews.[96] They could hardly have lamented the passing of an international committee which had never truly addressed itself to their special problem. After all the diplomatic motion emanating from Washington, Evian, London, and Berlin, the doomed Jews of Europe would probably have agreed with Adolf Hitler, who, seething with sarcasm, said on January 30, 1939: "It is a shameful example to observe today how the entire democratic world dissolves in tears of pity, but then, in spite of its obvious duty to help, closes its heart to the poor, tortured people." [97]

4. The Wagner Bill

T‍*he failure of* the United States to effect any major breakthrough in the placement of Jewish refugees at the international level before the war was hardly remarkable in view
of the unwillingness of this nation to accept more than its "fair
share" of these people. Other receiver states could not be
faulted for declining to strain their own resources when they
witnessed the unhelpful attitudes of the American government.

America's near-universal condemnation of Nazi brutality
as a result of Kristallnacht gave hope that this country might
bend its immigration laws to aid in the refugee crisis. Assistant
Secretary of State Henry Messersmith accurately assessed
America's indignation when he wrote Hull on November 14,
1938 that "unless we take some action in the face of the events
in Germany of the last few days, we shall be much behind our
public opinion in this country.[1] Republican leaders like Herbert
Hoover, Alfred Landon, Thomas Dewey, and Gerald Nye chas-
tised the Nazis, as distinct from the German people, for the
bloodiest pogrom in history.[2] They were joined by Democrats
Al Smith (who said "Democracy died in Germany on the
dustheap of the German Constitution")[3] and Interior Secretary Harold Ickes, who nearly precipitated an international
incident when he lambasted Hitler as "a brutal dictator"
at a Hanukkah banquet in Cleveland on November 18.[4] Protests were issued by John L. Lewis of the CIO and William
Green of the AFL, by Sinclair Lewis, Harry Emerson Fosdick,
Henry Sloane Coffin of the Union Theological Seminary,
Archbishop Michael Curley, of Baltimore, Episcopal Bishop
William T. Manning, Bishop Edwin Hughes of the Meth-

odist Episcopal Church, Archbishop John S. Mitty of San Francisco, and Bishop John Mark Cannon of Cleveland. On November 15, 1938, the *New Yorker Staats-Zeitung*, the foremost German-language daily in the U.S., hitherto silent about the persecution of the Jews in Germany, editorialized: "In the name of our dear ones do we protest against the desecration of the German name through fanatics in the ranks of the party in power who are trying to drag a great people into the mire of their degradation." [5] Also, the national executive of the American Legion, meeting in Indianapolis, issued a statement deploring "the unconscionable policies now being pursued by the German Government with respect to racial and religious minorities." [6]

For some, however, verbal protest was not enough. The National Conference of Christians and Jews set aside November 20 and 21 as days of prayer, mass meeting, and demonstration. The reverend Ralph W. Sockman of New York warned, "Christianity must save the Jews if it is to save itself." William Randolph Hearst, once an admirer of Hitler, recalled an earlier day when he had pressed for the severance of commercial relations with Tsarist Russia as a result of its abuse of Jews. Passive sympathy was not enough, argued Hearst. "We Americans must begin the great work, because we are free to speak. We are free to act." Senator William King of Utah demanded action—immediate severance of diplomatic relations with Germany—and the State Department was bombarded with letters urging this, or, as an alternative, economic sanctions against Germany.[7]

But the most amazing statement of all came from Henry Ford. The intractable squire of River Rouge, once the foremost purveyor of anti-Semitic literature in this country through his Dearborn *Independent*, and presently the most implacable foe of organized labor, issued a statement shortly after Kristallnacht which showed genuine sympathy for the oppressed Jews. Ford even went so far as to advocate bringing these people to the United States. The statement read:

> I believe that the United States cannot fail at this time to maintain its traditional role as a haven for the oppressed. I am convinced not only that this country could absorb many of the

victims of oppression who must find a refuge outside of their native lands, but that as many of them as could be admitted under our selective quota system would constitute a real asset to our country.

My acceptance of a medal from the German people does not, as some people seem to think, involve any sympathy on my part with Nazism. Those who have known me for many years realize that anything that breeds hate is repulsive to me.

I am confident that the time is near when there will be so many jobs available in this country that the entrance of a few thousand Jews, or other immigrants, will be negligible.

I believe that the return-to-the-land movement is one of the ultimate solutions of our economic problems and in this movement of the Jews of the Old World can play a significant part. I am wholly sympathetic with the movement to give the oppressed Jew an opportunity to rebuild his life in this country, and I myself will do everything possible toward that end.[8]

Ford's words reflected the initial American reaction to Kristallnacht. In December 1938 the American Institute of Public Opinion found that 94 percent of those polled disapproved of the Nazis' treatment of the Jews. At the same time an increasing proportion of Americans (56 percent in October; 61 percent in December; 66 percent in April 1939) favored some form of boycott against German products. By April of 1939, 78 percent of those polled approved a proposed 25 percent penalty tax on German imports.[9] Understating the situation somewhat, Key Pittman, chairman of the Senate Foreign Relations Committee, noted, "The people of the United States do not like the Government of Germany." [10]

Roosevelt reacted to Kristallnacht by issuing a typically dramatic statement. In his 500th press conference, held at the Washington airport on November 15, he announced that he was recalling Ambassador Hugh Wilson from Berlin. Roosevelt told reporters:

The news of the past few days from Germany has deeply shocked public opinion in the United States. Such news from any part of the world would inevitably produce a similar profound reaction among American people in every part of the nation.

I myself could scarcely believe that such things could occur in a twentieth century civilization.

> With a view to gaining a first-hand picture of the current situation in Germany, I asked the Secretary of State to order our Ambassador in Berlin to return at once for report and consultation.[11]

Asked if he had given any thought to a possible mass transfer of Jews from Germany as a consequence of Kristallnacht, Roosevelt hedged, saying first, "I have given a great deal of thought to it," then added, "the time is not ripe for that." Asked if he might recommend the relaxation of our immigration restrictions to permit the entry of Jewish refugees, FDR, ever cognizant of the restrictionist spirit of the Congress, answered, "That is not in contemplation; we have the quota system." [12]

Despite the president's apparent coolness to any alteration of that quota system, liberal journals repeatedly expressed hope that existing immigration laws might be modified along lines proposed by Samuel Dickstein, chairman of the House Immigration and Naturalization Committee. Such a plan would have suspended quota allotments during the emergency and established a reservoir of approximately 100,000 visas, drawn from those nations which were not using their annual quotas. *Commonweal, The Nation,* and *The New Republic*[13] were among several journals which endorsed the idea of emergency immigration allotments to help the German refugees. *The New Republic* was especially outspoken in support of such a scheme. An editorial on November 30 stated: "One would think that we might let in the entire 500,000 Jewish population of Germany in a single year without serious dislocation. It would be equivalent to an increase of about four-tenths of one percent in our existing population." [14]

Roosevelt dashed any hope that the government might be receptive to the idea of redistribution of unused quotas in his next press conference on November 18. After a verbal tilt with one reporter over whether Wilson had been "summoned" home, the president announced that he planned to send Congress no recommendations for change in existing immigration laws. The best he could offer the refugees ("not all Jews by any means," said Roosevelt) was an extension of visitors' permits by six months. Some 15,000 German nationals in the country would not be forced to return home. Labor Secretary Frances Perkins, who just the previous day convinced him that there was no need to alter the laws, assured Roosevelt that additional extensions could be tacked on indefinitely for those visitors whose lives might be imperiled by returning to Germany.[15] Roosevelt acknowledged that few, if any, additional refugees would profit by this idea, since Germany would not issue visitors' visas to non-Aryans. FDR also conceded that to qualify as a full-fledged immigrant, that is, to qualify for ultimate naturalization, visitors would have to return to their native countries and undergo existing quota processing from the beginning.[16]

Like Roosevelt's call to Evian, the president's announcement concerning visitors made good news copy for several days. Henceforth, however, all official efforts on behalf of the Jewish refugees would be addressed to, and would come at the expense of, other nations. Shortly after Kristallnacht, Henry Morgenthau began to badger Roosevelt with letters and reports about the possibility of settlement of great numbers of refugees in South and Central America, particularly in Costa Rica.[17] Apparently undaunted by repeated anti-Jewish expressions of the Latin American governments, Cordell Hull cabled American missions in that region on November 22 to seek further clarification from the governments on the question of accepting additional refugees. In making such overtures the secretary instructed American diplomats to point out what this nation was doing already within existing laws and to emphasize once more that no state would be expected to take more refugees than its absorptive capacity would allow. The responses, received within a week, indicated no retreat on the part of the Latins from their firm restrictionist positions. Only Peru, the Dominican Republic, and Haiti seemed truly interested in receiving Jews. The other replies ranged from Mexico's "wait and see," to Uruguay's "agriculturists only," to Colombia's "impossible to accept any more Jews," to Costa Rica's "considerable anti-Semitic feeling in this country." The Venezuelan government did not even bother to respond officially to the American query.[18]

Hull sent Roosevelt a comprehensive report on potential refugee havens around the world on November 28. This document bleakly outlined the difficulties which existed in such tropical regions as Tanganyika, Rhodesia, Nyasaland, Madagascar, and New Caledonia. As for the Latin states, Hull noted, "Only Peru seems to be willing to follow U.S. pressure." [19]

Jews found little to commend in the actions of the Latin American nations in the next six months. As Germany's Jews stampeded under the terror of new Nazi persecutions in the closing days of 1938, corrupt Gestapo officials and Latin consuls in Berlin collaborated in a lucrative trade of supplying them with inadequate or invalid passports. Jews bribed German peasants to obtain certificates which qualified them for admission to South American countries as legitimate farmers. They purchased property in the unexplored reaches of Brazil to qualify as immigrants with land holdings. Such tactics, however, often proved fruitless. The Latin governments changed regulations even as the refugees departed from Germany. Some nations suspended all immigration, and overcrowded vessels of the Hamburg-American Line cruised the Caribbean in search of port.[20]

On December 7, 1938, with the Rublee negotiations foundering (Schacht had not yet been to London), with the Latin states obstinate, and with no other reasonable alternative for settlement of the refugees in the offing, Roosevelt turned in desperation to the dictator of Italy.[21] He instructed Ambassador William Phillips in Rome to deliver a personal note outlining a startling solution to the problem to "my dear Signor Mussolini." After applauding Mussolini's "decisive action" at Munich, which allegedly had preserved peace in Europe, Roosevelt suggested that he might also resolve the Jewish question by opening the southwestern section of Ethiopia, known as the Plateau, to colonization by German refugees. Italy would profit through the exploitation of this vast region by a white colonial population. Germany, too, would profit because the emigrants would bring supplies, clothing, tools, and other items indispensable for their resettlement, along with German marks. The U.S. would even assume a share in the cost of the settlement.[22]

One can only imagine the hilarity that such a scheme must have provoked in Rome and Berlin.[23] For three years the American government had firmly aligned itself on the side of states which had censured Mussolini's imperial ventures. The U.S., at Roosevelt's urging, had proclaimed a moral embargo against Italy when the fascists invaded the kingdom of Haile Selassie in 1935. Two years later, when Mussolini intervened in Spain to assist Generalissimo Francisco Franco, the U.S. extended its embargo of arms and oil shipments to Italy. Yet here in December 1938 FDR was asking Mussolini's permission to capitalize on that same Italian aggression while acquiescing in the financial extortion so often condemned by State Department officials that fall.

Before Phillips could secure an audience with Mussolini, Schacht and Rublee entered into serious negotiations, and Welles subsequently canceled Phillips's instructions in a communiqué dated December 30.[24] It was too late, however, for the proposal afforded Mussolini an opportunity to chastise "the large democracies" (the United States, Soviet Union, Brazil) for their failure to accept greater numbers of Jews.[25] The scheme also was rebuked by the World Jewish Congress, which refused to have anything to do with an anti-Semite government such as the Italians.[26]

With this last extreme possibility eliminated, the question recurs of why Roosevelt did not champion some drastic change in America's immigration laws at this point. The answer lies in FDR's complex personality, which blended political pragmatism and human compassion. Ever sensitive to public opinion, he recognized that Americans' condemnation of Nazi persecution of Jews simply was not matched by their corresponding concern for its victims. With his personal popularity[27] already at an all-time low, Roosevelt could only have suffered politically from directing such a crusade.[28] He faced a hostile Seventy-sixth Congress, one charged with nativist and neo-fascist sentiment and filled with many senators whom he had unsuccessfully tried to purge that November. Even his closest Jewish advisers, Samuel Rosenman and Bernard Baruch, cautioned against increasing quotas for German refugees for fear of creating "a Jewish problem" in the United States.[29] Apparently for these reasons the president abdicated his leadership role in the refugee question to Congress. In the future those congressmen calling for immigration reform could count on only whispers of support from the White House.

Among the many bills designed to give relief to Jewish refugees which were considered by Congress in the winter of 1938–1939, the most celebrated was the Wagner-Rogers Bill. It was introduced in the Senate on February 9, 1939 by New York's Robert Wagner and in the House five days later by Edith Nourse Rogers of Massachusetts. The measure called for the admission of 20,000 German refugee children under age fourteen on a nonquota basis over the next two years.

The choice of terms (German refugee children instead of Jewish refugee children) was deliberate because the bill's sponsors did not want to provoke anti-Semites by calling for special exemptions solely for Jewish children. For this reason a special Non-Sectarian Committee for German Refugee Children was established. To underscore the nonsectarian nature of the legislation, the committee arranged to have only a handful of Jews appear before the various congressional hearings conducted on the bill in April and May of 1939. When Clarence Pickett, executive secretary of the American Friends Service Committee and chairman of the Non-Sectarian Committee, appeared before the congressional committees to outline placement procedures, he emphasized that the proposals dealt with "children of all faiths." Wagner also testified that he never would have authored the legislation if he had thought that it might suggest that selection be made on the basis of race or religion rather than need.[30]

There was little doubt in anyone's mind, however, that the children in need of rescue in Germany were Jewish and that the bill directly concerned their plight. The idea of admitting special numbers of German children was inspired by the success of the German-Jewish Children's Aid Committee. From April 6, 1934, when Max Kohler first broached the idea to Frances Perkins, to January 1939, 397 Jewish children had been resettled in the United States under special nonquota arrangements worked out with the Department of Naturalization and Immigration.[31] Social workers' evaluations of their adjustment to this country had been so favorable that, after Kristallnacht, suggestions for an expanded program had been made by playwright Sam Spewack to Lessing Rosenwald of the American Jewish Committee[32] and by James McDonald to the President's Advisory Committee.[33] There is even some evidence that Secretary of Labor Perkins surreptitiously lent her support to the idea.[34]

There were other connections between the Wagner Bill and the Jews of Germany. Wagner could argue that there were 75,000 "non-Aryan" children in Germany in 1939, but in the context in which such language was understood, the term "non-Aryan" was generally conceded to mean Jewish.[35] More specifically, the American Jewish Committee estimated that there were 20,500 children in Germany between the ages of six and fourteen whose parents could be considered observant or practicing Jews.[36] This figure was strikingly similar to the number of immigrants envisioned in the Wagner Bill. While Wagner labored hard to present the measure as a truly nonsectarian proposition, his efforts were unintentionally undermined by witnesses before the congressional committees who lapsed into the habit of speaking only of the sufferings of "Jewish children."[37]

In a sense the history of the Wagner Bill was symptomatic of the anti-alien, anti-Jewish sentiments which helped to shape American immigration policy in this era. Proponents of the measure were buoyed by the thousands of supporting letters which poured into Washington from every state. Endorsements came from Herbert Hoover, Albert Einstein, Robert Hutchins, Norman Thomas, Samuel Cavert of the Federal Council of the Churches of Christ in America, the American Unitarian Association, the National YMCA, the Methodist Federation for Social

Service, the executive of the Boy Scouts of America, the faculties of Columbia, Wellesley, Harvard, and Los Angeles City College.[38] Both the AFL and the CIO went on record as approving passage.[39] Wagner worked vigorously to read into the record the dozens of newspaper editorials from the *Boise Statesman,* the *Christian Science Monitor,* the *New York Herald-Tribune,* the *New York Times,* the *Boston Herald,* the *Washington Post,* the *Cincinnati Enquirer,* the *New Orleans Times-Picayune,* among others, all in support of his bill.[40] And yet the measure failed.

The bill failed in part because its opponents—John Trevor's American Coalition, Francis Kinnicutt's Allied Patriotic Societies, the Junior Order of American Mechanics, the American Legion, Senator Reynolds—were old hands at clouding immigration issues with procedural objections, sham humanitarianism, or outright bigotry. Representative Charles Kramer of California, no great friend of refugees himself, noted the ubiquity of these self-proclaimed patriots whenever Congress debated immigration legislation and charged that they "came out of their holes to lobby" when such bills were under consideration.[41] Like the mythological dragon's teeth, these nativists would throw up new obstacles just as Wagner, Pickett, and their colleagues struck down the old ones.

The principal objection of the restrictionists, including those who swamped Wagner with hate mail demanding that he withdraw his bill in favor of one introduced by Reynolds at the same time which would have suspended immigration indefinitely, was that the Wagner Bill was designed to help only the Jews.[42] Assisting the Jews, allegedly notorious "mental defectives,"[43] a clannish people who hired only their kinsmen,[44] and also the people who "originally financed Hitler,"[45] was not merely illogical, the opponents said, but also unfair to the thousands of persecuted Spanish children who had been forced to flee from France and had no special interest group agitating for their admission to the United States.

While the restrictionists lamented for the Spanish refugees, they also charged that the bill could serve as a precedent for "similar unscientific and favored-nation legislation in response to the pressure of foreign nationalistic or racial groups, rather than in accordance with the needs and desires of the American people." [46] Eventually the U.S., which according to James Wilmeth of the Junior Order of American Mechanics already contained 21 percent of the "alien population of the earth," [47] might be obligated to admit "many millions" from Europe and from Asia, persons imbued with "a heritage of hate," who would then drown American liberty in communism or Nazism.[48] A circular issued by Trevor's American Coalition warned that 20,000 children, mating within or without the original group and with each union resulting in four children who in turn became parents, could provide 640,000 offspring within five generations, truly an ominous subversive bloc.[49] Margaret Hopkins Worrell, national legislative chairman of the Ladies of the Grand Army of the Republic, went so far as to claim that she did not believe it possible to "Americanize" any immigrant over age four.[50]

Spokesmen for the bill patiently refuted each of these arguments. Clarence Pickett pointed out that there was no special urgency in the Spanish refugee situation because: (1) the civil war was ending and France "would not stand for the torture of children"; (2) Spanish children in France were being well cared for by French authorities until such time as they desired to return to Spain; and (3) Mexico had volunteered to take at least 20,000 Spanish refugee children.[51] As for shattering the dike of American immigration laws, Wilbur LaRoe, a well-known Washington attorney who served as legal counsel for the Non-Sectarian Committee, and Avra Warren of the Immigration Service both had testified that the figure of 20,000 children was "solely a maximum number." [52] And far from bringing in a haphazard selection of social undesirables, the Wagner Bill would offer this country its first intelligently planned immigration. Pickett stressed repeatedly that social workers would screen applicants in Germany and recommend that only the physically and mentally fit, those who seemed "good material for American citizenship," be admitted. The final safeguard against any child saboteur, Pickett pointed out, would still lie in the veto enjoyed by the American consul.[53]

94

If the entry of 20,000 children would not unleash a tidal wave of immigration, might it not, at least, have created an endless trickle? The restrictionists, dubbed by Utah's Senator King as "200 percent Americans," raised the humanitarian objection of separating children from their parents. In May 1939, Ohio's Republican Senator Robert A. Taft, a budding candidate for the Republican presidential nomination in 1940, told the Non-Sectarian Committee that such a separation might impose hardships greater than would result if the children remained with their parents.[54]

To preclude the possibility that those parents might one day use sentimental arguments in attempts to be reunited with their children, several congressmen demanded that specific requirements for adoption be written into the proposed bill. Others wanted Pickett's selection procedure clearly delineated in the legislation. Still others asked for written guarantees that the children would never become public charges. Quite understandably, then, did Monte Lemann, once a member of Hoover's Wickersham Committee and now a proponent of the bill, exclaim angrily that no bill ever written had fulfilled all the reservations of Congress.[55]

It is difficult to imagine how any non-Aryan child could have profited by remaining in Germany, a land about which author Quentin Reynolds had warned that the complete pogrom was not very far away.[56] As for guarantees from parents that they would not use their children as ploys by which to enter the U.S., Pickett had testified that the Non-Sectarian Committee would accept only children whose families were already ruptured, a common circumstance in Nazi Germany at the time. Another witness on behalf of the bill, Mrs. Benjamin Joffe of the Michigan Federation of Women's Clubs, emphasized that many desperate parents were willing to give up their children to save them.[57]

As for financial guarantees that the children would not become public charges upon entry into this country, Pickett pointed out that the Department of Labor, where questions of social and economic absorption were ultimately determined, was satisfied that they would not pose a relief problem.[58] According to Pickett and Non-Sectarian Committee Treasurer Newbold Morris, more than $250,000 had been pledged voluntarily to underwrite the costs of the operation. LaRoe repeatedly affirmed that "not a single child will be brought into this country under this bill, for whom satisfactory assurances as to its support have not been given in advance." [59]

The Non-Sectarian Committee also supplied guarantees of placement in good American homes where the children would be taught democratic ideals. LaRoe read letters from Protestants who volunteered to take the children. Morris mentioned 1,500 unsolicited offers of foster homes in forty-six states. Even Mrs. Calvin Coolidge agreed to sponsor twenty-five of these children.[60]

Such statements seemed merely to provoke the restrictionists, who painted touching images of millions of native American children wandering the streets, clothed in rags, diseased, starving, without any hope of adoption. Taft noted, for example, "20,000 American children could profit if such nice homes were available." [61] Trevor summed up this attitude when he ended his testimony with the bromide, "Charity begins at home!" [62]

Few, if any, opponents of the bill had carefully studied the existing child care situation in this country. James Wilmeth, although proud of the record of his Junior Order of American Mechanics in maintaining 206 orphanages, was unable to say whether current demand for adoptions outstripped the available supply of children. Francis Kinnicutt could do no better. Queried by Representative Anton Maciejewski (D.-Ill.) about exactly what the Allied Patriotic Societies did for American children, Kinnicutt stammered, "That is not exactly our function. Our function is in reference to legislation of this kind which affects our whole system." [63] Even Representative Charles Kramer, who expressed the fear that 20,000 refugee children might "be blown" into California by the dust storms of Kansas, admitted that no one had shown where those thousands of suffering American children were.[64]

Substantial evidence was available that the country was not only willing but able to accommodate the 20,000 children.

Katherine Lenroot, chief of the Children's Bureau of the Department of Labor, certified that there were approximately 250,000 children in charitable institutions and foster homes in the spring of 1939. An additional 20,000 would be an increase of 4 to 8 percent, which she stated the welfare agencies in the U.S. could easily handle. Catholic Bishop Maurice Sheehy also testified that there was no "surplus" in Catholic orphanages and that children were being adopted as rapidly as they could be obtained. Paul Beissler, president of the Child Welfare League of America, estimated that the demand for children was so great that there already were twelve applicants for every child in an American institution. Jacob Kepecs, executive director of the Jewish Children's Bureau, estimated that the ratio was at least twenty applicants for every child.[65]

In answer to the argument that the entry of the 20,000 might aggravate an already critical unemployment situation among America's youth, Gertrude Zimand of the National Child Labor Committee presented data showing that because of their differing ages, the children's entry into the labor market would be staggered over the fifteen year period between 1943 and 1958. Perhaps 1,500 children would reach employable age each year—an addition of one to every 4,500 unemployed youth in the nation in 1939.[66]

In their eagerness, proponents of the Wagner Bill used every conceivable argument to secure its passage. Southerners like Douglas Carroll, dean of the School of Commerce of the University of North Carolina, Homer Rainey, president of the University of Texas, Samuel C. Mitchell, professor of social history at the University of Richmond, and dirt farmer Hugh McRae from Wilmington, North Carolina, all testified that the South had been "shortchanged" in previous waves of immigration and that the region could be rejuvenated by an influx of industrious young people. Professional social workers like Cheney Jones, a member of the executive committee of the National Conference of Social Work and a foster father for 550 New England children, Paul Beissler, and Gaynell Hawkins, president of the Texas Social Welfare Association, warned that the birthrate in the U.S. was falling, that the U.S. needed children, that 700,000 fewer children had been born in this country than in 1931, and that at least 20,000 children died each year in domestic accidents. Beissler pleaded in vain that "the more we do in our field, the better we do it, and that affects all the children we care for." [67]

If the Wagner Bill was carried along by the eloquence of some of its supporters, it was doomed by the ambivalence of others. Once more Jewish leaders could not agree on any action for fear that they might evoke charges of double-loyalty and lead to the measure's defeat. Rabbi Wise labored behind the scenes to gain the endorsement of key politicians but publicly counseled caution.[68] Such timidity, however, was generally construed by the nativists as symbolic of indifference and weakness. If American Jews did not feel strongly enough about the bill to give it complete support, the nativists argued, why should American Gentiles act for them? As late as May 1939 some segments of the Jewish community, having pledged to Wise to "refrain from publicity" while the bill was under consideration, were having second thoughts. Ludwig Auer of the American-Hungarian Jewish community scored Wise for his failure to supply the forthright leadership required under the circumstances and for his failure to achieve any "concrete results" after obtaining pledges of silence from his peers.[69]

Officially, the principal spokesmen of major Jewish organizations in America remained silent, but when these individuals did speak out, they managed to do as much harm as any American Legion petition. Samuel Dickstein's comments about a steady tide of illegal immigrants coming from Canada were readily seized upon by restrictionists and converted into page-one news about "thousands" and "millions" of illegals streaming across our borders.[70]

Even more damaging was the effect of a story on June 9, 1939, which told how the Independent Order of B'rith Sholom was arranging to bring fifty Jewish children from Germany to Philadelphia on a nonquota basis. The announcement, which came just as the Wagner Bill was being readied for report, was immediately denounced as ridiculous by the National Coordinating Committee and the Non-Sectarian Committee. Joseph Chamberlain of the NCC sharply criticized Jacob Kepecs of the Philadelphia lodge of B'rith Sholom for creating the illusion that Jews could get around the nation's immigration laws if they had enough money and influence.[71]

In like manner, the well meaning representatives of America's largest labor unions did more harm than good when they testified before congressional committees. In May, Joseph Padway, counsel of the AFL, made his second appearance at the hearings and read a letter from AFL President William Green. Green indicated his "personal approval" for the bill and added that the membership of his organization also would be sympathetic to its passage. This clumsy attempt to weld Green's personal opinion (and Green was none too enthusiastic about the measure in any case) [72] to the rank and file membership of the AFL resulted in a merciless grilling of Padway by Congressmen William Schulte, Clifford Clevenger, George Allen, William Poage, and Charles Kramer.[73]

Was this a departure from the traditional restrictionist stand of the AFL? Wasn't the membership actually split on the question? [74] What would the AFL do five years hence when these children reached working age? What was its position on admitting Spanish refugee children? Chinese immigrants? Hadn't Paul Scharrenberg, another AFL legal expert, testified that same March that the organization "heartily favored" closing the gates to the U.S. for several years to permit the nation to set its own house in order? [75] By the time Padway left the stand, what was supposed to be his testimony in favor of the Wagner Bill had persuaded the congressmen that organized labor did not really know what it believed.

Equally useless was the testimony of CIO representatives. In this instance, at least, the position of this organization's president, John L. Lewis, was unequivocal. The gruff leader of the United Mine Workers had said, "Assuredly America should do its part in caring for some of the children who are victims of religious and racial oppression in Germany. I heartily approve of any practical action necessary for the accomplishment of this purpose." [76] John Brophy, director of the CIO, minced no words in lashing out at "cowardly thugs" who persecuted little children. He added that the Wagner Bill had the strong endorsement of his union in convention.[77]

Like Padway, however, Brophy was questioned and nitpicked by congressmen who asked if the CIO might welcome all six million potential refugees in Europe.[78] Never popular with conservative congressmen, the CIO was smeared as redlining in this and in simultaneous hearings conducted on Reynolds's sequence of bills before the Senate Subcommittee on Immigration.[79]

Unbelievably, spokesmen of the Junior Order of American Mechanics, by its own admission not a labor group, and M. W. Poulson of the Adams Hat Employees Association, 176 members strong and the only legitimate labor organization (a company union) to oppose the measure, were able to speak at equal length and on an equal par with the representatives of 8,000,000 American workers.

The most important setback to the Wagner Bill, however, was delivered neither by the indecisive Jewish community nor the Hugh Herbert-like spokesmen of organized labor, but by official Washington. James Patton, a Harvard graduate who was secretary of the New York JOAM, noted in the course of a three-hour debate with Representative William Poage in May that no high-ranking official in government—not FDR, Hull, Frances Perkins, Taylor, nor Rublee—had said one word about the bill, although it had been widely publicized for three months.[80]

This silence was most significant, for the unexpressed dictum in the executive branch was that the bill was solely a legislative matter and that the administration would in no way attempt to influence its outcome. Frances Perkins, who may have originated the idea for a child immigration bill, spoke out forcefully against Reynolds's proposed restrictionist legislation in February 1939 but said nothing about the Wagner Bill. During the Senate deliberations, her subordinates, James J. Houghteling, commissioner of Immigration and Naturalization, and

Edward Shaughnessy, deputy commissioner of Immigration and Naturalization, said little for fear of personal vilification by Reynolds.

Houghteling's exchange with the senator was especially enlightening. After the commissioner had contested Reynolds's charges that there were more than 300,000 "visitors" in the U.S., Reynolds asked if Houghteling wanted more visitors to enter this country. "Not under present circumstances," he responded. Asked if he then opposed the Wagner Bill, the commissioner said, "I am not taking any position on that." Asked for his personal opinion, he replied, "My official opinion is that it is a matter to be decided by the Congress." When Reynolds pressed him for a definitive answer, since the Department of Labor was so liberal with its words of censure where his bills were concerned, Houghteling begged off, saying, "I am not prepared to express a personal opinion at this time."

"You don't care to answer?" Reynolds stormed.

"I do not care to answer," concluded Houghteling.[81]

That same kind of verbal jousting frustrated Poage when he questioned Katherine Lenroot, another official in the Labor Department section, during the second session of public hearings on the Wagner Bill. When she spoke on behalf of the measure, she emphasized that she was merely presenting her personal views and not those of the administration. Representative William Poage (D.-Tex.) asked, "How can we get the views of the administration?"

"Through the usual channels," was her answer.

"There is not any usual channel," said Poage. "You are told to ask the Bureau of the Budget and they say they are not ready to comment on it. Agencies supposedly organized for the purpose of giving information do not give it. We cannot get a thing." [82]

It should not have been too difficult for any discerning person to evaluate the position of the administration. At the first hearing of the Joint Subcommittee on Immigration in April, Hull had paved the way for the restrictionists' objections when he warned of a potential tidal wave of immigrants if the

Wagner-Rogers bill should pass. Hull conceded that the bill "could open the door to similar or more radical departures from existing immigration legislation." [83]

More damaging to the bill's chances for success, however, was the Fourth White House Conference on Children held that same month, April 1939. When the restrictionists were seeking support for their charges that there existed numerous pathetic American children without shoes or crayons, food or shelter, the president and 500 educators and social workers gave them the needed evidence. Isidore Falk of the Social Security Board termed children "the economic orphans of our society" and added that 71 percent of the children in America were in homes "where the income is inadequate or just barely adequate." [84]

Then Roosevelt, who had been pressured by his wife, Eleanor, to come out for the Wagner Bill, addressed the throng in the East Room.[85] The fundamental concomitants of a happy child, he said, were home warmth, food, affection, a good education, and the knowledge that a secure job awaited him. "As we consider these essentials of a happy childhood our hearts are heavy with the knowledge that there are many children who cannot make these assumptions." Recalling the imagery of his second inaugural address, Roosevelt emphasized that the nation needed to do more for the children of the unemployed, of minority groups, of migrant families swept out of the Dust Bowl, for children without adequate shelter, food, clothing, medical attention, or education.[86]

Throughout the hearings, restrictionists and wavering congressmen incessantly returned to this theme of underprivileged American youth, and they could always cite the president as their authority.[87] Roosevelt never made public reference to the struggle for a German children's refugee bill. In fact, when Representative Caroline O'Day (D.-N.Y.) wrote him asking for an opinion on the measure, the president, ever wary of arousing the wrath of the economically dislocated American public, penciled in the following instruction to Secretary "Pa" Watson: "File, no action. FDR." [88] The restrictionists made much of contrasting this official administrative silence on the Wagner Bill with Roosevelt's beatitudes on behalf of native youth. More than anything else, such words as "one-third of a nation ill-housed, ill-clad, and ill-nourished" spelled doom for the Wagner Bill.

What then could be done in fairness to both American and German-Jewish children? Poage offered one compromise. He suggested that as many as 50,000 of these German children be admitted as visitors, with passes renewable to age twenty-one. At that time they could be eligible for citizenship and be charged against the quota. George Allen of Alabama swiftly vetoed the idea, pointing out that the proposal was illegal because a visitor must have the right to return to his native land.[89] When Congressman Kramer asked several witnesses what their thoughts were about admitting the children on a preferential basis within existing quotas, they all opposed the idea, saying it would destroy the purpose of the bill. Monte Lemann of the NSC commented, "You would be giving a stone instead of a piece of bread." [90]

In a last-ditch attempt to wrench the bill free from the Senate and House immigration committees, Wagner delivered an impassioned radio address nationwide on June 7. He began by relating the story of the S.S. *St. Louis*, which had been ordered out of Havana harbor six days before. He spoke of the misery of people in no man's lands, of the "unfortunate waifs"—Catholic, Protestant, and Jewish children—behind the barbed wire of concentration camps. He berated the American public for its evanescent concern over the fate of these people, saying, "One by one, these incidents impress themselves on our consciousness, until they disappear from the public prints, and a merciful curtain of obscurity is drawn over their ultimate outcome." For Wagner, the passage of this bill was crucial not merely as "a token of our sympathy" but also "as a symbol of our faith in the ideals of human brotherhood." [91]

Wagner's speech attempted to elicit widespread public support at the last moment for his measure. It failed to do this, and when the bill emerged from committee on June 30, it was with the amendment that the 20,000 children enter the country under existing quotas. What Pickett, LaRoe, Rogers, and Wagner had all opposed—giving 10,000 of the annual 27,000 German certificates to the children on a preferential basis instead of adding 10,000 to the 27,000—was to become a reality if the bill passed.[92]

His bill emasculated, Wagner lashed out bitterly against the amendment and stated: "The proposed change would, in effect, convert the measure from a humane proposal to help children who are in acute distress to a proposal with needlessly cruel consequences for adults in Germany who are in need of succor and are fortunate enough to obtain visas under the present drastic quota restrictions."[93] Because of Wagner's opposition, the amended bill never came to a vote.

This was not the end of the German refugee children question. Amazingly, the subject reappeared in the Senate Immigration Committee's report on Reynolds's bill to suspend immigration for an indefinite period. Among the many amendments tacked on to this doomed piece of legislation was the recommendation to admit 20,000 refugee children from Germany, Moravia, and Slovakia, provided they possessed genuine certificates proving they were under age fourteen and provided they did not become public charges. Wagner and his associates had chosen to destroy their own bill rather than see 20,000 of 54,000 available certificates go to children. Now the Senate was suggesting that 20,000 certificates go to children, and none go to adults.[94]

Both the Wagner and Reynolds bills were defeated in 1939, and it is ironic that in their last moments the two were joined. It was a fitting testimonial to the hesitance of the administration, the disorder within the Jewish community, and the hostility of the American people, 60 percent of whom had told George Gallup that they opposed the Wagner Bill.[95]

5. The Fifth Column

hree weeks after September 1, 1939, when Adolf Hitler unleashed his Panzer divisions against Poland, agents of the moribund Jewish Hilfsverein in Berlin cabled HIAS President Abraham Herman in New York: "Continuance of emigration possible and urgently requested." Similar communications were received from Jews singled out for special abuse by conquering Nazi and Russian armies in Poland, Latvia, and Lithuania. Now that they were confronted with the actuality, not merely the prospect, of nearly four million stateless Jews,[1] Herman and HIAS Vice-President Solomon Dingol submitted a plan of rescue to Representative Sol Bloom of the House Committee on Foreign Affairs, to IGCR Executive Director Robert Pell, and to the State Department.[2] The failure of any of these groups to take action on the HIAS proposal again illustrated the lack of coordinated effort toward refugee problems through the twilight of nonpeace for America between September 1939 and December 1941.

As yet uncommitted to a policy of extermination of the Jews, the German government was more than cooperative in permitting Jews to leave Germany in the days of the "Phoney War."[3] As late as June 1940, trains carrying frightened emigrants made regular runs from Berlin, Prague, and Vienna to Lisbon, Bilbao, and Vigo. From these Iberian ports refugees could depart for South America or the United States on a dozen neutral vessels with capacities ranging from 1,200 to 2,300 passengers.[4] It was estimated that 2,600 persons left Lisbon in this manner each month.[5] Many more could have made the journey to freedom on half-empty vessels, but for the decisions of American consular officials who would not or could not supply extensions on transit visas which might have expired before the emigrant reached Lisbon.[6] Some Jews, desirous of emigrating to Palestine, fled through the Balkans, chartered tramp steamers in the Black Sea, and sailed on to the Holy Land, much to the distress of the British.[7] Perhaps as many as 25,000 illegals flouted the White Paper and two subsequent suspensions of all immigration between 1939 and 1941.[8] The most adventurous refugees could make the 6,000-mile-trek by rail to Vladivostok, there to sail for Yokohama or Kobe, and ultimately the United States or South America. Between July 1, 1940 and June 1, 1941, 4,413 persons made this journey through Kobe bound for the Western Hemisphere.[9]

Here the refugees were hardly greeted with open arms. The United States, for example, first refused admission to passengers stuffed in the clammy holds of the freighter *Navemar* because they possessed deficient papers.[10] Another vessel, the *Quanza,* turned away from Mexico, was repulsed from Norfolk, despite the intercession of Nahum Goldmann with Cordell Hull.[11] Chile barred all immigration on October 11, 1939. Brazil closed its borders to Jews. Cuba raised its entry guarantee to $2,500 a person. While all this went on, the IGCR feebly explored the possibility of planting colonies of refugees in Yunnan, China, or Birobidzhan, Siberia.[12]

The U.S. government was outwardly sympathetic to the entreaties of the Joint Distribution Committee, the American Friends Service Committee, and other humanitarian agencies engaged in refugee work. The nation and its representatives knew that something was terribly wrong in Europe, that thousands of innocent civilians were starving to death in Poland's ghettos,[13] that thousands more were dying of disease and brutality in French detention camps.[14] Herbert Hoover predicted that as many as 18,000,000 Europeans would be without food in 1941.[15] Like so many other Americans, Hoover, although grief-stricken at the plight of the Europeans and particularly the Jews, nevertheless did not feel that this country should open its doors to refugees. In an address before the Jewish Welfare Fund in Chicago on February 11, 1940, the man who had fed Europe during World War I affirmed, "For one hundred and fifty years America was this refuge and this sanctuary. Sanctuary must be found elsewhere." [16]

About the same time, Hoover's successor, Franklin Roosevelt, was convinced that no plan of international cooperation was feasible.[17] Urged by his wife, Eleanor, FDR requested that U.S. Commissioner of Immigration James Houghteling explore the possibility of congressional liberalization of existing refugee laws. Houghteling reported that instead of becoming sympathetic toward the victims of Nazism, the congressmen were advocating more stringent alien control of the sort which ultimately was enacted in the Smith Law. Houghteling said that after he had sat in on all sessions of the Senate and House immigration committees, he found "a great deal of confusion in the minds of Congressmen on the subject of refugees and of hostility to the admission of any considerable number of aliens to compete for employment with American citizens." With eight million Americans still unemployed, Houghteling warned: "The tendency of a considerable part of Congress was toward the reduction of existing immigration quotas. The chance of any liberalizing legislation seemed negligible." [18]

Although the nation had begun to enjoy an economic resurgence directly related to defense production, the old fears that foreigners would push American laborers out of jobs remained very real in 1940. A study of 149 companies done by the National Industrial Conference Board, an employers' research organization, found that two-thirds of those queried refused to hire any alien workers. Those which did hire aliens generally did so only if no other applicant was available and only after a comprehensive examination of the alien's background.[19] Coincidentally, the Opinion Research Corporation indicated that 40 percent of those persons polled between 1940 and 1942 would refuse to hire a Jew, regardless of whether or not he were an alien.[20]

The federal government discriminated against aliens in civil service, where applicants were required to swear out affidavits that they were citizens or intended to apply for naturalization, and in the merchant marine, where citizenship was a prerequisite for all crew members on cargo vessels and for 90 percent of the crews aboard passenger vessels. At the same time nearly every state had laws barring aliens from certain occupations. In 1940 aliens were prohibited from practicing medicine in twenty-eight states, law in twenty-six, accounting in fifteen, pharmacy in fourteen, dentistry and optometry in eleven, banking in seven, and plumbing in four.[21] In several states aliens could not become teachers, barbers, engineers, pilots of vessels, registered nurses, architects, or even garbage collectors. In others aliens could not own land, hunt game, or fish.[22] Such laws had repeatedly been validated by the courts on constitutional grounds because regulating trades and professions was reserved to the states. Many justifications were offered—that training received abroad might not be applicable in the United States, that language could serve as a barrier to carrying out one's functions—but the impression remained that the United States still subscribed to the nativist rationalization expressed in an earlier case that "foreign born have not the same inspiration for the public weal, nor are they as well-disposed toward the United States as those who by citizenship are a part of the government itself." [23]

Hostility toward aliens, refugees, or Jews in the form of dismissals and job turndowns became so pronounced in 1940 and 1942 that Washington officials had second thoughts about the propriety of legal restrictions on their employment. In September 1940, Attorney General Francis Biddle warned that continued discrimination against aliens in employment could ultimately create a refugee problem within this nation, because such people could not return to their native lands even if they desired and since they were barred by law from obtaining government welfare aid. "To deprive them of their employment is often to deprive them and their dependents of their sole means of livelihood and to leave them helpless," Biddle said.[24]

For Roosevelt such economic discrimination was "as stupid as it is unjust, and on both counts it plays into the hands of the enemies of American democracy." [25] The government now moved to assure employers that aliens could work in defense plants, despite laws dating from July 2, 1926 and June 28, 1940 which seemed to indicate that employing them was illegal and punishable by imprisonment for five years and a fine of $10,000. All the alien needed was approval from the federal department involved in the work project.[26] Thousands of aliens obtained jobs this way, but thousands more had to fall back on the President's Committee on Fair Employment Practices headed by Malcolm MacLean, president of Hampton Institute, and civil servants like Governor Herbert Lehman of New York, Governor Charles Edison of New Jersey, and Mayor Fiorello La Guardia of New York City, who tried in vain to implement the laws equitably.[27]

This employment hassle notwithstanding, through the winter months of 1939 and 1940 the American government acted as if it fully concurred with Jay Allen's cynical appraisal that "there is no reason to talk of refugee problems anymore." Allen wrote, "Hitler has solved it with the continental concentration camp." [28]

Most Americans considered that with the outbreak of the world war all nonbelligerents who found themselves persecuted, dispossessed, or dominated by the Nazis technically could be lumped into the category of stateless or displaced persons. In the process they relegated the suffering of the Jews to a minor position. Even some Jews shared this attitude. William Zukerman, European correspondent for the New York *Jewish Morning Journal,* wrote that the suffering of the Jews was no greater than that sustained by any other population. After the fall of France, Zukerman predicted that Nazi anti-Semitism would now abate because it had "served its purpose" and because "very few people are now left who can be taken in by this obvious bluff." [29]

The popular view in the U.S. was that although conditions in French and British internment camps were bad, they were not intolerable. The fall of France changed that.[30] At the instance of German and Jewish refugee organizations, IGCR Director Herbert Emerson cabled the President's Advisory Committee on June 7 and called for the creation of a common reservoir of quota certificates and the immediate admission of sufficient refugees (many of whom had been battered about several countries already) to fill the quotas for 1940 and 1941.[31] The British and French ambassadors also called on Cordell Hull to assist the Allies by removing refugees who impeded military operations. The American Red Cross requested aid for some 2,000,000 refugees from Belgium, Holland, and Luxembourg who were currently in France.[32] The U.S. Committee for the Care of European Children, founded that spring and backed by such sponsors as Eleanor Roosevelt, Marshal Field III, Raymond Clapper, and Joseph Alsop, pressed for an emergency treasury of $5,000,000 and the admission of 70,000 refugee children to the U.S. in 1940.[33]

Only 120,000 immigrants, less than half the number permitted under existing legislation, were admitted to the United States in 1940–1941, as the government steadfastly refrained from redistributing unused quota allotments.[34] But Congress did set aside $50,000,000 for European relief in the summer of 1940.[35] Four measures were introduced in the House and Senate to facilitate the transport and admission of "refugee children" to the U.S., but none eventually passed. And Roosevelt, again demonstrating his proclivity to government by crisis, reorganized his refugee advisory committee as the National Coordinating Committee for Aid to Refugees and asked this body to draw up a list of eminent refugees who could receive temporary visitors' visas to America.[36]

In doing so, the president was responding to pressure from Mrs. Roosevelt, Thomas Mann, Joseph Chamberlain, and Albert Hirschmann, professor of international relations at Columbia University.[37] Such a list, containing the names of 3,286 persons of "superior intellectual attainment, of indomitable spirit, experienced in vigorous support of the principles of liberal government, and who were in danger of persecution or death at the hands of autocracy" was prepared for Alvin Johnson of the New School for Social Research, an institution rich in refugee faculty, and was made public by Sumner Welles in November.[38] The proposal was undermined, however, partly by the diffidence of American consular officials here and abroad.[39] Marc Chagall, Max Ernst, Jacques Lipchitz, Lion Feuchtwanger, Franz Werfel, and Konrad Heiden were among the fortunates, most of them Jews, who fled France under the terms of this special measure. In all, only 1,236 persons were rescued before January 1941 when the plan was aborted.[40]

Various proposals to bring children to this country in 1940 did not fare much better. This time there was no question but what the children involved would be "Aryan," or, more specifically, British. The scheme was based on the success of transporting approximately 38,000 British children to Canada in the first year of the war.[41] Within five weeks of the announcement on July 14, 1940 that the United States was considering issuing visas to children in England, 32,000 applications had been filed by British parents anxious to have their children removed from the pending threat of the Blitz.[42]

Despite the obvious racial, religious, and philosophical affinity with the American way of life that these children possessed, American restrictionists reverted to their standard arguments during congressional hearings on the proposal that August. What of financial guarantees? What of the sanctity of the quota system? Could such a measure pave the way for the admission of thousands of Chinese? Would the children be here permanently? Most significant, however, was the query of Representative Noah Mason. Sympathetic to the refugee measures of 1939 and 1940, Mason questioned simply how the children could safely cross the Atlantic.[43]

Apparently the House felt it had hit on a solution when it tagged the Hennings Bill as an amendment to the Neutrality Act of August 7, 1940. Under this provision, adopted by the Senate on August 19, American ships could be used to transport children under age sixteen out of the war zone, including France and Portugal. Cognizant of the dangers which American vessels had faced in World War I, Congress required that these rescue ships have huge American flags painted on both sides and on the decks. The ships would sail, however, only when all belligerents had guaranteed them safe conduct. These voluntary restrictions were reminiscent of the German demands on American shipping at the time of resumption of unrestricted submarine warfare in January 1917. Such demands had virtually impelled the United States, traditionally jealous about its rights to freedom of the seas, to go to war against Germany that spring. In 1940, however, American congressmen prided themselves on having achieved a relatively good compromise with Hitler. If he now declined such arrangements, Hitler would be fully exposed as "an advocate of genocide." [44]

Here again the nation's representatives in Washington were going no further than their readings of American public opinion would allow. In June, Gallup reported that 58 percent of the persons polled favored admitting British and French women and children for the duration of the war. Americans were reluctant, though, to have their ships involved in the project. In July and August a full 55 percent opposed the use of U.S. liners for transport purposes. But when the AIPO prefaced the question with hypothetical guarantees of safety from Italy and Germany, public opinion in this country shifted, with 63 percent now favoring the use of American ships to bring the refugees across the Atlantic. [45]

Some 4,200 children and 1,100 adults reached the United States, and another 6,000 reached Canada, before the massive rescue plan was abandoned in the fall of 1940. [46] The unmerciful sinking that summer of the Canadian liner *Arandora Star*, carrying a mixed passenger list of refugees and prisoners of war, plus the sinking of the S.S. *City of Benares*, with seventy-three children and six adult refugees aboard, on September 17, 1940 dispelled any notion that the Germans would permit unescorted vessels to traverse the ocean. Fully aware of such perils, the British government argued that it could not spare the necessary convoy ships, and Clement Attlee asked the U.S. to postpone plans for future passage. [47]

All but a handful of the children thus saved in 1940 were British, a fact which has led Arthur Morse to conclude that the rescue operations discriminated deliberately against the true refugee children of Europe, the Jews. [48] It also contributed to the yet extant myth that thousands of British children swarmed into the United States during World War II while refugee children faced extermination. [49] In fact, all of the British children could legitimately have entered under Britain's never-filled quota allotment of 65,000 a year. That they entered as legitimate immigrants may explain why the Department of Immigration and Naturalization has no special statistics available for British refugee children.[50]

Perhaps the saddest innuendo about the "menace of refugee children" that had to be refuted in 1940 was the charge that they were potential fifth columnists. Joseph Chamberlain of the National Coordinating Committee actually petitioned Roosevelt on behalf of the innocence of these young travelers that summer.[51] But the United States viewed a different world in that fearful epoch, one haunted by the effectiveness of Nazi military prowess and brutality, one in which Madrid, Oslo, Prague, and a score of other ancient centers of civilization had been betrayed by Nazi sympathizers from within. Fear of internal traitors, known as the fifth column, generated an irrational hysteria seldom equaled in American history. Members of the Jehovah's Witnesses were mobbed as "fifth columnists" for refusing to salute the flag. A foundry worker in Sparta, Michigan, was killed by his neighbor because "he was in the fifth column." In Sapulpa, Oklahoma, a Technocrat was jailed because he allegedly was a "fifth columnist." Jeff Davis, self-anointed king of America's hobos, appointed celebrated gate-crasher "One-Eyed" Connolly to watch for the fifth column on the rails. In New York state, a group of women banded together, like so many Mrs. Minivers, vowing to shoot on sight any German parachutists. An American Legion Post in Erie County, New York, promised to bar the fifth column from crossing the Niagara River.[52]

Despite the admonitions of John Haynes Holmes, pastor of the Community Church of New York, William Haber of the National Refugee Service, George Warren of the President's Advisory Committee, and Attorney General Robert Jackson, all of whom cautioned against lawlessness or vigilantism in the guise of upholding liberty, and despite Werner Guttmann's detailed exposé of Hitler's underground operations in the United States, many people still considered liberals, Trotskyites, aliens, Jews, Earl Browder, and J. P. Morgan as part of the fascist fifth column in 1940.[53] Anyone who was unknown or disliked could be labeled a fifth columnist by panicky Americans, who even before Pearl Harbor were deluging the Federal Bureau of Investigation with as many as 2,800 complaints daily about spies in the neighborhood.[54]

The fright-mongers and sensation-seekers did a thriving business in this atmosphere. Ex-Storm Trooper Otto Strasser painted a gloomy picture of impending fascist takeovers in Argentina, Chile, Ecuador, and even Mexico. Samuel Lubell, Donald Keyhoe, and John Daly brought the menace closer to home, charging that Hitler was forcing persons in this country who had relatives in European concentration camps to do his bidding.[55] Through the summer of 1940, Martin Dies, never particularly sympathetic to refugees or what he called the "sobbing sentimentalists" in this country who championed their cause, used the platform of the House Un-American Activities Committee to lash out at the fifth column. Dies, whose birddogging tactics earned commendation from Roosevelt (who also had warned Americans to be alert to the fifth column menace that summer), charged that there were six million communist and Nazi sympathizers in the U.S. working hand-inglove with one another and with the Gestapo and NKVD to destroy American liberty.[56] And finally, American fears were not eased when Colonel William Donovan, director of the Office of Strategic Sciences, told the press that foreign agents were free to function at will in the democracies.[57]

Not all Americans believed that aliens and Jews were fifth columnists, but many did, and one of those who did and had the power to do something about it was Breckinridge Long. Long was the small, wizened man whom Sumner Welles had recommended for the position of assistant secretary of state in January 1940 when George Messersmith resigned to become ambassador to Cuba. He was descended from Kentucky's aristocratic Breckinridge clan and had been a State Department functionary in the restrictionist heyday toward the end of the Wilson administration. Defeated in his only two bids for public office in his native Missouri, Long possessed little fondness for

114

the common man or the foreigner. In October 1940, James McDonald, chairman of the President's Advisory Committee, walked out on a meeting with Long after blasting him for his "vindictive mentality and superlative ego." [58] A similar judgment was passed by Tabitha Petran and William Walton in *PM*, who said of him:

> He is an old man, a narrow, limited man, whose wealth and inclination have kept him from ever having any sympathy for the people who get pushed around. He may no longer admire the fascist way of life, but he still retains a contempt for the little people, which makes his holding of any government position a danger to American democracy.[59]

For his generous contributions to the Roosevelt's campaign coffers in 1932, Long was rewarded with the post of ambassador to Italy. He served there for three years, hosting swank parties that were the envy of other embassies, lavishing praise upon the fascists for their efficiency in getting the trains to run on time, and generally making clear his approbation of the Mussolini regime. Even before Mussolini's forces invaded Ethiopia, Long advocated appeasement by offering huge slices of land in the contested region to the Italians. Afterward, he endorsed the fascist conquest and sent repeated cables to Washington which criticized the American embargo. He opposed Roosevelt's fireside chats on European affairs, warning of the president's criticism of Hitler's expansionist policies, "He must not say that. This is terrible. This will get us into war." He advocated a $100,000,000 credit in the form of food supplies for France. He opposed the language Roosevelt used in his "Hand that held the Dagger" speech, which the president delivered in June 1940 to condemn Italy's entry into the war against France. Long questioned the wisdom of the embargo on steel, oil, and iron to Japan in November 1940 and spoke out against Lend Lease in the winter of 1940–1941.[60] The assistant secretary was one of that great host of persons unable to see the dimensions of the fascist threat to America, and his counsels, in retrospect, generally were in error.

In 1936, Long was recalled from Italy, ostensibly for reasons of health, but newspapers blamed his constant indiscretions. After holding a number of legal positions in private life for three years, he reappeared in the government as the American member of a Commission for the Advancement of Peace with Italy. Then in 1939 he was appointed as an adviser on international trade and war emergency matters in the State Department's Special Division on War Problems. Here he so impressed Welles with his geniality that when Messersmith's departure created a vacancy at the top level in the State Department, Hull and Welles both pushed for Long's promotion to assistant secretary.

In his four years as assistant secretary Long supervised twenty-three of the forty-two divisions in the State Department, including those related to overseas relief, transports, civilian internees, prisoners of war, and the all-important visa section. Long's attitudes toward the refugee were narrow and unsympathetic. On one occasion Long directed the Visa Division to turn down the applications of a group of 292 German-Jewish refugees in England because "they are pacifists." In a comment reminiscent of the faded days of his youth in the era of A. Mitchell Palmer, Long explained, "They would have the same attitude about this country as was indicated in the last war. If this country is not worth fighting for, it is not worth coming to." [61] On another occasion, when under pressure from the many religious and nationality groups that were badgering his office for special favors, he stated, "Personally, I would feel much easier about the future if we could get rid of all groups, blocks, and special interests." [62]

The group that especially harassed the assistant secretary was the Jews. Far from being the anti-Semite suggested by Morse, however, Long was extremely cordial to the Jews and opened his office on repeated occasions to spokesmen of every faction.[63] Whether cynically or not, he even offered that it would help their cause if these factions coalesced behind a single leader. Long recognized that the major portion of visa applicants from Europe in the period before Pearl Harbor were Jews, and it is difficult to find a single anti-Semitic statement in any of his personal notes or memorandums.[64] In fact, Long apparently was genuinely concerned about the fate of European Jewry. An example is his instruction to Avra Warren of the Visa Division on the question of extending visas to rabbinical students in Lithuania in 1940. "I want to do everything we legitimately can to help these people out of the predicaments they find themselves in, at the same time observing the requirements of our law," Long wrote.[65]

This rigid adherence to the letter of the law was what inevitably earned Long the enmity of the Jewish community and other nationality groups as well. He personally crippled efforts to save the British children during the summer months of 1940, charging that there were no American vessels available for this purpose and saying that "the very surest way to get America into this war would be to send an American ship to England and put 2,000 babies on it and then have it sunk by a German torpedo." [66]

Long's refusal to approve visas for the scholars and scientists stranded in France solely because they had no French exit visas (which, of course, the Vichy government would not issue without an American entry visa, ad infinitum) nearly provoked a mass resignation of the President's Advisory Committee in the fall of 1940.[67]

Long even abandoned his initial efforts on behalf of Jewish rabbis and students, persons who could legitimately have qualified under existing legislation as nonquota immigrants. He explained that all plans under consideration for the rescue of European yeshivot were inadequate since they did not carry "any definite assurance" that the persons to whom passports would be delivered would actually be the persons whose names appeared on the various consular lists.[68]

Once more the gorgon of the fifth column reared its ugly head, for Long was not immune to the fear about spies and saboteurs that was sweeping the country in 1940. On June 17, 1940 he noted in his diary (p. 108) that alien agents could merely walk across the American-Canadian border, a "sieve" he called it, to do their nefarious work. On the same day he confided to Avra Warren that American nationality laws were lax and had to be tightened up.[69] Later that month, the fall of France having conjured up for him "all my childhood fears—

Genghis Khan, Cyrus, Xerxes, the Pharohs [sic], Caesar, Mahomet, Napoleon, on the march," [70] he was able to convince the attorney general to issue a special ruling, confirmed by executive order, that future immigrants would be admitted on the basis of "reasonable need." But henceforth such need was to be determined from the viewpoint of the American nation: whether the U.S. would profit from the admission of such immigrants, and not whether the alien himself was to be the determining test for admission.[71]

Long advocated alien registration and favored a narrower interpretation of the nation's LPC clause in granting visas. Through the fall of 1940 he fretted about the 2,000 "saboteurs" currently employed in the shipping and aircraft industries, persons known to the Dies Un-American Activities Committee, who could not be removed for fear of antagonizing the already-fractious labor unions.[72] In November he lamented, "We're still having a good deal of trouble with refugees," and blamed the President's Advisory Committee for having forced most of the State Department's mistakes, including the granting of a visa to one individual who was, in Long's words, "an expert dynamiter with a subversive intent." [73]

Seeing spies everywhere, Long departed from the State Department's tradition of silence on legislative matters and submitted a draft text on exclusion of aliens whose admission would be "inimical to the interests of the United States" to Attorney General Francis Biddle.[74] There is even some reason to believe that Long's eventual acquiescence in the scheme to rescue elite scholars was purchased at the price of promises from the attorney general, solicitor general, and other representatives of the Justice Department to champion a tightening up of immigration examination procedures at the end of 1940.[75]

Long's determination to make a complete review of an immigrant's credentials before admitting him to the United States was sustained by his subordinates, some of whom various analysts saw as suave anti-Semites. Journalists Petran and Walton charge in their *PM* article (p. 7) that Long readily admitted that Consuls Leland Morris in Berlin and James Stewart in Zurich were anti-Semites who were loath to issue visas to

Jews, yet he did nothing to remove them from their crucial posts during the period before the United States entered the war. Functionaries of the State Department who counseled Long also showed little sympathy for the Jewish refugees.

The cool, young, legalistic head of the Visa Division, Avra Warren, echoed Westbrook Pegler's fulminations in November when he vetoed a Harold Ickes suggestion to permit 12,000 "German" refugees in Portugal to colonize the underpopulated Virgin Islands. Warren, like Pegler, warned that many of these applicants were subversives or operatives of the Nazi government.[76] Warren also rejected as impractical a scheme to set up a haven for refugees in Alaska, arguing that "nearly all of them belong to a particular race" and that their admission in large numbers would eventually create "serious problems." [77]

Warren's assistant in the Visa Division, Robert Alexander, supported his superior's views on refugees. He consistently opposed the idea of lumping all unused quota permits into what he referred to as "a jackpot for the Jews." [78] Alexander even intimated that the Jews in this country were consciously or unconsciously in league with Hitler, and contended that their emotional antics only served to impede the success of the Allied war effort.[79]

Like views were held by Long's executive assistant, George Brandt, a man who had served as a delegate to Evian, who would play a key role in deliberations at Bermuda, and who would withhold information of Nazi genocide from the public. Such views were also entertained by the European Division Chief, Elbredge Durbrow, who dismissed reports of mass extermination issuing from Europe as atrocity tales. And finally, similar views were held by Robert Border Reams, a Pennsylvanian who had risen in the ranks of the Foreign Service to become Long's principal adviser on Jewish questions in the Division of European Affairs by 1942. Reams was most influential in reinforcing Long's view that most refugees coming to the United States were fifth columnists in disguise. "Naturally it can't be made public knowledge, but some are getting in and some have been apprehended as agents," Reams later commented.[80]

This gnawing fear that somehow the U.S. was being duped into admitting Nazi and Bolshevik agents preyed upon Long through the winter of 1940–1941. Despite his labors on behalf of more stringent reviews of visa applications, he was disturbed by reports reaching his desk from Cordell Hull that consuls abroad should be as lenient as possible in processing refugees.[81] Hull indicated that the Nazis were sending 450,000 Jews in sealed cars to Lisbon, and the secretary wanted them moved out as swiftly as possible "within existing quotas." [82]

Long was even more distressed when he received a nine-page letter from Ambassador Laurence Steinhardt in Moscow in early May. Steinhardt, who later earned the plaudits of Jewish relief groups for his work as minister to Turkey, blasted "the so-called humanitarian agencies" which were being "derelict in their duties as Americans" in sponsoring "so-called refugees." He charged that in the past eighteen months "many who will engage in activities inimical to our interest" had entered the U.S. under fraudulent pretenses. "We have direct evidence, that a substantial proportion of these so-called refugees from the Soviet Union and Soviet-controlled areas are approached by the G.P.U. to act as agents in the U.S.," he wrote. The ambassador called on Long to restore the discretionary powers of consuls, who by this time were so confused they could only deny admission to someone "naive enough to tell us he is going to blow up the DuPont powder works." Steinhardt added, "I feel strongly that when our country is facing perhaps the greatest crisis in its history, its security from foreign machinations is of a great deal more importance than the entry of this, that, or the other immigrant, no matter how good a case he or she can make out on humanitarian grounds." [83]

To check this flow of subversive personnel Long recommended the expansion of the Visa Division to include 300 persons and the establishment of five interdepartmental review boards to pass on the merits of each visa application in Washington, not leaving the decision totally in the hands of the consuls.[84] Such a time-consuming review would, according to Long, discourage "the insidious infiltration of whispering agents . . . the agents of trouble and discord . . . the saboteurs [who] throw monkey wrenches into the machinery . . . all with the object of creating discord and dismay and of rendering nugatory efficient organization." [85]

It is doubtful that Long's viewpoints would have become policy but for the drastic deterioration of German-American relations in the spring of 1941. The transfer of fifty destroyers of World War I vintage to the British Navy in September 1940, the convening of joint Anglo-American military staff talks in January 1941, the enactment of Lend-Lease in March 1941, and the acquisition of bases in Greenland in April 1941 all pushed the United States farther toward undeclared war with Germany.

Then on May 21, 1941 an unarmed American mechant ship, the *Robin Moor*, bound from New York to Capetown and carrying noncontraband cargo, was sunk by a German submarine operating well outside the blockade zone proclaimed by the German government on March 25, 1941. Although all passengers and crew were permitted to take to lifeboats, this first sinking of an American vessel so incensed the public that Roosevelt was able to proclaim an unlimited national emergency on May 27.[86]

In June the United States seized Italian and German vessels "idled" in American harbors. Shortly after, Hitler's invasion of Russia prompted the freezing of Axis funds in this country and the closing of their consulates. The Nazis and fascists retaliated by closing down American consulates in Germany, Belgium, Luxembourg, Holland, Norway, Denmark, Yugoslavia, Greece, Italy, and occupied France. With these closings, Spain, Portugal, and Vichy France, which feared that the chances of refugees being admitted to the U.S. would be constricted, began to restrict the issuance of transit and exit permits. On October 1, 1941 the German government, already in a verbal and shooting war with the United States, removed much of the fear that refugees might act as spies by prohibiting the departure of Jews from the Reich and Government General of Poland. Most of the exit portals of Europe, therefore, were sealed against the Jews well before Pearl Harbor.[87]

What the Nazis attempted to do in Europe, the State Department matched in this country. On June 5, 1941 the department issued a telegram to all consuls directing them to submit all visa applications of persons with close relatives in occupied territory to Washington for final approval. Long later explained to Roosevelt that the department made this recommendation because of a confidential memorandum received from J. Edgar Hoover, FBI director. According to Hoover, refugees leaving Vichy France were being required to submit four photographs instead of the usual three when applying for exit permits. The extra picture was added to the files of the Second Bureau, which was responsible for French espionage activity. Permission to leave France, Long stated, was granted on the condition that the emigrant, who left the proverbial close relative behind as insurance, would serve as an agent of the fascist government in Vichy upon reaching the United States.[88]

Here at last was the concrete evidence of espionage that Long needed to stem the flow of immigration. It is no coincidence that the Bloom-Van Nuys Bill, introduced by Long's good friend Representative Sol Bloom and enacted on June 20, 1941, bore many trademarks of Long's philosophy. This law provided for five possible levels of review of every immigration application. The first was the consular level, where the American official could reject an applicant if he maintained close ties with someone in a hostile country or if there were other evidence that his entry would endanger the U.S. All consular decisions had to be confirmed by an interdepartmental committee in Washington, comprised of representatives from the departments of State, Navy, Army, Justice, and the FBI. Beyond this, unsuccessful applicants could run the gauntlet of appeals to a special committee of review, a board of appeals, and ultimately to the secretary of state.

The law, and subsequent State Department clarifications, required consuls in the south of France and Iberia to serve as amateur psychiatrists or seers. In his memorandum to Roosevelt, Long defended the measure by saying that visas would be denied only after "meticulous inquiry" into the background of the refugees. Applicants would be considered undesirable if "they had agreed to be agents for one of these governments or *who might under circumstances existing and because of their mental philosophy serve as agents*" (Italics added). What this last phrase really meant was never sufficiently defined. Consular officials interpreted such directives as having only one meaning, however, and that was to slow down immigration processing.

Long and his staff prided themselves on pushing through "the relative rule," as the Bloom-Van Nuys Bill was known, to hinder the entry of potential fifth columnists. Subsequently, Robert Alexander drafted a statement for Long which pointed out that the government faced three alternatives in the middle of 1941: (1) suspend all immigration for the duration of the unlimited national emergency; (2) repeal all restrictions on immigration so that refugees and spies could pour into the country on an indiscriminate basis; or (3) pursue a middle course between the first two possibilities, keeping the doors ajar, but utilizing intensive screening to protect internal security from enemy infiltration. This had actually worked to the best interests of the nation, Long and Alexander felt assured, and they cited the attorney general's favorable report on their actions to Hull dated November 27, 1942 as proof.[89]

There is no way of estimating how many desperate persons found themselves jeopardized by the State Department's insistence on complete typewritten copies of three immigration forms, done in sextuplicate, for ultimate review by slow-moving officials in Washington. In some instances consulates in Europe were not equipped with the typewriters made mandatory by Long's Order #946, and the Joint Distribution Committee was forced to rush the machines overseas. Even then the wait might be four or five months before the applicant, fearful that his transit visa in France, Spain, or Portugal might expire and that he would then be returned to Nazi-occupied territory and certain death, would learn that he had been rejected because of a narrow interpretation of the relative rule. In August 1942, Hull noted that 10,649 visa applications out of a total of 69,604 had been refused in the previous fiscal year.[90] Such a figure is misleading, however, as both Assistant Secretary Long and Visa Division Chief Warren both were proud of the fact that roughly one-half of the applicants turned down by the State Department before the U.S. entered World War II had been rejected because of the relative rule.[91]

Albert Einstein, a personal friend of the Roosevelt family, wrote Mrs. Roosevelt on July 26 to remonstrate against the callousness of the State Department's immigration practices. He wrote:

> A policy is now being pursued which makes it all but impossible to give refuge in America to many worthy persons who are the victims of Fascist cruelty in Europe. Of course this is not openly avowed by those responsible for it. The method which is being used, however, is to make immigration impossible by creating a wall of bureaucratic measures alleged to be necessary to protect America against subversive, dangerous elements.[92]

The Einstein letter, like the urgings of the earlier Princeton Conference on Refugee Problems and Needs in which Mrs. Roosevelt had participated, had no effect on policy.[93] At the time FDR and Hull were more concerned with the impending rupture with Japan, with the embargo on oil shipments to that nation, and with defensive measures designed to protect American possessions in the Philippines.

If American idealists were dismayed at the State Department's constricted interpretation of the relative rule, the pragmatists on the President's Advisory Committee on Political Refugees were outraged. Chairman James McDonald, speaking for the entire committee on September 4, 1941, issued a statement to Roosevelt which contradicted everything Long had told the president. "The so-called relative rule," wrote McDonald, "should be cancelled or substantially modified. Our experience with refugees has convinced us that it is unnecessary, illogical, ill-adapted to the purposes claimed for it, and cruelly burdensome on the refugees affected by it." Rather than elaborating the visa process, McDonald argued, it should be simplified. Washington need only be consulted as a final resort, rather than as a preliminary step, to approval.[94]

The attack on Pearl Harbor banished all hopes for the modifications which McDonald and the committee favored. Instead, there was talk in December 1941 of reviving the Hobbs

Bill, a measure which would have interned all aliens in concentration camps where "good" aliens could be sifted from the
"bad." [95] On December 7, Roosevelt enjoined persons of Japanese ancestry in this country to refrain from acts against the
public safety and issued restrictions on travel, possession of
firearms, cameras, and shortwave radios. These steps were
preparatory to removing 100,000 of these aliens and Nisei from
the West Coast to eighteen "relocation centers" in Utah, Idaho,
and Colorado by the summer of 1942. By January 7, 1942 further restrictions were imposed on all alien nationals who may
have fled the "enemy" states of Germany, Italy, Austria, Hungary, and Korea. Even Jews who were technically stateless
emigres were instructed that they were now classified as
"enemy nationals" and were required to obtain affidavits of
two persons who could vouch for their loyalty. Not until November 1942 did the Alien Enemy Control Unit, set up in the
first days of the war by the Department of Justice, remove such
restrictions on the stateless and the Italians.

The State Department prided itself on having spared the
nation from what Long termed "the pernicious activities against
the United States by German agents in the guise of refugees"
between 1939 and 1942. Testifying before Congress in the
winter of 1943, Long said, "I think the records of the FBI will
show that there was quite a good deal of that at one time and
that there were in this country certain persons to whom those
persons were under instructions to report when they arrived." [96]
In his memoirs Hull revealed that he also subscribed to the
theory that without the vigilance of the State Department an
unchecked influx of refugees would only have resulted in widespread espionage before Pearl Harbor and catastrophe afterward. [97]

The facts do not support such viewpoints. Far from finding
a sinister anti-democratic conspiracy among refugees, the FBI
testified to the loyalty of America's immigrants. J. Edgar Hoover indicated as much in a letter to Representative William G.
Stratton in April 1947. Hoover wrote, "The experience of the
FBI in coping with foreign agents, spies and saboteurs has con-
clusively illustrated that the great mass of aliens are loyal to

America, devoted to the principles of democracy. The vast majority of aliens have remained true to the land of their adoption." [98] Only 23,000 "enemy aliens," representing less than one-half of 1 percent of all aliens of enemy nationality in the U.S. in 1940, were ever taken into custody for questioning. Only a fraction of these ever received jail sentences—generally for minor violations of immigration regulations. Moreover, these so-called enemy aliens distinguished themselves in all kinds of endeavors which were beneficial to the war effort. Between July 1, 1940 and June 30, 1945, some 300,000 foreign-born served in the U.S. Army, among them 109,000 noncitizens and 30,000 "enemy aliens." Thousands more labored in defense plants or contributed their ingenuity in promoting the Allied cause.[99]

It may be argued that Hull and Long did not have the benefit of this hindsight and that the Nazi menace seemed quite real when they were faced with making decisions in 1940 and 1941. But the government did have access to reports of the provost marshal general from World War I, telling of the overwhelming loyalty of immigrants then. Four million aliens, 60 percent of whom had not even sworn out their declarations of intent to become naturalized citizens, registered for the draft in that first war. Thousands distinguished themselves on the Allied side in a war where the issues were not as clearly defined as in World War II.[100] Moreover, the State Department had the analysis of the new immigration and naturalization commissioner, Earl Harrison, issued three months before Pearl Harbor, that aliens were reliable persons with strong ties in the U.S. and that aliens at no time ever conducted themselves en masse as "enemies" of the United States.[101]

In the final analysis the State Department's reasoning for restricting immigration between 1939 and 1942 had little basis in fact. Despite Long's efforts to the contrary, Nazi sympathizers came and went in and out of the U.S. with relative ease. In 1940, for example, the U.S. admitted French anti-Semite Pierre Massin, John Makkari, author of Hungary's anti-Jewish laws, Gerhard Westrick, a Nazi businessman from Germany, and several anti-Jewish Czech laborers from Bata (subsequently deported for their anti-democratic behavior in this country), while legitimate refugees from totalitarianism perched anxiously at the tips of semi-free Europe.[102] Even after Germany declared war on the U.S., several persons who had emigrated to Hitler-occupied lands during the late years of the depression were brought back to the U.S. on the S.S. *Drottning-holm*.[103]

The U.S. made no effort to bar Frederich Ried, German consul in New York, from taking his post in the summer of 1940, although Brazil had expelled him for the subversive conduct which now sent shivers up and down the spines of State Department personnel. Ried boasted openly of having founded 1,000 schools for Nazi activity in Brazil before being ousted from that country.[104] His story was not unique, and Breckinridge Long complained throughout 1940 that the German consulate and embassy were spy-infested and that diplomatic visas were being granted to individuals who were not members of the German Foreign Service.[105] The German embassy in Washington remained open until June 30, 1941. Italy and Japan maintained their centers of foreign intrigue in the capital until December of that year. And Vichy France, whose Second Bureau caused Long and the FBI so much consternation, maintained its embassy in Washington until November 1942.

Although the State Department was alarmed by the thought of refugee conspirators, it is significant that of thirty persons indicted for sedition by the attorney general's office in the spring of 1942, not one was an alien.[106] Even more significant was the fact that many months before Pearl Harbor, the FBI and various municipal police had shattered every one of the major Nazi espionage networks in the United States, including those operations headed by Wilhelm Lonkowsky, Ludwig Crown, Guenther Rumrich, Baron Duquesne, Franz von der Osten, and Paul Borchardt.[107] Hans Thomsen, German chargé in Washington, lamented in 1941, "American authorities knew of the entire network, which was no work of art in view of the naive and, to a certain extent, stupid manner in the way these people carried on." [108]

Irrational panic, fanned by nativism and anti-Semitism,

resulted in the constriction of American immigration at a time when sanctuary for refugees of all faiths was both desirable and possible, when French ships sailed regularly from Marseilles to Martinique, when the British Blue Star Line carried on a steady passenger trade to South America, when Sweden offered to charter vessels from Göteborg to the United States, when C.I.T., the Italian Travel Agency, and steamship lines in Portugal and Spain stood by ready to transport emigrants to the Western Hemisphere at $500 to $1,000 a person.[109] On the American government's reluctance to evince interest in any of these facilities *The Nation* Editor Freda Kirchwey wrote:

> The record is one which must sicken any person of ordinarily humane instinct. It is as if we were to examine laboriously the curricula vitae of flood victims clinging to a piece of floating wreckage and finally to decide that no matter what their virtues, all but a few had better be allowed to drown.[110]

Not until the spring of 1944, when the operations of the Visa Division were transferred to Adolph Berle, would the policies of Breckinridge Long and his associates be liberalized.[111]

6. A Partnership
of Silence

S*tephen S. Wise* was the most important Jewish leader in the United States during the Second World War. In his quest for justice for his people, the Budapest-born rabbi wore many hats during this critical period—president of the American Jewish Congress, chairman of the American Emergency Committee for Zionist Affairs, chairman of the Executive Committee of the World Jewish Congress, cochairman of the Zionist Organization of America, chairman of the United Jewish War Effort, chairman of the American Jewish Conference, and cochairman of the Commission of Rescue of the American Jewish Conference. Wise had long been a leader in the fight to establish a Jewish homeland in Palestine. He took pride in the fact that he had sensed the danger inherent in Hitler's rise to power in 1932 when German-Jewish leaders were saying, "Er wird nie zur Macht Kommen." [1] Wise advocated boycotts and protest demonstrations against Hitler long before such tactics became stylish in the U.S. He championed relief and rescue of refugees during the 1930s and was instrumental in bringing about the short-lived unity among Jewish groups on the eve of the war. His well-publicized friendship with FDR, whom he addressed affectionately as "Boss" or "Chief," dated back to the president's unsuccessful senatorial race in 1914. The doors of the White House were always open to Wise, whom Roosevelt had appointed to his Advisory Committee on Political Refugees. To his comrades at the American Jewish Congress, Wise was a "hero" who labored night and day to organize fifteen massive rallies at Madison Square Garden and who constantly badgered the State Department, Roosevelt, and Treasury

Secretary Henry Morgenthau for more action on behalf of his tortured people in wartime.[2]

Because of his power and prestige Wise was the man with whom anyone receiving confirmation of the rumored Nazi extermination plot against the Jews in 1942 would wish to communicate.[3] Once in possession of such catastrophic news, European Jews hoped Wise might influence the president to force the Allies into taking decisive measures to save the rest of Europe's doomed Jews. Failing this, perhaps Wise would be able to rally the American public to break down existing immigration barriers. Perhaps the rabbi, in desperation, would implement Gandhi's well-known techniques of Satyaragraha, lead a march on Washington like that threatened by Negro leader A. Philip Randolph, engage in a hunger strike, or call for civil disobedience to effect some outward expression of concern for the Jews on the part of the United Nations. To preclude such activism, Arthur Morse intimates, the State Department deliberately deceived the rabbi and withheld information confirming Nazi genocide from Wise for three months in the fall of 1942.[4]

State Department records seem to bear out Morse's contention that Wise personally, and the American Jewish community collectively, were at first kept unaware of the department's terrible information. On August 10, 1942, Howard Elting, Jr., American vice-consul in Geneva, mailed Hull a two-page memorandum on a discussion held with Gerhart Riegner, secretary of the World Jewish Congress, in Switzerland. Riegner claimed that an unnamed German businessman, who had supplied him with accurate information on two previous occasions, had verified the Nazi plan to exterminate all four million of Europe's surviving Jews that fall through the use of Zyklon B gas—Prussic Acid. Riegner, in what Elting termed "a state of great agitation," requested that all Allied governments and Jewish organizations, particularly the World Jewish Congress which Wise led, be informed of his report. Elting, although astonished by Riegner's statements, emphasized that the young Jewish attorney appeared to be "a serious and balanced individual, and that he would never have come to the consulate with the above report if he had not had confidence in his informant's reliability and if he did not seriously consider that the report might well contain an element of truth." Elting recommended that Riegner's request to relay this news to Wise be honored.[5]

However, Elting's superior in Bern, Leland Harrison, was more skeptical. When he cabled the essence of the Riegner message to the State Department on August 11, Harrison attached a disclaimer, attributing the report to "war rumor inspired by fear and what is commonly understood to be the actually miserable condition of these refugees who face decimation as a result of physical maltreatment, persecution, and scarcely endurable privations, malnutrition and disease." [6] The State Department's European Division director, Elbredge Durbrow, went further. He recommended that Wise and other Jewish leaders not be informed of Riegner's "fantastic" allegations. Even if true, he reasoned, the United States could do nothing at the present time to help the victims.[7]

Paul T. Culbertson, Durbrow's assistant chief in the European Division, took a different view. He drafted a communication to Wise along the lines indicated in the Riegner message.[8] This note, which attempted to dismiss Riegner's tale as "unreliable war rumor," was never sent. The original is still on file, bearing three pencil slashes across the body with the statement "Do Not Send" and the initials "ED" of Durbrow.[9] Instead of provoking the American Jewish community into fits of frenzy over an atrocity tale, the State Department wired Geneva on August 17 to "recommend" that no further unconfirmed reports be transmitted by "third parties" and that all reports be limited to information involving "definite American interests." This cable was signed by Sumner Welles and Cordell Hull, and initialed by Durbrow and J. H. Hickerson of the European Division, among others.[10]

Despite this admonition, American officials in Switzerland felt they could not sit on information supplied by Riegner in the fall of 1942. On September 28, Paul C. Squire, American consul in Geneva, mailed a set of reports to Hull. They did not arrive until October 23, indicative of a slowdown in the transmission of such information at this critical juncture. In these documents Riegner identified his source as a man called "Frank," someone who maintained close political and military connections in the Government-General of Poland. By this time Riegner had received additional confirmation of the extermination scheme from several other sources. From a Swiss university professor, he had obtained a memorandum of a German officer attached to the OKW (Wehrmacht High Command), detailing how the Nazis were proceeding against the Jews. This Wehrmacht officer, allegedly a member of a group opposed to the Hitler regime, told of cattle trains from the West streaming through Germany loaded with Jews, many of them already dead of suffocation or starvation. He told of mass killings, often done by physicians who injected air into the veins of their victims, and of research by other physicians, who were studying new uses for corpses, such as in the production of soap, glue, and lubricants.[11]

Riegner also supplied Squire with photostats of two letters written in code from Jews in Warsaw to friends in St. Gallen, Switzerland. The first was dated September 4, 1942. Translated from the broken German, it reads:

> I spoke to Mr. Jaeger, He told me that he will invite all relatives of the family Achenu with the exception of Miss Eisensweig from Warsaw to his countryside dwelling Kewer. I am alone here; I feel lonely . . . As to the citrus fruit I hope that I shall receive them in time (for Sukkos) but I do not know whether I shall then find anybody of my acquaintances. I feel very weak. A week ago I yet spoke to Mr. Orlean. Mrs. Gefen telephones very often. Uncle Gerusch also works in Warsaw; he is a very capable worker. His friend Miso works together with him. Please pray for me.[12]

State Department interpreters confirmed that there were numerous code words in the above message, including Mr. Jaeger (Germans); the family Achenu (our brethren, the Jews); Miss Eisensweig (probably those working in the iron industry); Kewer (tomb, grave); Zitrus fruchte (citrus fruits used on Succos near the end of September); Gerusch (deportation); Miso (death); Mrs. Gefen and Mr. Orlean (references to the countryside). The implication which these government officials gave to the message was that Jews in Warsaw, with the exception of those in vital industries, were being deported to be killed in the countryside of Poland and that this was to be accomplished before Succos.[13]

Riegner's second letter, dated September 12 read in literal translation from the garbled German:

> I too was in sorrow, for I am now so lonely. Uncle Achenu has died. Excuse my fashion of expression. I suppose that I shall receive the advised citrus fruit these days. As the Uncle is now dead, I do not know to whom to give them. I am very sad that I cannot use them and that they will have to dry miserably. Those fine fruits. My regards to Mr. Tschlenoff and please tell him that all his work and pains are in vain completely. I shall write about it in my next letter.[14]

Once more State Department translators noted that the Mr. Tschlenoff referred to was the representative of the Jewish OSE, specializing in medical support for the ghettos in Poland. The import of this letter, then, was that few Jews remained alive in Warsaw and that those who did survive were doomed anyway.[15]

The U.S. government, in conjunction with eleven other nations engaged in the struggle against the Axis, formally acknowledged the existence of this mass murder plot on December 17, 1942, in a declaration which warned that "those responsible for these crimes shall not escape retribution." [16] Any thought that this might change the prevailing attitude at the State Department was dispelled early the next February. For the previous five months Riegner had continued to supply Washington with verified accounts of atrocities in Poland and Rumania, contributing to this government's realization of the horrid reality of Nazi genocide.[17] On February 10, however, Harrison received another cable signed by Welles for Hull which ordered, not merely recommended, that all further communications from Riegner be barred from official correspondence. This cable, bearing the code number 354, read:

In the future we would suggest that you do not accept reports submitted to you to be transmitted to private persons in the United States unless such action is advisable because of extraordinary circumstances. Such private messages circumvent neutral countries' censorship and it is felt that by sending them we risk the possibility that steps would necessarily be taken by the neutral countries to curtail or forbid our means of communication for confidential official matter.[18]

Who actually devised this cable and why he was so concerned about Swiss sensitivities about genocide cannot be determined. Two months after it was sent Welles cabled Bern again, asking for additional reports from Riegner, precisely the kind of material Harrison had been ordered not to send earlier. From discussions with Hull, Henry Morgenthau concluded that neither the secretary nor Welles had been responsible for Cable 354.[19] Nevertheless, this cable, issued two months after the United States had officially condemned Nazi genocide, typified the desultory manner in which the State Department treated news of Jewish persecution during the war.

Twice—on February 16 and 23, 1940—Assistant Secretary Adolph A. Berle, Jr., tried to prod Hull to action, basing his claim of brutal deportations of Jews to concentration camps on reports from Alexander Kirk in Warsaw. Berle said, "We should register a protest. We did so during the far less significant, though more dramatic, riots of a year ago November; and I see no reason why we should not make our feelings known regarding a policy of seemingly calculated cruelty which is beginning to be apparent now." Berle stressed that the U.S. had protested Nazi oppression in 1933 and 1938 and had even spoken on violation of American commercial rights by the British blockade in the early days of World War II. All the more reason, he argued, to register an impartial protest in the face of the current pogrom.[20]

Berle's request for such a protest was squelched by Breckinridge Long. In a two-page memorandum to Hull, initialed by the European Division's J. H. Hickerson, Long expressed "every sympathy with the poor people involved," but went on to point out that such a formal protest would be redundant. The United States had through its admission of "a great many of these poor people" already registered its tacit disapproval of this persecution. "It is hardly necessary for us to make public expressions of our feelings. Everyone in this country already knows, and the civilized governments of the world are already cognizant of, our feelings in the matter," Long said. Far from doing any good, he reasoned, such a protest would only embarrass the U.S., would be exploited for political gain in the Allied camp as a condemnation of Germany, and would impair any opportunity the U.S. might still have to help the victims. He noted further that Germany might take offense at what he, Long, agreed was purely an internal affair. "We have known since the publication of *Mein Kampf*, and since the accession of Hitler to power, that these poor people would be subjected to all kinds of improper treatment," he added.[21]

If the State Department recognized Hitler's plan to persecute European Jewry in 1940 after the mere reading of *Mein Kampf*, it is difficult to explain the department's skepticism of the verification of genocide in 1942. Even before the first Riegner message had been relayed in August, sufficient evidence existed to establish at least a prima facie case for the existence of a plan to exterminate the Jews. On June 2, 1941, Jan Ciechanowski, ambassador of the Polish Government-in-Exile in Washington, delivered a White Paper to Hull, charging the Nazis with "compulsory euthanasia" against the Jews.[22] A year later, in June 1942, the same Polish government in London, drawing its information from reports smuggled out of occupied territory by underground channels, broadcast the news that 700,000 Jews had been murdered in Poland and Lithuania that year.[23] On June 17, the Jewish Telegraphic Agency announced the execution of hundreds of Jewish and Russian war prisoners in poison gas experiments at the Liebenau Monastery in Wurttemburg.[24] In July the same agency confirmed that 20,000 French Jews and more than 100,000 Austrian Jews had been deported to the East, half of them dying enroute to Poland.[25] Israel Goldstein, president of the Synagogue Council of America, submitted a long report to Hull on July 17 which detailed the slaughter. Goldstein supplied Hull with information on the machine-gunning of masses of

Jews in Galicia, on mobile gas chambers used to exterminate thousands "in a less painful fashion" in the region of Lublin, on the forced starvation of a half million Jews in Warsaw, on 25,000 Jews murdered in the Pinsk-Vladimir-Vitebsk region of Russia, on another 25,000 dead in Odessa, on the cleansing of Slovakia of its last several thousand Jews.[26] Four days later Herschel V. Johnson of the American legation in Stockholm sent Washington a résumé of a discussion held with Wieclav Patek, director of the Consular Section of the Polish Legation in Stockholm. According to Patek, 60,000 Jews in Vilna, another 100,000 in Kiev, and 84,000 in White Ruthenia had been massacred by special Nazi battalions of death.[27] Patek's figures were corroborated by Soviet Commissar for Foreign Affairs, V. M. Molotov, in an official note to the Allied governments a few days later.[28] On August 6, four days before Riegner met with Elting, the reliable American Friends Service Committee through its operatives in Vichy France reported that thousands of Jews were being transported from occupied regions of France to Southeastern Poland, "where conditions of life are such that few can survive." [29]

Through the summer of 1942 scores of reports poured into the State Department from refugees, Swedish businessmen, the *WRN* (the leading Polish underground newspaper), the Jewish Telegraph Agency; the Jewish anti-Fascist Committee in Kuibyshev even monitored radio broadcasts from Berlin, all telling of the same thing—that the Jews were "spurlos" (missing), that they were being transported to Poland in the most inhumane of conditions, that "their fate was no mystery." [30] Far from publicizing such communications, the State Department consistently elected to suppress them.

On September 1, 1942, Shloime Mendelsohn, the representative of the American Jewish Congress in London, tried to contact Rabbis Wise and Perlszweig by cable to urge them to hold a press conference at which the rabbis would confirm the existence of the Nazi extermination plot. Mendelsohn suggested that the Allies issue a formal condemnation of genocide, that the Vatican be asked to intercede on behalf of the captive

Jews, and that, failing all this, Hitler be warned that the Allies would engage in reprisals against the person and property of German nationals abroad.[31] The cable, sent through State Department wires, was stopped at the desk of Foreign Activity Correlation. Appended to it were two notes. The first read, "We will *suppress* if you approve." The second read, "Here is a cable message somewhat in line with ones I have previously referred to you. Pass or suppress?" These queries were directed to Berle, who had wanted to speak out against Nazi persecution two years before. For unknown reasons, the Mendelsohn cable was never sent.

Even after American officials in Stockholm verified the existence of the death camps in the so-called Lublin Reservation on November 25, 1942, the American government issued no formal pronouncement on the extermination of the Jews for three more weeks. The reason for this procrastination, Morse implies, was anti-Semitism in the State Department. Such an answer is, however, an oversimplification of the problem, as well as an insult to many officials engaged in the decision-making process. Morgenthau's memoirs leave little doubt that the Secretary of Treasury considered Hull, Welles, and Long genuinely sympathetic to the plight of the Jews, if somewhat incompetent to meet the problem.[32] Some of the lesser officials in the department perhaps harbored anti-Jewish feelings, but such personal feelings likely were of secondary importance when compared with other factors that led to a suppression of atrocity reports.

For one thing, the nation had already waged one great crusade in this century and suffered extreme disillusionment in that humanitarian cause. Only too late did the American public realize that stories of German rapine and death factories in Belgium were propaganda tales spun by the British. The historical revisionism of the 1920s had left Americans with a greater sense of skepticism where atrocity stories were concerned. It is noteworthy that in January 1943, a month after the Allies condemned Nazi genocide, fewer than half of the American people believed the Nazis were deliberately killing the Jews.[33]

As late as December 1944, when Allied troops had already over-run some camps, most Americans still believed that fewer than 100,000 Jews had been exterminated.[34]

Even if the reports coming from Europe were partially true, what difference could that make to people hardened by the massacre of 500,000 Armenians in World War I, 150,000 Ukrainian Jews during the Russian Civil War, millions of Russian Kulaks who starved to death or were exterminated in Stalinist purges in the Thirties, thousands of Spanish Republicans bombed to death in 1937 and 1938, and millions of Chinese victimized by the Japanese since 1931? It was generally believed that in this war the Jews had no monopoly on suffering. As late as July 10, 1942 the *Times* (London) charged that the Germans were "aiming at extermination" of Poles, whereas what the Jews were suffering was a "plight." The idea that the Nazis would truly attempt to eliminate six to ten million people in a concerted plan of human slaughter, however, seemed absurd. That it was rejected as implausible by staid government officials 6,000 miles from the death camps should not seem remarkable; the victims did not even believe it to the very end.

Through 1942 the Nazis took extraordinary precautions to guard against any disclosure of the truth about "resettlement in the East." They sent forged postcards from relatives long since gassed to the ghettos of Poland, telling of the glories of nonexistent pastoral wonderlands. It is a testimonial to Nazi security that few persons succeeded in escaping from the death camps. Those who did failed to rouse the remaining Jewish populations, lacking in arms and will, to resistance. The doomed Jews, programmed for their own destruction by centuries of social antipathy and abuse, broken by disease and hunger, but still dedicated to the principle of the essential goodness of man, simply would not believe that such an inhuman plan could spring from German civilization.[35]

The State Department alone cannot be faulted for failing to condemn Nazi genocide in 1942, when everyone in the world had already witnessed a decade of this same brutality, when Dachau was transformed from a quaint village in Bavaria to the symbol of concentration camp ruthlessness, when the world had witnessed three years of Nazi rule in Poland where Jews were rationed fewer than 200 calories of food a day, when the world had known for one year of Nazi slaughter in Russia and Rumania where, as Ambassador Franklin Gunther had reported to Hull, thousands of Jews were massacred and strung up on meat hooks.[36] The final act of the Jewish tragedy in Europe was being performed in the open, and yet the global audience seemingly needed a printed libretto to comprehend this fantastic scene.

The cautious bureaucrats who surrounded Cordell Hull in 1942 reasoned that nothing could be done to help Europe's Jews. Publication of such unconfirmed reports could only evoke frustration and hysteria and ultimately detract from the war effort. Too late, with several hundred thousand Jews dead, did these functionaries realize that they had miscalculated in their evaluations of the reports. Too late did they realize that they had overrated the emotional level and preparedness of the American Jewish community. Nothing had to be concealed, nothing feared, from this relatively docile group, for it had already possessed piecemeal confirmation of Nazi genocide plans. Wise had received Riegner's message long before December 1942, and he and the leaders of the Jewish community had remained silent.

To argue that the American Jewish community and Wise had deliberately been kept uninformed by the State Department, that Jewish organizations operating independently of official cable lines had gathered sufficient data to submit a twenty-page report on German atrocities to the White House on December 8, 1942, and that this dramatic report ultimately impelled the government to take action in concert with its allies would make relatively pleasant reading—if true.[37]

But it is indisputable that Wise, like many other Jewish leaders in America, not only knew about the death camps in the summer of 1942, five months in advance of the forementioned petition, but actively collaborated with the department in keeping verified accounts of mass murder from the public. Wise admitted as much when he wrote Roosevelt a "Dear Boss" letter on December 2, 1942. Requesting a word of solace and hope for the Jews, Wise said, "I have had cables and underground advices for months, telling of these things. I succeeded, together with the heads of other Jewish organizations in keeping them out of the press, and have been in constant communication with the State Department, particularly Under-Secretary Welles." [38]

The rabbi had been equally well-informed, though somewhat less laconic, earlier that summer when he addressed a cheering throng at Madison Square Garden in one of the now-famed "Stop Hitler" rallies. Three weeks before Elting had his first meeting with Riegner in Switzerland, Wise and other Jewish leaders protested the murder of "more than a million Jews already brutally done to death by the Nazis." Hitler, they argued, would not be satisfied till every Jewish community in Europe was transformed into a vast cemetery, and they even detailed his scheme for gassing the Jews in a resolution which concluded "The Jewish people will not permit itself to be exterminated." The resolution read, in part:

> In the whole long history of man's inhumanity to man, there is no record of persecution more charged with brutality and horror than the record of the special persecution of the Jews by the Nazis. *The extermination of the Jews* has been the first goal of Hitler in his mad race to dominate the world. He has waded through Jewish blood and tears. Jews have been branded, segregated in ghettos, made the inevitable victims of hunger and plague, deprived of all possibilities of life and labor. Multitudes have suffered the agonies of a slow and painful death by the methods of forced labor, in concentration camps, or as *victims of experiment in poison gas factories* (Italics added).[39]

Such comments were not mere exercises in rhetoric. The choice of the word "extermination" was deliberate, for the very first sentence of the underground report of the Jewish Socialist Party in Poland smuggled out of Europe in May, 1942 read: "From the day the Russo-German war broke out, the Germans embarked on the physical extermination of the Jewish population on Polish soil, using the Ukrainians and the Lithuanian fascists for this job." This report went on to detail the massacres of 50,000 Jews in Vilna; 30,000 in Lwow; 25,000 in Lublin; 15,-000 in Stanislawow, Rowne, and Brzezany; 9,000 in Slonim; 6,000 in Hancewicze; and 5,000 in Tarnopol in the fall of 1941. It revealed the first primitive forms of execution used: men were driven to cemeteries or fields where they were forced to dig trenches and then were shot by machine guns, and women and children were shot down in the streets. And it told of the gassing operations of Nazi death camps at Chelmno ("twelve kilometers from the town of Kolo") and Maidanek ("Majdanek Tatarowy, a suburb of Lublin").[40]

The report so startled Shmul Zygelboim and Ignacy Schwarzbart, Jewish representatives on the Polish National Council in London, that they pressed the Exile Government and Great Britain for a condemnation of what Schwartzbart called "the threatened annihilation of European Jewry." On July 9, 1942, Stanislaw Mikolajczyk, minister of home affairs in the Polish government in exile, finally told the press of the systematic destruction of the Jewish population of Poland, but his claim of 700,000 deaths was not readily accepted by other segments of world Jewry. Yitzhak Gruenbaum, head of the Jewish Agency's Department for the Diaspora in Palestine, discounted the stories of mass murders in Poland and Lithuania because the numbers reported were larger than the known number of Jews in those areas.[41] At a conference of Jewish publicists held in August 1942 under the auspices of the World Jewish Congress, Leon Kubowitzki of the WJC dismissed the report of the Bund, saying, "Such things do not happen in the twentieth century." [42] A week later, the editorial board of the militant *Jewish Frontier* also rejected the idea of a Nazi extermination scheme as "the macabre fantasy of a lunatic sadist." [43] Marie Syrkin later called this reluctance of American Jews to recognize genocide in the face of overwhelming testimony "a monument to our gross stupidity." [44]

Long before December 1942, however, Wise possessed the

Jewish Bund report and more. He actually received the first of Gerhart Riegner's messages on August 28, shortly after Elting's letter relating the discussions with the World Jewish Congress representative in detail reached Washington by mail pouch. Riegner had contacted Labour Member of Parliament Sidney Silverman, chairman of the British Jewish Congress. Silverman relayed Riegner's information to Wise while officials in the State Department debated the merits of notifying him.[45]

According to Lillie Shultz, Riegner's "incredible" news was discussed in a closed session of the AJC's executive board. It was decided that Wise should go to Washington and attempt to verify Riegner's news through the State Department.[46] In his autobiography Wise indicates that he did consult Welles shortly after receipt of the Riegner message and was asked not to release the story until the Allies checked further into the matter. On November 4, 1942, Welles called in the rabbi "to confirm and justify your deepest fears."[47] Ten weeks had elapsed since Wise first received Riegner's report. Another month would go by before the Jewish leaders would request some formal condemnation by the American government.

Wise agonized between his responsibility to inform humanity that Jews were being singled out for expeditious slaughter and his promise to Welles to keep silent about it. In September 1942 he poured out his grief in a letter to longtime comrade John Hayes Holmes, minister of the Community Church in New York City:

> I have had the unhappiest days of my life. Please remember, dear Holmes, that in addition to all your suffering over everything connected with the war, I have something more, namely the uniquely tragic fate of my people. You will be tempted at once to ask, why do I think of it as "uniquely tragic?" "Is it any worse than the fate of the Czechs or Yugoslavs or Poles?" Yes! Think of what it means to hear, as I have heard, through a coded message—first from Geneva, then from Berne, through the British Foreign Office—that Hitler plans the extermination at one time of the whole Jewish population of Europe; and prussic acid is mentioned as the medium.
> The other day something came to me which has left me

without sleep: that 100,000 Jews within the Warsaw Ghetto have been massacred by the Nazis and their corpses used to make soaps and fertilizers . . . . Moreover, Jews, unarmed and defenseless, have been unable to do anything for themselves; and the world has done little if anything for them. . . .

. . . .

I don't want to turn my heart inside out, but I am almost demented over my people's grief.[48]

Elie Wiesel, author of several volumes relating to the Holocaust and a graduate of the Nazi concentration camp system, addressed the forty-ninth General Assembly of the Union of American Hebrew Congregations in 1967 and asked: "How could he [Wise] pledge secrecy when millions of lives were involved? How was he not driven mad by the secret? How could other Jewish leaders pledge silence? How is it they did not cry out in despair?" And when Welles released Wise from his pledge, what happened then?

> Not much. Not much at all. Did he and the other Jewish leaders proclaim hunger strikes to the end? Did they organize daily, weekly marches to the White House? They should have shaken heaven and earth, echoing the agony of their doomed brethren; taken in by Roosevelt's personality, they, in a way, became accomplices to his inaction.[49]

Shultz dismisses Wiesel's arguments by claiming that no one who lived through incarceration in a concentration camp can have any patience or objectivity in dealing with the record of Jews who were not caught in the death-trap of Europe. "Human beings have only so much capacity," she said, "and Wiesel and his kind cannot understand that. We were heroes, fighting Hitler. It is horrifying that we did not succeed, but wrong to judge us." [50]

One Jew, not caught in that death-trap, would have disagreed. Chayim Greenberg, editor of *Jewish Frontier,* was one of those like Kubowitzki, Syrkin, and Wise who originally dismissed the reports of genocide as rumor. Subsequently, however, he altered his view and authored a scathing indictment of American Jewry for the *Yiddisher Kempfer.* This article, entitled "Bankrupt," appeared in the February 1943 issue of that journal, but was not translated into English until 1964. Hence, much of the hoped-for impact upon Greenberg's contemporaries was lost.

Like Wiesel, Greenberg wondered how American Jews had managed to maintain their sanity in the face of the news from Europe. He wrote:

> A horny shell seems to have formed over the soul of American Jewry to protect and defend it against pain and pity. We have become so dulled that we have even lost the capacity for madness and—may God not punish me for my words—the fact that in recent months Jews have not produced a substantial number of mentally deranged persons is hardly a symptom of health.[51]

Greenberg chronicled the failures of all segments of the Jewish community in America to do its elementary duty toward the millions of Jews who were captive and doomed in Europe. Chief among these was the failure of American Jewry to organize some kind of general staff, to bridge the gaps between cliques of Zionists and anti-Zionists, Congressists and anti-Congressists, Orthodox and Reform, synagogue Jews and secularists, labor and management. "Every 'Committee' cherishes its own committee-interests, its sectarian ambitions, its exclusively wise strategy and its 'power position' in the teapot of Jewish communal competition," he wrote (p. 8).

Greenberg blasted the American Jewish Committee, which had held its annual conference in January 1943 and had passed a number of resolutions but had said nothing about the massacre of the Jews in Europe. He blasted the Jewish Labor Committee for its "non-cooperation, non-action, and keeping apart from common attempts to accomplish something." He blasted the Orthodox Jews who refused to collaborate with other groups unless one of their members was assigned an important post (p. 6). But most of all he lambasted the American Jewish Congress and Wise.

Greenberg noted that the American Jewish Congress had established a special planning committee to deal with rescue activity and had assigned an emissary to stay in Washington on a more or less permanent basis to maintain contacts with various government departments. But the rescue committee itself had delegated responsibility to a subcommittee (chaired by "a very busy man") which had met only once in more than two months, and the emissary in Washington was "a foreigner who cannot always exert the necessary influence in our capital," according to Greenberg. Although one stated goal of the rescue committee was to enroll Christian clerics in the struggle to save Jewish lives, Greenberg pointed out that there had been little such effort in the United States and no effort whatever to seek the intercession of the Vatican to stop the slaughter. He concluded: "The AJ Congress, the only Jewish organization which did not remove the subject of the extermination of the Jews of Europe from its agenda has proven to be criminally slow and lacking in tempo and temperament in its rescue work" (pp. 8–9).

Indeed, Wise had had much difficulty in balancing his responsibilities as an American with his duties toward the Jewish people after 1938. Until then he had been the Young Turk among Jewish leaders, the most outspoken radical in condemning Hitler. But in June 1938 he altered some of the procedures and toned down publicity campaigns for the World Jewish Congress elections at the request of Roosevelt and Henry Messersmith, who worried that the affair might be construed by "someone in Des Moines" as proof of the existence of the Elders of Zion.[52] Later that year, right after Kristallnacht, Wise wrote Holmes that "I am trying to keep Jews silent until after tomorrow's funeral of the victim of the crazed Polish Jewish boy."[53] And during the debate over the Wagner-Rogers Child Refugee Bill in 1939, Wise again counseled silence on the part of the Jewish community.[54] A Zionist News Service bulletin of October 13, 1972 has further charged that the American Zionist Emergency Council, headed jointly by Wise and Rose Halprin, was responsible for turning down a request for aid to Jews stranded in Rumania in November 1939. The refugees, who included twelve-year-old Albert Mandler, now commander of Israel's Sinai forces, were turned down because the Zionist Council felt it could not assist "undesirable elements" to enter Palestine.

It was as if Wise preferred to throw verbal darts against other Jews, like "the Warburg Gang," "Skunkolsky" George Sokolsky, and Jerome Frank, whom, Wise argued, was suffering from "dementia assimilata," [55] rather than to speak up on behalf of the troubled millions in Europe. At the same time Wise expressed concern that he, too, might be suffering from the malady which he claimed afflicted Frank. He wrote to Felix Frankfurter on September 16, 1942, "I don't know whether I am getting to be a *Hofjude*, but I find that a good part of my work is to explain to my fellow Jews why our Government cannot do all the things asked or expected of it." [56] Wise's actions throughout 1943 and 1944 did little to relieve him of that particular anxiety.

Wise was helpful in bringing about a short-lived unity among Jewish groups in the United States, much on the order of that suggested by Greenberg, by the end of the summer of 1943.[57] But his domineering leadership of the American Jewish Conference (Greenberg had already chided the American Jewish Congress for its "own prestige ambitions" and its jealous attempts to corner all "credit" for relief and rescue operations) resulted in the collapse of this united front in a name-calling debacle two months later. When the conference took a strong stand in support of a Jewish commonwealth in Palestine, Judge Joseph Proskauer of the American Jewish Committee announced that body's intention to withdraw. Because this decision had been reached by the AJ Committee's executive council without consultation of the full membership, other Jews announced the severance of their ties with the AJ Committee.[58] Thus, within two months of its formation, the American Jewish Conference had witnessed one act of secession within another act of secession. Such episodes typified the absence of American Jewish unity during the war.

Even more distressing from the viewpoint of the Jews in Europe was Wise's consistent opposition to the American Friends of a Jewish Palestine, the Committee for an Army of Stateless and Palestinian Jews, the American League for a Free Palestine, and the Emergency Conference to Save the Jewish People of Europe. These committees all were organized in the

United States after 1939 by two Palestinian Jews, Peter Bergson, whose real name was Kook, and Samuel Merlin. Members of the terrorist *Irgun Zvai Leumi*, these men succeeded in gaining the nominal support of thirty-three senators, 109 representatives, fourteen current governors, fourteen ambassadors, sixty mayors of important American cities, 400 rabbis of various degrees of orthodoxy, twice that number in Christian ministers, 500 university presidents and professors, a score of American generals, colonels, admirals, and rear admirals, hundreds of stage and screen personalities, and even several members of Roosevelt's cabinet by 1943.[59]

Nevertheless, Wise's American Jewish Conference condemned the leaders of these groups (including Ben Hecht, Max Lerner, Emil Lengyel, Louis Bromfield, Pierre Van Paassen, and Will Rogers, Jr.) as "opportunists" who represented a small political party in constant friction with the constituted Jewish leadership of the country and whose only purpose was to spread chaos and demoralization in Jewish life.[60] For Wise, who shared the Jewish Agency's distaste for the Irgun's methods, Bergson's manifold operations in this country were a distinct embarrassment, "a wretched plot," as he told Sol Bloom.[61]

Wise thus served to buttress the State Department's unwillingness to allow Bergson's Committee for an Army of Stateless Jews to send a field representative to Turkey to help with Jewish relief in the Balkans. Throughout the summer of 1943, Hull and Long tried to put off Bergson, Dean Alfange, and Joe Davidson with such excuses as the impossibility of dispatching a civilian to the Middle East when military priorities were yet to be handled or the argument that the U.S. already had a qualified ambassador in Turkey (Steinhardt) and did not need someone else peering over his shoulder. Meanwhile, the State Department was busily checking out Bergson's background to see if he should be deported.[62]

Ultimately, in October 1943, Breckinridge Long did agree to send a Jewish representative to Istanbul to unclog the flow of refugees.[63] The excellent work which Bergson's choice, Bloomingdale Vice-President Ira Hirschmann, did was accomplished despite undermining by Emanuel Celler, Wise, and Nahum

Goldmann of the World Jewish Congress. Nine days before Hirschmann's papers were approved, on October 6, 1943, the last two men sat in the offices of Breckinridge Long, and, in Long's words, "excoriated" Bergson's group as "a body composed of a lot of persons, many of whom were not Jews," and all of whom failed to represent the thinking of most Jews in this country.[64] That the State Department did finally approve Hirschmann's mission is less a testimony to the efforts of Wise and his colleagues than it is to the discomfort caused by Bergson's provocative newspaper advertisements. When Long agreed to send Hirschmann, he asked if the newspaper campaign, principally through the *New York Times*, would now cease. Bergson gave no guarantee that it would.[65]

This affair did not mark the first time that Wise and other reputable Jewish leaders in the United States had attempted to derail a rescue scheme proposed by activist-minded pressure groups. In February 1943, Ben Hecht, the well-known playwright who served as cochairman of the Committee for a Jewish Army, received information from Switzerland that the Rumanian government had offered to allow 70,000 Trans-Dnistrian Jews (the survivors of a pre-Nazi population of 130,000 Jews in this region) to leave Rumania at a cost of 20,000 *lei* ($50) each for transport to the border. The total sum involved—$3,500,000—could easily be raised by several Jewish organizations. Hecht had Bergson and Merlin confirm the report through underground sources, and then he authored a four-column advertisement in the *New York Times* of February 16, 1943, which flashed in two-inch high letters: "FOR SALE to Humanity. 70,000 Jews. Guaranteed Human Beings at $50 apiece." [66]

Hecht's advertisement was addressed to "the Four Freedoms, in care of the United Nations." He argued that Rumania's offer was bona fide "for this month only," that it had been endorsed by the prestigious *Manchester Guardian* on February 9, that the inhabitants of Palestine (both Jews and Arabs) would welcome these troubled people, that no spies had been found among the 300,000 German Jews who had emigrated to Palestine since the rise of Hitler. If any spies were included in

148

the number in Rumania, Hecht said, "You can shoot them." In fact, the only persons who could possibly object to the transaction were the Nazis and the Arabs who were collaborating with the Nazis in Berlin.

One week later, on February 23, an angry Wise released the following statement to the press: "The American Jewish Congress, dealing with the matter in conjunction with recognized Jewish organizations, wishes to state that no confirmation has been received regarding this alleged offer of the Rumanian Government to allow seventy thousand Jews to leave Rumania. Therefore, no collection of funds would seem justified." [67] Wise wrote a longer letter to the Reverend Holmes in which he referred to the publicized sale of Rumanian Jews no less than three times as "a hoax on the part of the Hecht group." According to Wise, even if such a proposal had been made, the costs were prohibitive. Not $3,500,000, but a minimum of $30,000,-000, would have been required to assemble these Jews in Bucharest, put them in trucks, and send them on their way.[68]

Wise was wrong in this judgment. Bergson telephoned Assistant Secretary Berle for the desired confirmation, and Berle admitted that the State Department had received news of such an offer from its reliable source in Bern, Gerhart Riegner, on February 10, 1943.[69] Despite its knowledge of what was transpiring in Eastern Europe, the State Department for reasons which are unclear did not act on the offer in the summer of 1943. One result of this delay was the development of a bitter rivalry between the State Department and the Treasury Department, in the course of which officials at the State Department dashed off caustic memorandums charging the Treasury Department with overreacting to the crisis, while Morgenthau and his associates charged the State Department with hypocrisy when it argued that ransoming the Trans-Dnistrian Jews would aid the Nazi war effort. Referring to an earlier conversation with Hull in which the secretary had indicated that such funds would remain blocked in Switzerland until the end of the war, Morgenthau recalled bitterly, "The State Department was usually among those who scoffed at economic warfare in other connections." [70]

While the subject of the Trans-Dnistrian Jews was being debated behind closed doors, Wise came to Washington in July to propose an amplification of the rescue scheme. Wise had been aware of the Riegner message since March 31, and he became a last-minute advocate of purchasing safe conduct for Jews of Eastern Europe. Where only months before he had done irreparable harm to the Trans-Dnistrian proposal by belittling the efforts of the activists, he now called for the removal of Jews from Poland to the relative safety of Hungary and Rumania in return for large sums of money deposited to blocked accounts in Switzerland. In his meeting with Roosevelt, Wise emphasized that the Nazis could not use the money during the war and that the victorious Allied armies would prevent them from using it after the war. According to Wise, Roosevelt called in Morgenthau to give his assent to the scheme and encouraged the rabbi to rouse public support.[71]

On August 14, 1943, Roosevelt officially notified Wise that financial arrangements to save the Rumanian Jews had been made.[72] It took the State Department seventeen more days to get a cable to Harrison in Bern notifying him that Washington desired to issue a license to the appropriate authorities in Europe. By now, however, the British had discovered the negotiations and had requested time to study the matter. It was not until December 17 that the State Department received a cable from its embassy in London giving the British view on this rescue proposal. The British Foreign Office, ever mindful of the explosive Palestine situation, was said to be concerned with the difficulty of disposing of large numbers of Jews, should they be released from enemy territory. For this reason it was reluctant to approve of preliminary financial arrangements with the Nazis, "though these were now acceptable to the Ministry of Economic Warfare." [73] Morgenthau commented, "The letter was a satanic combination of British chill and diplomatic double-talk, cold and correct, and adding up to a sentence of death." [74]

The State Department did not need the sanction of the British government in this affair, and this point was clearly indicated by John Pehle, director of the Treasury Department's

Division of Foreign Funds, in a telephone conversation with Breckinridge Long in October. Pehle noted that the British had not asked our prior consent to spend £3,000 to feed British subjects on the captive Guernsey Islands. If the negotiations fell through, he charged, "the State Department will be held responsible for their failure." [75] Evidently the State Department agreed, for on December 18, the day after the British made known their opposition to the Trans-Dnistrian rescue plan, Long cabled Riegner that he could proceed with his operations in enemy territory drawing on a fund of $25,000, one-tenth the amount of money Riegner had originally requested.[76]

Because of this eleven-month delay, most of the Jews who might have been extricated from Rumania were exterminated. Subsequently, Wise was to blame the State Department. "Let history, therefore, record for all time," he wrote, "that were it not for State Department and Foreign Office bureaucratic bungling and callousness, thousands of lives might have been saved and the Jewish catastrophe partially averted." [77] The passage of years apparently had exculpated Wise and other Jewish leaders who had scoffed at the Bergson-Hecht group and denied the existence of a bodies-for-cash proposition for six vital weeks in the spring of 1943. Ben Hecht, however, challenged Wise's statements when he wrote, "But in 1943, we, who called out the plight of the Rumanian Jews to the world, were discredited by the Zionist unions, the established Zionist leadership and their associated philanthropies, as scandalmongers. Our attempt to get the Jews out of Rumania before the Germans came was scotched." [78]

It would seem that Wise's worst fears, that he might become a "court Jew" or shtadlan for the administration, were realized. This could be attributed in part to the concentration of so many chairmanships in his person. Wise more than any other figure represented American Jewry and as such he was patronized by Roosevelt, Hull, and other top-ranking government officials. Because of his longtime friendship with the president and Roosevelt's nodding approval of virtually everything Wise suggested, because he was privy to confidential information that smacked of policy-making, Wise naturally considered himself a person of importance and responsibility. In these crucial years to European Jewry, Wise believed that his larger responsibilities compelled him to silence.

Never a notably humble man, Wise had continually saluted himself for appreciating the true menace of Hitler long before others had gloatingly recalled the mob scenes that greeted his near-messianic appearance in Warsaw's ghetto in 1936.[79] Wise also carried on a running feud with his ZOA co-chairman, Abba Silver, which, according to Silver's intimates, was as much a conflict of egos as anything else.[80] When Silver called Wise "senile" in 1943, the latter retorted, "How charming it is. Working for a great people is to work by the side of the littlest men." [81]

No less an authority than Sigmund Freud had commented once, partly in jest, on Wise's self-image. Asked by Freud to name the five most important Jews in the world, Wise rattled off the names of Freud, Einstein, Weizmann, Brandeis, and Bergson. When Freud asked him, "What of you?," Wise replied, "Oh,no,no,no,no." Freud then commented, "I would have believed you if you had said 'no'—but not 'no,no,no,no.' " [82]

It is still questionable whether Wise could have been as influential in shaping government policy as he or Elie Wiesel desired him to be. Certainly he was no more successful in keeping the gates of Palestine open to the Jews during wartime than he was in his belated efforts at rescue of the Jews of Poland and Rumania.[83] Moreover, his decision to play down the persecution of Jews after 1938 and to cooperate with the State Department in suppression of the news of Nazi extermination plans are decisions open to legitimate challenge. They certainly confirmed government officials from Roosevelt through lower state functionaries in the view that Wise had no intention of creating public ripples during wartime.

Why didn't Wise endure a hunger fast, or lead a march on Washington, or devise some other appropriate expedient, perhaps even suicide, as Wiesel suggests, to dramatize the need for action for his people? Such alternatives must be assessed in their historical and cultural perspective. Were they feasible in 1943? Were they even considered by Wise? Gandhi and A. Philip Randolph had surely demonstrated that fasts and mass marches were within the range of possibility at the time. And the suicide in May 1943 of Shmul Zygelboim, one of two Jews serving on the Polish National Council in London, was intended to dramatize the passivity with which the world permitted the extermination of the Jews.[84]

But what were the practical results of these actions? Gandhi was thrown into prison by the British as a Japanese sympathizer. Randolph's threatened march on Washington, before the United States entered the war, never reached fruition, and his Brotherhood of Sleeping Car Porters was bought off by tokenist concessions from the AFL. Wise could hardly have expected to achieve much more in an America which was at war in 1942–1943, where anti-Jewish sentiment was regenerate, where racism had resulted in the mauling of Mexican-American "Zoot Suiters" in Los Angeles and the killing of twenty-five Negroes and nine whites in Detroit.[85] Civil disobedience on the scale advocated by Wiesel, who viewed these events twenty-five years later, when such behavior is not uncommon during peacetime, would have been regarded by Americans in 1942–1943 as seditious behavior designed to immobilize the government and thereby jeopardize the lives of American fighting men abroad.

Intimates of Wise indignantly reject the notion that he ever seriously considered suicide. The concept of self-immolation, originally an oriental concept, was not as widely known in 1942 as it is today. Moreover, the idea of taking one's own life is not merely a violation of the Mosaic Code, but of subsequent Halakhic pronouncements, known well to Wise, against self-destruction except in times of grave personal peril. And finally, Wise could note that Zygelboim's suicide was a futile act, one which failed to elicit any outpouring of sympathy from the democracies, let alone force marked changes in Allied policy toward the Jews of Europe.

What then was left for Wise? Personal intervention with the president, public rallies, fund-raising drives, and Zionism. That these were not enough was not necessarily the fault of Wise, who may or may not have been gullible in his dealings with government officials. Rather, the fault lay in the force of circumstances, the deep-rooted divisions in the Jewish community —among socialists, capitalists, assimilationists, Zionists, revisionists, reform and orthodox—which produced the feelings of antipathy demonstrated in Wise's relations with the Hecht group and the American Jewish Committee. Perhaps the fault lay even more in a society which had created an atmosphere in which a leader of a minority did not feel free to speak the terrible news he had learned of persecution abroad for fear of generating that same persecution at home.

7. The Bermuda
Conference

*B**y the end* of 1942 the world knew that Hitler's shrill railings against the Jews were no longer vain threats. At first the reaction was one of sorrow and pity. In Jerusalem, rabbis congregated at the Wailing Wall to recite Psalms 73, 79, and 142 and to read the Yizkor Prayer composed on the occasion of the Chmielnicki massacre in 1648. In New York City several thousand persons gathered at the aged B'nai Jeshurun Temple, where American Jews had protested the Damascus pogroms of 1840, to hear the shofar, the ritual ram's horn, sounded, as a reminder of fearful days. In Sweden, Apostolic Vicar Bishop Johannes Mueller designated December 20 as a day of prayer for the Jews. In Costa Rica, Chile, and several other South American countries where Jews had not been wanted before the war, the Confederación Trabajadores Latino-Americanos proclaimed a fifteen-minute work shutdown on December 11. In Britain's House of Commons, the source of the baneful White Paper, members of Parliament stood in silent tribute to the Jews for one minute on December 17.

It did not take long, however, before the shock of this news was transformed into anger, and pressure mounted from all sides to rescue the remnants of European Jewy. Protest demonstrations were organized in London, Tel Aviv, Johannesburg, Melbourne, New York, and Chicago. In the vanguard of these demonstrations were gentile churchmen, the Archbishops of Canterbury, York, and Wales; Bishop William Manning of New York; Archbishop Michael Curley of Baltimore; Denis Cardinal Dougherty of Philadelphia. The leading newspapers in the United States, including the *Los Angeles Times, Miami Herald,*

New York World-Telegram, Boston Traveler, Cleveland Plain Dealer, New York Times, and *Philadelphia Bulletin,* among others, and a few journals in Great Britain (particularly the *Manchester Guardian*) clamored for something to be done to stay what the *Charlotte Observer* termed "Hitler's beastly, bloody-handed followers." [1]

During the winter of 1942–1943 the president, the State Department, and the Congress were subjected to a ceaseless barrage of inquiries and' suggestions from Jewish and non-Jewish organizations like the Refugee Economic Corporation, the American Friends Service Committee, the Joint Distribution Committee, and the Union for the Protection of the Rights of the Human Person (among whose members were former French Premiers Paul Reynaud and Edouard Daladier, the economist Sidney Hook, the Archbishop of Canterbury, and Harry Lorin Bisse, managing editor of *Commentary*). Groups such as these demanded immediate action by the Allies, something dramatic that would truly polarize the belligerents and demonstrate how morally superior was the Allies' cause.

The most intriguing proposal, however, was raised by Bergson's Committee for a Jewish Army of Stateless and Palestinian Jews. Chaired by the Dutch author and philo-Semite Pierre van Paassen, this group called for the creation of a special Jewish Legion, numbering from 80,000 to 200,000 soldiers, to serve under the Supreme Allied Command in the Middle East. Such a proposal could not be written off merely as a flight into fancy. There was a precedent for such an army in the Zion Mule Corps and the Royal Fusiliers, a Jewish unit commanded by Joseph Trumpeldor and Vladimir Jabotinsky, which had distinguished itself at the battles of Gallipoli and Jerusalem during the First World War. There was much support for the idea in Palestine, where 85,800 men and 50,400 women volunteered for active duty with the British when the war broke out. [2] There was a great deal of support for the idea in this country among Senators Edwin Johnson (Colorado), James Davis (Pennsylvania), William Smathers (New Jersey), Robert Taft (Ohio), and William Green, Father Flanagan, Paul Tillich, Cedric Hardwick, Lowell Thomas, Rear Admiral H. E. Yarnell,

Melvyn Douglas, and William Allen White, all of whom served on the Advisory Board of the National Committee for a Jewish Army.

Despite the ceaseless abuse heaped on the Committee for a Jewish Army and its sister organization, the Emergency Conference to Rescue the Jews of Europe, by Wise and other leading Jews in the country, these groups waged extensive propaganda fights in the press,[3] emphasizing the strategic worth of a Jewish fighting force to the Allies. Operating in the Middle East, a region which was home to many of them, these Jews would release British troops for use elsewhere. They would protect Britain's vital oil supply and patrol lines of communication to India and the Far East. They might even help stabilize an area which had been the source of great trouble for the Allies in 1941 and 1942.[4]

National Committee Executive Chairman Alfred Strelsin volunteered to go to Britain in the summer of 1942 as an official emissary of the American government to broach the subject of a Jewish legion. The idea was vetoed at the time by Assistant Secretary of State Adolph Berle, who noted that this government had never sanctioned such an army and then went on to evaluate Strelsin as someone who "does not strike me as a heavyweight."[5] It is doubtful that anyone associated with the Bergson-Hecht groups would have been welcomed by the British anyway, since the militants had harassed the British government with speeches, pamphlets, and advertisements criticizing that government's stringent implementation of the White Paper on Palestine.[6]

Such criticism of British policy in the Middle East, even if they were the opinions of private citizens, worsened the diplomatic frost which had developed between the United States and Great Britain in January 1943. The two nations were already feuding over proper treatment of Vichy French officials in North Africa,[7] and the British government felt that any attack by the U.S. on its Palestine policy was especially inappropriate, since the Americans had stolidly refused to drop their own immigration barriers in wartime. London boasted that 400,000 refugees had been welcomed since the rise of Hitler and challenged the United States to prove that it had done as much.

It was in this testy atmosphere that Lord Halifax issued a memorandum to the State Department on January 20, 1943, calling for an Anglo-American conference on refugees. The idea was not new. Jewish leaders ranging from Hecht to Wise had long called for such a special meeting. The idea had even been endorsed by Herbert Emerson in his capacity as chief of the somnambulant IGCR.[8] The Halifax note was significant, however, because it set the tone for all future negotiations between the two governments. While maintaining that the refugee problem could not be regarded as solely a Jewish problem, Halifax ascribed a special position to the Jews. The Germans, he charged, might seek to embarrass the West, whose absorptive capacity was allegedly strained to the limits, by releasing "a flood of Jews." There was, therefore, "a distinct danger of stimulating anti-Semitism in areas where an excessive number of foreign Jews are introduced." The British suggested that areas of refuge be restricted to neutral countries in and near Europe and that efforts be made to discourage "false hopes among the refugees."[9]

The Department of State was amenable to holding a conference on refugee matters and leaned over backwards in an effort to mollify Great Britain in the next few weeks. On February 25, Hull issued a three-page note to the British ambassador, proposing that such a meeting be held in Ottawa. The secretary omitted any reference to the Jews, preferring to express the view held by Halifax that the refugee problem transcended the confines of any particular group of people. As if to match the British's claims about their humanitarianism, Hull pointed out that American consular officials had issued 547,775 visas to nationals of countries presently dominated by the Axis. He agreed that "temporary sanctuaries" for refugees should be located as close to the refugees' native lands, if for no other reason than the shipping problem facing the Allies. Moreover, the secretary emphasized that this conference should be "exploratory," should make its recommendations to the nearly defunct IGCR.[10]

In many ways this note was a microcosm of the Anglo-American Conference on Refugees which finally met at Bermuda in April 1943. Hull's statement, like the conference itself, was cautious, even defeatist in tone. Little could be expected of discussions which did not commit either government, which were heavily underwritten with rationalizations about shipping shortages or the lack of appropriate refuges, and which attempted to ignore the special situation of the Jews in Europe. Hull's note, moreover, contained statistics which were both inaccurate and misleading. And finally, the release of the note to the press on March 3, before the British had had an opportunity to digest its contents or make an official response, provoked the first of several procedural hassles between the two allies before the conference even began. Because of the publicity given the Hull note, Foreign Secretary Anthony Eden found himself peppered with questions in Parliament about "the conference at Ottawa." The British were annoyed by this diplomatic slip but instead of contrition, Ambassador Ronald Campbell received a lengthy dressing down about the British's mistakes from Undersecretary Welles on March 4.[11]

In the next few weeks the British were extremely sensitive about untoward publicity and the prospect that unnamed pressure groups might descend on the conferees at Ottawa or any other site in North America. Thus, at the end of March they suggested shifting the conference to Hamilton, Bermuda, 1,500 miles out in the Atlantic. The State Department, already belabored by the Polish-American Council, the National Council of Women, the American Committee for Zionist Affairs, Wise's American Jewish Congress,[12] and the Bergson-Hecht group to allow one of their representatives to participate in the upcoming discussions, readily agreed to the switch.

Bermuda was definitely "hermetically sealed," as Representative Emanuel Celler charged later.[13] There was no approach to the island, save by air, and then only by way of a closely guarded airstrip. F. Goodwin Gosling, the man in charge of accommodations at the Horizons Hotel, announced on April 7 that the hearings would definitely be "private." [14] CIO President Philip Murray, distressed over this situation and the failure of either government to accord delegate status to a representative of a legitimate relief organization, publicly expressed his dismay on the April 24. Quoting from a letter written to Undersecretary Welles, Murray asked that "the voice of the people's organizations" be heard lest the Bermuda meetings "behind closed doors" recreate the errors of "the future Evian Conference." [15] Similar sentiments were expressed by the Massachusetts State Senate, which passed a resolution calling on Hull to permit officials of the Joint Distribution Committee to appear at Bermuda,[16] and by former Czech Minister Jan Masaryk, who said that "because the Jews have been singled out more than the rest of us . . . the voice of the Jewish people should be heard whenever some plans or some hopes are being discussed." [17] The State Department did not relish such advice, as Breckinridge Long revealed when he wrote that their activities might lend credence to Hitler's charges that "we are fighting this war on account of and at the instigation and direction of our Jewish citizens." [18]

Actually, the British killed any chance of unofficial representation being accorded to a Polish, Quaker, or Jewish group. On April 7 George Hayter, embassy first secretary in Washington, informed Long's executive assistant, George Brandt, that the Foreign Office had rejected such a bid from the Jewish Board of Deputies in London. The British position was that allowing this would compel the two governments to accommodate virtually every organization that had a view on the refugee problem. This would create precisely the division and the flood of rhetoric which the British had hoped to avoid when they suggested remote Bermuda. The British demanded, and received, assurances that the Americans would not put them on the spot by taking an opposite position.[19]

The chief of the American delegation, Harold Willis Dodds, while admitting he took his own records of the conference, now claims that there were "several highly emotional" representatives of Jewish organizations aboard the plane that carried the Americans to Bermuda. Dodds, then president of Princeton University, said that another American delegate, Sol Bloom, was so upset by the presence of these persons on the flight that Bloom said he would not have agreed to participate in the conference if he had known "they" were coming. Dodds says that Jewish organizations were heavily represented at Bermuda.[20]

In fact, no "they" traveled with the delegates. State Department Records show that Hull and Consul General William Beck in Hamilton were extremely punctilious about expenses, travel arrangements, and accommodations for the American contingent in 1943.[21] Only five representatives of the press— Robert Vivain of Reuters, H. O. Thompson of the United Press, Richard Massock of the Associated Press, Ida Landau of the Overseas News Agency, and Lee Carson of the International News Service—were permitted to travel with the official delegation.[22] While these individuals may have been sympathetic to the Jews, they hardly constituted official representation for Jewish pressure groups. The only Jewish official to offer personal testimony at Bermuda, and then merely before the American delegation in a vapid Sunday session, was George Backer, a member of the board of the Refugee Economic Corporation and president of ORT, the Society for the Propagation of Artisanal and Agricultural work among Jews. And Backer's dignified replies to a barrage of hypothetical questions show an admirable restraint, not the hyperemotionalism of the Jews which Dodds recalled at Bermuda.[23]

Also in the American delegation were Scott Lucas, the powerful Democratic senator from Illinois; R. Borden Reams, Long's special assistant on Jewish Affairs; Robert Alexander, the member of the State Department's Visa Division who had drafted many of Long's statements on refugee matters; George Warren, executive secretary of the President's Advisory Committee on Political Refugees; George Brandt, and nine other minor assistants, code clerks, stenographers, and typists.

The American contingent could not be regarded as overly sympathetic to the Jewish cause. Reams, Brandt, and Alexander all were openly hostile to further Jewish immigration to this

161

country. But the delegation's principal spokesmen, criticized by Republican leaders as "partisan" selections, lacked any real eminence in the field of foreign affairs.[24] Dodds had served as a special adviser to the governments of Nicaragua, Chile, and Cuba, but he had not held a diplomatic post in seventeen years and was virtually uninformed about the intricacies of the Jewish question. His selection as chairman of the delegation was something of a fluke, coming only after Supreme Court Justice Owen Roberts, envoy to the Vatican Myron Taylor, Yale University President Charles Seymour, and Isaiah Bowman of Johns Hopkins all had begged off the task.[25]

In like manner, Lucas was selected because he was the Senate floor leader of the Democratic party, a man eager to enhance his reputation for a possible vice presidential bid in 1944. Again, however, he was not the first choice of the government in the list of prospects drawn up by Long in March. Senator Claude Pepper, the Florida liberal, had headed that list.[26]

But it was Bloom's nomination that especially aroused the wrath of Jewish groups in this country. The son of an immigrant Polish Jew, Bloom had risen through the ranks of Tammany to become chairman of the House Committee on Foreign Affairs on the basis of seniority. Bloom enjoyed first-name relationships with Franklin Roosevelt, Cordell Hull, and Stephen Wise. Bloom, a man of limited means, had established a reputation as a faithful Democrat, a faithful American. Coauthor of the "relative rule" legislation of 1941, he would subsequently serve as a delegate to the United Nations Charter Conference at San Francisco in April 1945. As Harold Dodds put it in a recent interview, "He was as loyal Jew as I've ever met." For Breckinridge Long, who had so much difficulty in finding senators or professors to man the delegation to Bermuda in 1943, there was only one choice from the House of Representatives and that was his old friend, Sol Bloom.[27]

Why, then, did many American Jews object to Bloom's selection? The Independent Jewish Press Service stated that he had been picked only because he was a member of the Jewish faith. Most Jews would have preferred either Celler or Dickstein to Bloom.[28] The IJPS summed up their displeasure:

Congressman Bloom is known as an amenable Chairman of the House Foreign Affairs Committee, who could be relied upon by the State Department to go along with any program it would offer. Thus, in the case of Bermuda, when the report is made public, Congressman Bloom can be trotted out to stifle the criticism that will be forthcoming from responsible American Jewish public opinion. To the country at large, the State Department can say: "Now, look here! The Jews are unreasonable. Their criticism of Bermuda is unfounded. A fine, upstanding Jew in the person of Sol Bloom was part of the Conference. Surely he could be counted on to defend the interests of the Jewish refugees. And he says that Bermuda was just fine. You see, American Jews are much too unreasonable and unfair. 'White' Jews who are real Americans know that we are doing the best we know how." [29]

In the next few lines the IJPS admonished Bloom "not to permit himself to become the stalking horse he was intended to be when the debate on the Bermuda Conference takes place in the House or elsewhere." Dodds commented that Bloom proved his dedication to this country by agreeing that nothing should be placed above winning the war, not even rescue plans for Jews in Europe, though Dodds acknowledged that Bloom made the pledge "with tears on his face." Because of this patriotic zeal, Dodds maintains the U.S. delegation at Bermuda was never divided on a single issue.[30] Subsequently, Bloom never broke step with this picture of unanimity. In so doing, he earned the contemptuous abuse of the Jewish militants, who labeled him "a *shabbos goy* for the State Department," "a party to the conspiracy of silence about the catastrophe that had befallen your brothers." Snapped a spokesman for the Nation Committee for a Jewish Army: "We would not be happy in your place, Mr. Bloom. We would have nightmares; our ears would be split by the cries of all the Jews that have perished since Bermuda; and we would feel blood, Jewish blood on our hands.

"Blood on *your* hands, Mr. Bloom?" [31]

What those who freely condemned Bloom did not know was that he alone among the two delegations attempted to keep the door open on possible negotiations with the Nazis for the release of great numbers of Jews. Only Bloom tried to force the conferees into serious discussions on the prospect of trans-blockade feeding of Jews.[32] Only Bloom felt compelled to ask the question that was in every Jew's mind—what would the British do in March 1944 if all 75,000 landing permits for Jews were not used, and were to cease under the terms of the Jewish immigration to Palestine outlined in the White Paper?[33]

In every instance Bloom was quashed in no uncertain terms by Dodds. On three occasions Dodds all but told the congressman to stop asking about negotiations with Hitler. And Dodds dismissed Bloom's proposal to feed persons in concentration camps as "wholly outside the realm of the conference."[34] His questions about Palestine were intercepted by Dodds, who tried to apologize to the bemused British, saying on their behalf that such matters were internal in nature.[35]

Examination of the minutes of these initial sessions destroys any illusion about unity among the Americans. Bloom very correctly asked the questions that the American Jewish community wanted asked. It is regrettable that he did not have the stamina to sustain his position, but it is doubtful whether Celler or Dickstein could have fared much better.

If the American delegation was not all that Jews might have wished, it was the result of deliberate choice. Hull and Eden originally agreed to send "top rank" emissaries to the conference, but Hull's ready acceptance of Richard K. Law as the chief of the British delegation at the end of March created another diplomatic tangle. Law, the son of former Prime Minister Bonar Law, was merely Parliamentary Undersecretary for Foreign Affairs, a post which British Ambassador Campbell pointed out was not "top rank." Campbell expressed the fear to Long that the U.S. might designate someone of higher rank and thereby embarrass the British once more. Long assured him that the State Department would keep the delegates on a par with one another.[36] A month in advance of the exploratory conference to deliberate the fate of millions, both sides were committed to sending less than their best qualified men to Bermuda.[37]

The problem of delegates apparently resolved, it remained for the United States and Great Britain to agree on a working agenda. In this, again, a large number of humanitarian organizations, Jewish and non-Jewish, eagerly volunteered suggestions to the State Department. Wise, still a bit uncomfortable about the choice of Bermuda as the site of the conference and the government's reluctance to permit Jewish delegates to attend, sent Welles a lengthy proposal from the American Jewish Congress, World Jewish Congress, and the abortive Joint Emergency Committee for European Jewish Affairs. After pointing out that the world community was rapidly becoming disillusioned with the inaction of the Allies, Wise recommended that: (1) negotiations be opened with the Axis through neutral sources to secure the release of Jews; (2) sanctuaries be established, among others, in Sweden, Switzerland, North Africa, and Jamaica; (3) U.S. immigration laws be revised to permit the entry of additional numbers of refugees; (4) transport be provided by thousands of troop and cargo vessels returning from England and North Africa with empty bottoms; (5) a new Nansen passport be devised for the stateless; (6) the United Nations undertake to feed the Jews, whose death rate was ten times that of any other conquered people.[38] Virtually identical recommendations were made by the Fellowship of Reconciliation Refugee Committee, Clarence Pickett of the American Friends Service Committee, the Union for the Protection of the Human Person, the National Boards of the YWCA and the Federal Council of Churches of Christ in the U.S., the National Negro Congress, and some 283 scholars who signed a petition addressed to President Roosevelt urging action against genocide that spring.[39]

Two weeks after Wise wrote to Welles the undersecretary received another intriguing letter, this one from Harry Fleischman, national secretary of the Socialist Party of America. Fleischman said that the Socialist National Executive Committee favored abrogation of U.S. immigration laws for the duration, to permit Jewish refugees to come to this country to be interned in "humanely conducted camps." The socialists also favored opening Palestine "where possible" to Jewish immigration.[40]

For the New Zionist Organization of America, a Bergson-Hecht front which was distinct from the venerable ZOA of Wise and Silver, such settlement of Jews in Palestine was not merely possible, but desirable. The New Zionist Organization took out several full-page ads in the *New York Times* and quoted extensively from James McDonald, who favored Palestine as a solution to the Jewish refugee problem. McDonald, the head of the President's Advisory Committee on Political Refugees and hence a man whose word carried much authority, believed that transportation to Palestine presented little obstacle because the distance from Eastern Europe to the Holy Land was not great. He noted that Jewish refugees would face minimal adjustment problems in this region because of their common linguistic and religious ties with Palestinian Jews. The climate was moderate, and existing social service, industrial, and farm enterprises were eager to absorb the new population. As for any fear that the Arabs might object to this new influx of Jews, McDonald said, "The war emergency has tended to lessen, to some degree, the points of acutest friction. The great overshadowing danger to Palestine threatens all alike in such a way as to dwarf the lesser points of internal difference." [41]

One recommendation of the militants was not swiftly embraced by non-Jews. This was the idea of retribution, with the United Nations vowing to mete out punishment to the Nazi murderers at the end of the war. The idea had been bandied about diplomatic circles in Washington and London for nearly a year without clear definition.[42] Now, in 1943 some Jews expanded the concept to include direct threats against Germans, no matter where they lived. Even after the Bermuda conference opened, the State Department was receiving letters calling for retaliation against German citizens and pro-Nazi sympathizers in Allied countries and demanding the use of poison gas or massed bombing assaults on civilian population centers in Germany itself unless the massacres were halted.[43]

If any of the petitioners—Wise, Fleischmann, Pickett, or Bergson—had hoped to influence the State Department, they were sadly mistaken. Such letters were usually handled by subordinates in the Division of European Affairs. A form letter, accompanied by Hull's original statement on the conference back in February, would be sent, explaining how grateful the department was for the suggestion, how it would be given every consideration, how the secrecy of the negotiations precluded any fuller exposition at this time.

This is not to say that the recommendations were totally ignored. On April 20, 1943, Berle submitted a résumé of all those proposals to Long. Berle broke them down into three categories: (1) reprisals against a German city as each new massacre was reported; (2) a solemn declaration by the U.N. that the German people would be held accountable for the massacres when the war was over; (3) rescue of the surviving Jews through Spain and the Balkans. Berle rejected the first scheme on the basis of discussions with Air Corps officials, who felt that the Allies needed to concentrate all available strength on purely military objectives. To divert any air power for costly reprisal raids would inevitably slow up the war effort. Berle added, "It also puts us on a moral plane with the Germans, which I think we should not wish to do." As for the prospect of moving refugees through Spain and the Balkans, Berle was not too optimistic, but indicated that perhaps Cyrenaica could be used as a refuge *if* the refugees could obtain transport on their own. The only point that the assistant secretary felt merited instant approval was the denunciation of genocide. Holding the German people as a whole responsible for the atrocities, he reasoned, would force a mass protest in Germany which could "force stoppage of the massacres." Long agreed with all that Berle had said except the last point. When he passed the résumé on to Hull, he commented that any Allied declaration referring to German responsibility would impel all Germans to fight on with renewed unity and desperation.[44] As a result, it would be another year before the Allies would issue such a threat.

Thus, as the American delegation flew off to Bermuda on April 16, it left with vague instructions about considering the plight of "unfortunates" still within Nazi control and those in danger of being overtaken and subjected to persecution once more.[45] A last-minute resolution, introduced by Senator Edwin Johnson of Colorado and the National Committee for a Jewish Army, which would have charged the delegates with "immediate and stern action to save the remaining millions of the Jewish people of Europe," was tabled by administration forces in Congress.[46] At La Guardia Field, just prior to takeoff, Dodds and Bloom expressed what was to become the dominant tone of the negotiations when they told the press, "If the Nazis let anybody out of Europe, it will be for good military reasons only."[47]

On Monday, April 19, 1943, the clandestine Polish National Army (AK) Radio transmitted the following message to the Allied governments in London and Washington:

> A few hours ago armed contingents of the S.S. with armored cars and artillery began the total massacre of the survivors of the Warsaw Ghetto. The Ghetto put up a desperate and heroic resistance. This resistance was led by the Jewish Combatant Organization to which nearly all the fighting groups adherred. From the Ghetto a continuous bombardment and loud explosions can be heard and the whole area is covered with a ball of flame. A few aircraft are circling above the scene of the massacre. The result of the battle has naturally been discounted. The whole city is in a great state of excitement. This evening, a banner has been flown with the inscription: "We shall fight to the end." The people of Warsaw are following this unequal struggle with admiration and with manifest sympathies for the Ghetto in its death throes. Appeal immediately to the International Red Cross to visit the ghettos, the concentration camps of Auschwitz, Treblinka, Belzietz, Sobibor and many other concentration camps in Poland.[48]

Thousands of miles from the scene where S.S. General Jurgen Stroop commenced a twenty-eight-day operation against the ragged survivors of the Warsaw Ghetto, the Anglo-American Conference on Refugees opened at Bermuda. Despite the obvious urgency in the situation, the handful of newspapermen present at Hamilton soon took to calling Bermuda "the no-news conference."

The daily press briefings, for example, deteriorated into little more than exercises in platitude. After the opening session Dodds said: "There can be no doubt of the good will and intention of the British and American Governments, nor of the delegates representing these Governments. What can be done, will be done." [49] The next day he and Law emerged from an eight-hour session behind closed doors to announce glumly that they were "unable to give immediate succor" to the refugees.[50] The two did, however, testify that agreement had been reached "on several salient points" and that "substantial progress" has been made in the first day's discussions, which had been "entirely harmonious." [51]

"We are getting to the heart of the problem now, after an analysis, trying to decide what is practicable," Dodds told newsmen on April 22. Although the conference had already rejected the possibility of any mass transfer of refugees by this time, chiefly at Dodds' instance, the chief American delegate exuded confidence about the outcome of the deliberations. "I think we all feel we are making progress and that we shall not have lived in vain," he said.[52]

The press was kept uninformed about the actual course of the negotiations, however. Throughout the ten days of the conference they were titillated with the prospect that Palestine, North Africa, Madagascar, Mauritius, French Equatorial Africa, the Diredawa section of Ethiopia, Kenya, Mogador, Argentina, Mexico, Jamaica, or the Isle of Man might serve as a haven for refugees.[53] These reports were dutifully transmitted to the United States and Great Britain. They were designed to impress the populations of both nations with the humanitarianism and energy of the conferees and were inevitably shrouded in vagueness for reasons of security. Once more officials claimed that fuller exposition of proposed rescue schemes might jeopardize them. Alexander Uhl represented the views of skeptics when he commented that it was "unlikely that the conference will pull anything out of its hat that will embarrass anyone." [54]

Uhl's statement reflected a concerned world's growing impatience with the Bermuda conference. Dodds had barely finished reading his opening remarks, extolling the hospitality and clime of Bermuda, when the *New York Times* lashed out against the conference calling it "pitifully inadequate." The editors went on to say that "it would seem that even within the war effort, and perhaps even in aid of it, measures can be devised that go beyond palliatives which appear to be designed to assuage the conscience of the reluctant rescuers rather than to aid the victims." [55]

On the same day Colonel Morris J. Mendelsohn, president of the Revisionist New Zionist Organization of America, charged that the only reason the British had suggested a refugee conference was to divert attention from their failure to open Palestine to the Jews.[56] The *Washington Post* agreed that Palestine was the crux of the Jewish question in a particularly intemperate editorial which stormed: "Upon the British rests the onus as a result of the stupid White Paper policy of having prevented a large number of refugees from getting to the one nearby place where they would have been welcomed and needed." [57]

To Frank Kingdom, once co-chairman of the Emergency Committee to Save the Children of Europe and presently head of the International Relief and Rescue Committee, Bermuda was "a shame and a disgrace." He argued that vigorous action could not be expected from an American delegation which included "no individual who has shown any valid interest in refugees." [58] To Rabbi Israel Goldstein, president of the Synagogue Council of America and head of the Jewish National Fund, Bermuda was "not only a failure, but a mockery." He charged that nothing had come out of the meetings "because the democracies do not want the victims of Hitler's charnel houses. The job of the Bermuda Conference apparently was not to rescue victims of Nazi terror, but to rescue our State Department and the British Foreign Office from possible embarrassment," Goldstein added.[59]

The most scathing indictment of the conference while it actually was going on came from the pen of Ida Landau. Writing in the *New York Post* on April 23, she charged (p. 4):

The Bermuda Conference is foundering in its own futility.
. . . We did not need an international conference to tell us
about the difficulties of the job. We needed one to take a
positive approach toward the admittedly difficult problem of
rescuing now, while there is still time, as many as possible of
fascism's tortured captives. . . . If the delegates to the Bermuda Conference are going to pursue their deliberations in an
attitude of doleful defeatism, we say they might better go
home now. They can make a better contribution to the war
effort by puttering in their victory gardens.

Criticism of this sort was not limited to one side of the
Atlantic. While *The Times* (London) and the *Daily Worker*
applauded the intent of the negotiations, they both doubted
that much could be expected in view of existing circumstances
in the world. On April 22, however, the *Manchester Guardian*,
long the British gadfly on refugee questions, blasted the excuses
emanating from Bermuda as "all too familiar (p. 20)." The
Jewish journals in Palestine reached even more heated verdicts.
To the labor daily *Davar* and its sister paper *Haboker*, the conference was "a screen to conceal inactivity," "a second version
of the Evian Conference," though without Jewish suppliants at
hand.[60] At the same time the New Zionist daily *Hamashkif* and
the moderate *Hatzofeh* bemoaned the absence of Jewish representatives from the conference and suggested that by its silence,
the conference might actually encourage the Nazis to proceed
with their massacres.[61]

If the Americans and British had hoped to pull off a propaganda coup by calling such a conference—and a reading of the
communiqués from Reams to Hull and the eagerness with which
the State Department officials devoured newspaper commen-
taries from across the nation indicated that this was so—then
they were understandably disappointed by the near universal
anathema passed upon Bermuda.[62]

Three factors account for the tremendous outpouring of
abuse heaped on the delegates as they went about their delicate
work at Hamilton: the refusal of the American delegates to
discuss the possibility of changes in U.S. immigration laws to
accommodate refugees; the British refusal to consider Palestine
as a haven for Jews; and the reluctance of either side to give

vent to a public expression of sympathy for the singular condition of the Jews in Europe.

In 1943 immigration to the United States totaled 23,725, the lowest figure in 110 years except for 1933. In 1943 alone, 130,000 legal entry certificates went unused. While thousands of Jews were gassed daily in Europe, only 4,705 Jews entered the United States that year.[63] It had frequently been suggested, therefore, that the unused visas, particularly the 65,000 assigned to the British and the 27,000 to Germany, be reassigned to other nationals seeking refuge.[64] Failing this, Congress might be persuaded to make some other special dispensation for the Jews. Such an action had some precedent, for it was generally assumed that Section 3 of the Immigration Act of February 5, 1917 (providing for literacy tests for all immigrants to this country) had specifically exempted Jews from its restrictions. Moreover, Congress had indicated its willingness to amend the Johnson Act whenever the need arose. On May 26, 1926, a special act (44 *Stat.* 657) permitted Spanish nationals to enter Puerto Rico in excess of the 1924 quota. On June 13, 1930, waves of American citizens from China were granted similar immunities (46 *Stat.* 581). On April 29 and again on December 23, 1943, Congress passed a series of laws enabling agricultural workers from Latin America to enter the country to assist in food production. Under these provisions (57 *Stat.* 70 and 57 *Stat.* 643) 300,000 Mexicans were temporarily admitted to the U.S. to help with the harvesting of crops. And finally, on December 17, Congress repealed the Chinese Exclusion Acts, which had set America on the road to restrictionism back in 1882.[65] Although all of these actions were merely tokenist and responsive to America's self-interest, they did indicate that, given proper direction, Congress need not be recalcitrant in changing the nation's immigration laws to accommodate what small number of refugees might be able to flee Europe.

Even within existing limits of the Johnson Act, the United States might have offered to do more than it did. Refugees might have been welcomed under a series of nonquota loopholes in the law, which provided for the admission of "ministers, professors, their wives, and unmarried children under eighteen, and students at least fifteen years of age." [66] This would have entailed a liberal definition of what constituted a minister or student. Any such relaxation of screening procedures was out of the question to Hull and Long. Instead, Dodds received oral instructions upon his arrival at Bermuda not to permit the slightest mention of the subject of America's immigration laws.

Dodds is naturally reluctant to identify the individual who told him this (there is no mention of this instruction in any of the Bermuda records), but he affirms that the ultimate source of authority was Roosevelt himself. "We got direct word from the White House that we could not discuss increasing the quotas with the British," Dodds revealed. Dodds realized that this stripped him of his major bargaining lever, by which he had hoped to persuade the British to open the Dominions, the colonies, or Palestine. Moreover, such instructions were a direct contradiction of what Jewish leaders who had conferred with Roosevelt early in April had been led to expect of Bermuda. On the eve of his departure for the conference Dodds met with the ubiquitous Wise and was told how the Jews "expected great things" from the refugee conference. Thoroughly disillusioned even before the serious negotiations began, Dodds decided to do his best and to go through the motions of serving the interests of his country and of the refugees. But he vowed never to work for FDR again.[67]

There can be no doubt that Roosevelt and Hull were responsible for removing the subject of America's immigration laws from the agenda. In a letter prepared for Roosevelt one week after the conference ended Hull reaffirmed his belief in the sanctity of existing quotas. He wrote:

> I cannot recommend that we open the question of relaxing the provisions of our immigration laws and run the risk of a prolonged and bitter controversy in Congress on the immigration question. I cannot recommend that we bring in refugees as temporary visitors and thus lay ourselves open to possible charges of nullification or evasion of the national origins provision embodied in the quota law.[68]

Roosevelt's terse response agreed with the secretary's analysis. "I do not think we can do other than comply strictly with the present immigration laws," Roosevelt wrote, "I agree with you that we cannot open the question of our immigration laws. I agree with you as to bringing in temporary visitors. We have already brought in a large number." [69]

Hull was swayed by the fear, almost endemic to the State Department by this time, that a horde of aliens, all potential saboteurs, would swarm into the country to damage the war effort. Roosevelt, however, may have been motivated more by the distressing public opinion soundings taken during this period which indicated that Jews were the most unpopular racial or religious group in this country, fully four times as unpopular as Germans or Japanese.[70] In July 1942, months before the government officially acknowledged the existence of the death camps in Europe but well enough into the war for Americans to know of the sufferings of the Jewish people, one American in six told pollsters that Hitler was "doing the right thing" to the Jews.[71] Other analysts, noting the criticism of Jews as draft dodgers and wartime profiteers, suggested that during the war perhaps as much as 40 percent of the adult American population would have supported a hypothetical anti-Semitic movement, or at least sympathized with it.[72] Little, then, should have been expected from Bermuda because many Americans were unconcerned about what happened to the Jews. Government policies in a democracy, after all, reflect the needs, aspirations, and desires of its constituency.

Harold Dodds was to serve as a convenient mouthpiece for government inaction and little more. He demonstrated this position in his opening address to the delegates at Bermuda, an address which was merely a rehash of Hull's innocuous letter of February 25. Dodds paid tribute to Great Britain for the burden it had assumed toward the innocent victims of "the cruel Nazi philosophy," but in the same breath he felt compelled to cite America's humanitarian achievements as well. Among other things the United States had: (1) condemned the racist policies of the Axis governments; (2) appropriated large amounts of public and private funds for the relief of the oppressed; (3) applied American immigration laws "in the utmost liberal and humane spirit of these laws"; (4) called the first intergovernmental conference on refugees at Evian in 1938; (5) granted 547,775 visas to natives of Axis-dominated lands since Hitler's rise to power; and (6) made special provision through the International Red Cross for the care of several thousand refugees then in Spain awaiting evacuation.[73]

Dodds now admits his speech was little more than a smokescreen. "Frankly," he stated, "a bit of it was phoney. We tried to make the case that we were doing nicely. But they [the British] were doing better, though, proportionately. We also were encountering some restless public opinion." The only novel proposal which Dodds made to the British was for the revival of the Intergovernmental Committee on Refugees.[74] This, too, had been authorized by Hull, who reminded Dodds that "the IGCR is the result of President Roosevelt's thought and a development out of his original policy, and it seems appropriate that in view of his present and continuing interest in the same objective that this product of his thought should be used as the agency [for refugee relief]." Hull maintained that there were already thirty-two nations which belonged to the IGCR, and that any new program of international action might result in the alienation of some of these.[75]

Hull spoke of the IGCR as if it were a healthy creature, but many of the thirty-two nations he mentioned were under Nazi domination and in no position to give aid to the committee. Many others, particularly the South American nations, had once expressed official horror at the news of Nazi genocide but now maintained barriers against "undesirable immigration" from Europe.[76] Still others, like Switzerland and Sweden, already considered themselves saturated with 100,000 to 200,000 refugees and were getting no assistance from the IGCR for their support.[77]

There was no IGCR in April 1943, simply a token staff in London whose director, Herbert Emerson, had already conceded his committee's incapacity to handle any refugee problems at the time.[78] Myron Taylor, who had chaired the U.S. delegation to Evian and who normally followed the administration line in refugee questions, spoke out against the committee's revival in 1943, recalling the tremendous "covert dueling" between public and private funding agencies which had hampered its earlier efforts and would undoubtedly do the same during the war.[79] The British also doubted the personal capabilities of Herbert Emerson, whom they would have replaced with a younger man.[80]

Nevertheless, when Dodds made the suggestion concerning the IGCR, the British eagerly snapped at the bait. Here was precisely the kind of "concrete," yet harmless, proposal which might salve the critics of its Palestine policy. If any land seemed most appropriate as a refugee haven, it was Palestine. Most of the refugees were Jews. Most of them wanted to get to Palestine. And Palestine had been rendered accessible by countless Jewish illegals aboard decrepit tramp steamers or along the primitive Turkish rail facilities.

The official British position on Palestine, repeatedly affirmed by the Churchill government after the *Struma* affair, was that Jews fleeing the Nazi vise would be admitted to the Holy Land—but only in numbers up to 75,000, the maximum permitted under the White Paper of 1939. As late as April 7, 1943, Churchill, who once had suggested that the Chamberlain government "file a petition in moral bankruptcy" when it enacted the White Paper, cleaved to that same policy. He indicated that no Jewish refugees would be turned away from Palestine, but their numbers would be subtracted from the total permitted before March 1944 when all Jewish immigration would have to cease. None of these emigrants, however, would receive any assistance from His Majesty's Government in making their way to the Middle East.[81]

Unlike the Americans, the British did permit some discussion of their Achilles heel, the Palestine situation, at Bermuda. According to Dodds, "Balfour [the Balfour Declaration of November 1917 promising the Jews a national home in Palestine] came up time and time again." Each time, however, the British stood firm. When, for example, it was suggested to Admiralty Undersecretary George Hall that British victories outside Tunis had relieved the German threat in the Middle East to the point where Palestine might now serve as a refuge for Jews, Hall stated flatly that there would be no departure from his government's execution of the White Paper.[82] When it was pointed out that 29,000 certificates for Jews were still available under that edict, the British responded that there was no way the Jews could travel to Palestine. The few neutral sailing ships in the Mediterranean would be inadequate for the purpose, even if they could be hired.[83] British experts, contradicting the ORT's Backer who spoke optimistically of bringing 500 persons out of the Balkans on Turkish railroads, contended that these facilities were also inadequate.[84]

In reality, the British were not so much concerned about the problem of transport as they were about the kind of refugee who might come to Palestine. Through the war Great Britain granted asylum in the Middle East to an unlimited number of non-Jewish refugees. Before the end of the war some 45,000 Greeks, Poles, and Yugoslavs had passed through detention camps at El Shatt, El Arish, Khataba, Moses Wells, and Tolumbat in the Egyptian Delta and Sinai. Another 9,000 of these "Aryans" were granted outright sanctuary in Palestine, while 4,800 Greeks were admitted to Cyprus.[85]

The British Foreign Office dreaded the thought that Hitler might actually release his captive Jews. A. W. G. Randall of the Refugee Department, a delegate to Bermuda, later betrayed the geopolitical dilemma of the British government when he asked Moshe Shertok (Sharrett) of the Jewish Agency: "Where should we be if the Germans should offer to dump a million Jews on us? Where would we put them?" [86]

The answer was Palestine, but this was precisely what the British hoped to avoid. With protests from every Arab state against further Jewish immigration already in London and Washington, with Arab sympathies to the Allied cause openly in doubt, and with the Grand Mufti of Jerusalem preaching a *Jihad* for the Nazis from a Berlin radio station, the last thing that the British could afford was the heightening of tensions in the Middle East by the migration of more Jews into that area.[87]

However, the British can be faulted for their discriminatory rescue operations. Instead of denying access to Arab countries to all refugees from Hitler, the British defended their acceptance of non-Jews with the rationalization that at least some persons were being saved. On April 20, Law proposed removing 200 Polish families from Iran to Cyrenaica and an additional 5,000 Greek refugees from Cyprus to the Gaza region of Palestine. No Jews were to be considered in this scheme.[88] The next day Law suggested that relief be given to some 21,000 refugees who were detained in miserable camps like Miranda de Ebro, but who might be useful to the war effort. Approximately 12,000 of these were French nationals, 3,000 were Poles and Czechs, and 6,000 were stateless or "enemy national" Jews. Law proposed that all of those refugees except the Jews be assisted to North Africa.[89] That was too much for Dodds, who wired Hull that such action would antagonize "pressure groups and humanitarians." [90]

It is sardonic that the Jews should have occupied so much of the attention of the delegates. Officially, they were nonpersons at Bermuda. In his opening remarks about the work that the United States was doing, Dodds failed to mention the plight of the Jews at all. While he praised the American consular services, the IGCR, and the Red Cross, he never brought up the vigorous relief operations of the World Jewish Congress, HIAS, the Jewish Labor Committee, the American Friends Service Committee, the Unitarian Services Committee, the National Refugee Service, or the Joint Distribution Committee, which had assisted 60 percent of all refugees from Europe, regardless of creed.[91]

Nor was there a single reference to the Jews in the final public communiqué issued by the delegates to Bermuda on April 29. This bland document read:

> The United States and United Kingdom delegates examined the refugee problem in all its aspects including the position of those potential refugees who are still in the grip of the Axis powers without any immediate prospect of escape. Nothing was excluded from the analysis and everything that held out any possibility, however remote, of a solution of the problem was carefully investigated and thoroughly discussed. From the outset, it was realized that any recommendations that the delegations could make to their governments must pass two tests: would any recommendation submitted interfere with or

delay the war effort of the United Nations and was the recommendation capable of accomplishment under war conditions? The delegates at Bermuda felt bound to reject certain proposals which were not capable of meeting these tests. The delegates were able to agree on a number of concrete resolutions which they are jointly submitting to their governments and which, it is felt, will pass the tests set forth above and will lead to the relief of a substantial number of refugees of all races and nationalities. Since the recommendations necessarily concern governments other than those represented at the Bermuda Conference and involve military considerations, they must remain confidential. It may be said, however, that in the course of discussion, the refugee problem was broken down into its main elements. Questions of shipping, food, and supply were fully investigated. The delegates also agreed on recommendations regarding the form of intergovernmental organization which was best fitted, in their opinion, to handle the problem in the future. This organization would have to be flexible enough to permit it to consider, without prejudice, any new factors that might come to its attention. In each of these fields, the delegates were able to submit agreed proposals for consideration of their respective governments.[92]

At the time of the conference the only group of people who were being detached by force from their homes and occupations, segregated from their neighbors physically as well as socially, and marked for annihilation were the Jews. Only the Jews were being killed for no better reason than that they existed. As Senator William Langer later commented, "While singled out for suffering and martyrdom by their enemies, they seem to have been forgotten by the nations which claim to fight for the cause of humanity." [93]

More than ten million Jews lived in European states in 1939 that were to be overrun by the Nazis. By September 1943 fewer than three million of these remained, and 1,995,600 had emigrated or "been evacuated"; 1,800,000 had been "removed" to the interior of the Soviet Union; and three million were dead, exterminated.[94] Yet when the British delegates Peake and Hall were queried as to the number of refugees involved in these discussions, they said there were only 80,000 in the perimeter of Axis-dominated Europe—30,000 Poles in Iran,

15,000 Greeks in and around Cyprus, 20,000 mixed Europeans in Spain, 18,000 in Switzerland, and several thousand more in Sweden.[95] These figures do not differ substantially from those which Hull sent to FDR on May 23, 1943.[96]

Once more, as at Evian, the governments of the two great democracies could be accused of failing to come up with any practical rescue proposals, of underplaying the extent of the refugee problem, of refusing to acknowledge the special persecution of the Jews under Nazism. Once more, as with the suppression of the news of genocide, this was done not in malice but in the belief that special efforts on behalf of the Jews would signal vicious reprisals against them in Europe. This feeling is what reduced Sol Bloom to silence. As he wrote later:

> The announcement that we were going to aid a particular group might lead to intensified persecutions, perhaps to demonstrate that meddling from the outside could only intensify its wretchedness, perhaps to induce the payment of a huge ransom; or, quite possibly, the enemy would take unusual pains to sink a ship filled with helpless men, women, and children, thus hoping to discourage further attempts at rescue.[97]

The reluctance of the Allies to risk such a voyage was regarded by most critics of the Bermuda conference as a ruse to conceal the basic shortcoming of this meeting. "What lies behind Bermuda?" asked Alexander Uhl of *PM*. "Are we really as charitable and generous as we like to think we are?" His questions were answered by *Nation* Editor Freda Kirchwey, who wrote:

> In this country, you and I, the President and the Congress and the State Department are accessories to the crime and share Hitler's guilt. If we had behaved like humane and generous people instead of complacent, cowardly ones, the two million lying today in the earth of Poland and Hitler's overcrowded graveyards would be alive and safe. We had it in our power to rescue this doomed people and yet did not lift a hand to do it—or perhaps it would be better to say that we lifted just one cautious hand, encased in a tight-fitting glove of quotas and visas and affidavits and a thick layer of prejudice.[98]

8. Holding the Keys

The problem is too mighty grown
For our democracies alone.
We do not solely hold the keys
To open door to refugees.
In war we must decline to give
Admission to the fugitive.[1]

By the spring of 1943 the war had taken a decided turn in favor of the Allies. In the Far East supplies were rolling regularly over the Hump to Chiang Kai-shek's headquarters in Kunming. Orde Wingate's Chindits and Frank Merrill's Marauders were causing havoc behind Japanese lines in Burma and Indo-China. General Douglas MacArthur was planning the first Allied assault upon territory which had belonged to Japan before the war in the Pacific began—Rabaul and the Bismarck Archipelago. The Russians had repulsed the Germans from Kharkov, and Stalingrad stood as a scarred headstone to the 1,000,000 men lost to Nazi legions on the Eastern Front that year. On May 12, the Mareth line broken, the Afrika Korps in disarray, Americans pouring across North Africa from the west and the British ripping into Tunis and Bizerte from the east, Erwin Rommel ordered the capitulation of 300,000 troops rather than emulate the suicidal fight of von Paulus at Stalingrad, as Hitler ordered. By summer the Allies were poised to strike at Sicily, the first step preparatory to the liberation of Europe.

In the midst of rising optimism and oft-sounded phrases about the necessity for unity, some Americans were startled to open the pages of the *New York Times* on May 4, 1943 and see a six-column headline in two-inch block letters which read, "To 5,000,000 Jews in the Nazi Death Trap, Bermuda was a Cruel Mockery." The article, actually another advertisement purchased by the National Committee for a Jewish Army, accused Great Britain and the United States of giving Hitler a free hand with his extermination plans. It went on:

> Wretched, doomed victims of Hitler's tyranny! Poor men and women of good faith the world over! You have cherished an illusion. Your hopes have been in vain. Bermuda was not the dawn of a new era, of an era of humanity and compassion, of translating pity into deed. Bermuda was a mockery and a cruel jest.[2]

Two days later Scott Lucas, fresh from his labors at the Bermuda conference, rose to harangue his colleagues in the U.S. Senate about the inflammatory advertisement. He denounced its presumption in judging the conference before a complete report could be issued and went on to charge that the advertisement had been purchased without the knowledge of the illustrious personages, including thirty-six senators, whose names were appended to the text. Most of all, Lucas was mortified by innuendoes that he, a lifelong friend of Jews, was callously indifferent to their plight.

As far as publicity was concerned, the final communiqué from Bermuda stated that nothing would be divulged to the press which had not previously been cleared through diplomatic channels. The cables passed back and forth among Long, Hull, and Dodds on the last two days of the conference indicate an American sensitivity to "heavy pressures" and "public relations" at home, but a willingness to go along with the British demand for secrecy.[3] Apparently, the British were concerned that the Americans would tell everything, as Hull had done with his memo of February 25, and thereby expose the dearth of achievements at Bermuda. Dodds shared this feeling and advocated keeping the results confidential for as long as possible. Thus, while Lucas was assuring his comrades in the Senate that additional clarification of the final communiqué would be forthcoming "shortly," the public was not fully enlightened as to the nature of the discussions until 1963, with the opening of the State Department records on the conference.

Lucas's second point, concerning the illegitimate exploitation of names of notables, led to some interesting soul-searching on the part of his colleagues. Lucas claimed to have polled all the senators involved and ascertained that none had prior knowledge of the advertisement's contents. To emphasize the point he read a letter.from Senator Edwin Johnson, chairman of the National Committee for a Jewish Army, to Peter Bergson, the group's publicity director. Johnson rather paternally admonished Bergson for impugning "an esteemed colleague" and urged greater care in framing future releases. After he read this, Lucas was asked to yield by a battery of senators, including E. H. Moore of Oklahoma, Albert Chandler of Kentucky, Harry Truman of Missouri, Alexander Wiley of Wisconsin, James Davis of Pennsylvania, and Burnett Maybank of South Carolina, all of whom wished to disassociate themselves from the advertisement and to express confidence in Lucas.[4] The integrity of the senatorial club had to be preserved.

Just three weeks before this same group of senators, along with Mississippi's Theodore Bilbo and Ohio's Robert Taft, had made no outcry when the National Committee for a Jewish Army splashed an eight-column headline which read "What is the Shocking Truth About Saving the Lives of the European Jews and What Are the Untruths?" across the pages of the *Times*. No one objected then, even though the senators again were unaware of what they had endorsed, because the intemperate language of that first advertisement had been directed solely against the British government, which was charged with deliberate inaction and wanton ineptitude where Jewish lives were concerned.[5]

As for Lucas's alleged philo-Semitism, his declaration on the Senate floor might be construed as somewhat misleading. In questionable taste, the man who had nagged Backer with hypothetical questions about the prospect of Hitler's dumping Jews on the West, who had fretted for the "aching hearts" of American mothers whose boys were dying on the battlelines, now affirmed:

183

I yield to no man, regardless of his race, creed, or color, in my humane sympathy for those people who are now locked on the inside of Europe's conquered lands. I believe that I understand the heartbeats of the underdog. I believe that I understand what it means to make one's own way in this life. I believe that I understand something about suffering in the early days of life. Some of my best friends I have in this country, Mr. President, are members of the Jewish faith.[6]

In commenting on this affair, which apparently was resolved with Bergson's public apology to Lucas on May 8, the Independent Jewish Press Service decried the fact that the Jewish organization's bungling of the episode had permitted Lucas and the government to assume the roles of the wronged innocents and thus to gain the offensive in stifling criticism of the Bermuda conference. Perhaps, the IJPS noted sarcastically, this incident would serve as a warning to Jewish organizations which actively solicited senatorial signatures for semi-weekly advertisements without first briefing the senators as to the nature of the press release. The wire service looked to the upcoming American Jewish Conference to rectify the situation and coordinate the efforts of Jewish organizations in the United States and added, "Perhaps one of the first achievements of the American Jewish Conference will be to force suspension of letters to Senators asking them to approve the Skidolsky Unterstitzung Society in its latest card party and bazaar of the Organized Association for Upholding Jewish Honor." [7]

Despite its rather facile handling of this incident, the U.S. government, like the British, remained under heavy attack from Jewish and non-Jewish sources in the next several weeks. The Jewish National Conference, World Jewish Congress, Palestinian Zionists, American Polish-Jewish Federation, American Synagogue Council, and Sons of Zion all roundly scored what they considered to be the failures of Bermuda.[8] Governors of seven states set aside May 2 as a "day of compassion" for the Jews of Europe, and protest demonstrations were staged in cities from Boston to Oakland.[9] Writing in the monthly publication of the School of Social Work of the University of Chicago, Ben Hecht grieved:

Four million Jews waiting for death
Oh, hang and burn out—Quiet Jews!
Don't be bothersome; save your breath—
The World is busy with other news.

Oh World be patient—it will take
Some time before the murder crews
Are done. By Christmas you can make
Your Peace on Earth without the Jews.[10]

Still more eloquent was the anonymous poet "Sagittarius," who blasted the conference in Britain's socialist journal, *The New Statesman and Nation*. The magazine had warned months before the conference that history would one day censure the Allies for their inaction, their sanity, in the face of such horror.[11] Sagittarius wrote:

Where the Bermudas ride remote
This noble (but uncheerful) note,
Voice of inaction and delay
Echoes beyond the Mexique Bay,
(From whence a more inviting strain
Welcomes Republicans from Spain),
And may (perhaps) be heard afar
In Poland's steaming abattoir,
Where (doubtless) those about to die,
Would (were it possible) reply,
Approving of the long-term plans
Of would-be good samaritans.[12]

Such expressions of condemnation in Great Britain were not totally anomalous. Although most British newspapers endorsed the Government's refugee policies, the acerbic *Manchester Guardian* continued to flail away at Churchill's refusal to open Palestine with unlimited immigration for Jews.[13] And on May 19, 1943 the House of Commons subjected Anthony Eden, Peake, and Law to barbed questions and accused the ministers of having failed to appreciate the urgency of the refugee problem and of having draped the conference with "the dreadful spirit of defeatism and despair." [14]

It is hardly coincidental that on May 19, 1943 the American government, with the approval of the British, released the

185

long-sought clarification on the outcome of the Bermuda conference. This new State Department bulletin repeated what had been said previously about wartime security and the requirement of strict secrecy about certain matters. But it did relate that the delegates at Bermuda had: (1) agreed upon financial measures to cover the cost of maintaining refugees in neutral nations; (2) discussed a number of temporary havens to which refugees could be transferred and maintained "if and when shipping could become available"; (3) declared their intention of providing for repatriation of refugees upon termination of hostilities; (4) submitted a plan for an expanded and more efficient intergovernment refugee organization with increased authority to meet problems created by the war; (5) rejected any consideration of negotiations with Hitler "since his entire record has left no doubt that he would agree to such solutions as would be of direct aid to the Axis war aims." [15]

The State Department must have been satisfied with this amplification of the Bermuda protocol, for in June when it received a four-page letter from Wise outlining a host of rescue proposals and pointing to a growing passion in the Jewish community for revenge against the Germans in one form or another, Long dismissed the note as indicative of "a considerable degree of acquiescence in the recommendations of the Bermuda Conference." As for the rescue suggestions, Long, who never took Wise seriously, claimed they were "now of less emphasis." [16] The next day he wrote in his diary that even though "the recommendations of the Bermuda Conference have not been carried forward," the refugee question had calmed down. "Our information indicates that pressure groups now see the correctness of the position we have maintained from the beginning." [17]

If anything, pressure to force the government to take more decisive action to rescue the Jews of Europe continued to mount in the summer and fall of 1943. Gigantic rallies sponsored by the revisionist Emergency Conference to Save the Jews of Europe packed Madison Square Garden and Carnegie Hall in June and July. State legislatures in Connecticut, California, Illinois, Missouri, Pennsylvania, and Texas passed resolutions calling for freer immigration to Palestine. Norman Thomas, chairman of the executive commission of the Postwar World Council, wrote Roosevelt to complain of "the small and sorry results of Bermuda as contrasted with accomplishments at the recently concluded food conference."[18] Later Thomas told the press, "We are willing to fight Hitler partly because of his anti-Semitic cruelty, but we have not been willing to take any bold and aggressive action to rescue Jewish refugees or even temporarily to modify our immigration laws in this historic land of asylum."[19] This was exactly what the governing boards of both the national Democratic and Republican clubs urged in September. Appearing before a news conference on September 9, Democrat William Fullen and Republican Thomas Curren recommended a suspension of immigration restrictions for all aliens fleeing religious persecution.[20] The White House received numerous letters from rabbis, governors, and laymen of all faiths who demanded an end to what Pierre Van Paassen termed "the scandal of Christiandom," "the driving of an ancient people to haunt the corridors of time as ghosts and beggars and to wander about, waifs in every storm that blows."[21]

To silence such critics the administration fell back upon its standard rationalization—the war effort. Time and time again its spokesmen hammered home at the theme that everything must take a back seat to the primary task of defeating the Nazis and the Japanese. In a recent interview Harold Willis Dodds made reference to this rationalization five times. The same was true in conversations with presidential adviser Benjamin Cohen. Lillie Shultz, when defending Wise, also spoke in terms of actions compatible with winning the war. Adolf Berle, addressing a throng of 20,000 gathered in Boston to pay tribute to the Jews of Europe in May 1943, said, "The only cure for this hideous mess can come through Allied armies."[22] Hull also emphasized the importance of ultimate victory in his July message to the Emergency Conference to Save the Jews of Europe. "You will readily realize that no measure is practicable unless it is consistent with the destruction of Nazi tyranny; and that the final defeat of Hitler and the rooting out of the Nazi system is the only complete answer," he said.[23] In September 1943, the secretary tried to assuage the Zionist Organization of America Convention in Columbus, Ohio, by using this same approach and promising that the government would take "every feasible step" consistent with winning the war to ameliorate the plight of the Jews in Europe.[24]

Some congressmen, however, did not feel that pursuance of the war and rescue of the Jews were mutually exclusive. On Capitol Hill, Dickstein and Celler lashed out against the government's inaction since Bermuda.[25] In the Senate, North Dakota's lightly regarded junior Senator William Langer repeatedly clamored for more information about what had transpired at Bermuda and what was being done for the Jews six months after Bermuda. In October, Langer charged that "I submit that by doing nothing, we have acquiesced in what has taken place over there." [26] Finally, in response to these verbal recriminations, and against the recommendation of the State Department, Senator Guy Gillette, joined by fellow senators Clark, Ellender, Guffey, Van Nuys, and Taft and Congressmen Baldwin and Rogers, introduced a series of resolutions calling for the establishment of a special commission to save the Jews of Europe.[27]

On November 26, 1943, Breckinridge Long was summoned before the House Committee on Foreign Affairs (chaired by his friend Sol Bloom) to defend the government's refugee policy. Long nearly overwhelmed his inquisitors with statistics about the many achievements of the Roosevelt administration in refugee work during the war. Beginning with a recitation of Hull's oft-cited figure of 547,775 refugees whom Long claimed had been admitted to the U.S. since the rise of Hitler, the assistant secretary went on to tell how the U.S., with Britain, had (1) welcomed scores of persons, including the complete faculties of yeshivas, who had made their way across Siberia to Japan before the war broke out in the Pacific; (2) arranged for the transport of 1,200 stateless persons from Spain to North Africa in 1943 and persuaded the Franco government to keep

Spain's borders open as a way-station for refugees escaping to permanent havens; (3) found asylum for 6,000 Poles in Persia and 5,000 French children in neutral Sweden and Switzerland; (4) sought shipping through neutral nations like Spain and Portugal; (5) requested the International Red Cross to investigate atrocities against the Jews; (6) issued warnings to Nazi puppets in the Balkans not to assist in the extermination process; and (7) underwritten the expenses of the Intergovernmental Committee on Refugees on an equal basis with Great Britain.[28]

Under congressional examination Long once more revealed his insensitivity to the suffering of the Jews. Questioned by South Dakota's Karl Mundt about the *Struma* incident, he said, "It was a terrible thing to happen, but it was one of those things that do happen." He added hastily, "I do not consider it [the refugee question] as concerned with the Palestine question." [29] Long implied that Jewish pressure groups in this country had actually hampered rescue operations and exaggerated the sufferings of Jews to the exclusion of other racial and religious groups which were under the Nazi heel. When Congressman Mundt suggested that any new rescue commission be chartered to aid Jews and non-Jews alike, Long, who opposed the idea of a new commission allegedly because it would duplicate the work of the IGCR, said, "The State Department has maintained that attitude all through, but the situation has come to a state of publicity where I think the Jewish interests have emphasized the fate of Jews as such." [30]

That last statement was made almost a year after Nazi genocide against the Jews had been confirmed. It did not take the American Jewish community long to react. The Commission of Rescue of the American Jewish Conference issued its own statement that Long's testimony "can be read only with mixed feelings in which bewilderment and regret dominate over satisfaction." [31] The conference chided Long on his attitudes toward Jews, the inaccuracy of his immigration statistics, the worthlessness of the IGCR, the impossibility of feeding refugees in Nazi-dominated lands, the unavailability of shipping and the unavailability of havens, and, in the words of AJ

Conference Secretary I. L. Kenen, concluded that he was not only a bigot, but an inaccurate one at that.[32]

Like all Jews the conference members were offended by Long's innuendoes about Jewish pressure to secure preferential treatment for their brethren in Europe. The delegates from the largest Jewish bodies in the United States called for aid to all victims of Nazism regardless of race, but again emphasized the uniqueness of the Jewish tragedy. They added, "It is difficult to understand Mr. Long's repeated implication that specific aid to Jews excludes help to other people or that there is no distinction between the problems of rescuing Jews from Hitler Europe and rescuing refugees in general." [33]

The Rescue Commission of the conference challenged Long's statement that 547,000 refugees had been admitted to the U.S. since 1933. Such a figure did not belong in discussions about the rescue of Jews, as its use in conjunction with the State Department's efforts on behalf of yeshiva students, Jewish children, and stateless persons created the illusion that the United States had saved a half million Jews from the Nazi death-trap. Statistics indicate that only 163,843 Jews reached the United States between 1933 and 1943. Of these, 43,089 were admitted under visitors permits and had to reenter the country under regular quota restrictions. In the process some were counted twice by overzealous government officials. If Long sought to give a true picture of American immigration, he could have spoken of the needlessly cumbersome regulations which had limited immigration in 1943 to 5.9 percent of the number permitted under the 1924 law.[34]

Earl G. Harrison, commissioner of Immigration and Naturalization, conceded that Long's figures were misleading when he later told a refugee relief banquet that no more than 200,000 actual refugees had been admitted to the United States in the previous decade.[35] Even Long subsequently admitted that he had erred in his testimony on this point. Writing to Travers, Chief of the Visa Division, in December, he affirmed his belief that 547,000 visas had been issued, but added, "Which of those persons actually entered the United States is a matter that is not apparent from the records of the Department of State, as we do not keep such records." [36]

Long attempted to defend himself by having his subordinates draw up lengthy memorandums on the technical problems involved for European emigrants who were supposed to use their visas within the allotted calendar year. Long would not retract his testimony, however, save to issue a short note to Bloom conceding that he had made an innocent mistake and "more properly should have said, 'We have authorized visas for [547,000 persons] to come to this country' instead of 'We have taken into this country [547,000 persons].' " [37]

Long's hopes for the IGCR were equally unrealistic and perhaps even insincere. To speak of turning over the refugee question once more to an agency which had been described by its director, Herbert Emerson, as "moribund, honorary and not competent" was an action which could hardly be viewed with jubilation in the Jewish community. Myron Taylor, chief U.S. delegate at Evian, had cautioned against its revival. Emerson had called for the establishment of a new international refugee authority the previous year. Jews could not be expected to have confidence in a man who was criticized at Bermuda as incapable of handling the expanded duties of the IGCR. As late as August 1942, Emerson was still speaking in the prewar jargon of the danger of "flooding countries with large numbers of Jews" and of the necessity of resolving the Jewish problem through minority treaties with Central and East European nations. [38]

Twenty-nine countries sent representatives to the new organizational sessions of the IGCR at London in August 1943. Grandiose pledges of funds were made and an American, Patrick Malin, lately of the American Friends Service Committee, the International Migration Service, and OFRRO, was named vice-director. [39] For all its talk, however, the IGCR had little practical value for the remainder of the war. Three weeks before Long informed the House Committee on Foreign Affairs of the potential of the IGCR, Emerson had informed Hull that the committee had no authority to negotiate with anyone but neutral or Allied states, and this held out no hope for those behind barbed wire in Europe.[40] When Long implied that it could rescue refugees from occupied lands, the head office of the IGCR in London swiftly denied this and said that the assistant secretary's statement was "absolutely incorrect." [41] Until it was superseded by the International Refugee Organization in July 1947, the IGCR continued to function, engaging in some token relief work, but concentrating on planning for the postwar disposition of refugees.[42]

A third point in Long's testimony which rankled many Jews was his insistence that the democracies were powerless to send food or other supplies into Nazi-dominated lands to assist the Jews. The idea of trans-blockade feeding had been broached on several occasions by Jewish groups before the Bermuda conference but had been rejected by the American delegation as "wholly outside" the realm of that conference.[43] A suggestion from World Jewish Congress President Nahum Goldmann in September 1943 that the government cooperate in a $10,000,000 food relief project through the International Red Cross was similarly rejected.[44] The State Department, however, objected to this form of relief for European refugees for reasons which on the surface appeared valid. A special departmental memorandum on refugees prepared for Undersecretary Edward R. Stettinius, Jr., by R. Borden Reams in October 1943 noted that such a food project would destroy the effectiveness of the Allied blockade of Europe; lead to the feeding of European Jews, "many of whom were actually enemy aliens"; contribute to the Nazi war effort because there would be no effective control over the disbursement of food parcels.[45]

The fear that the Germans might, in fact, confiscate relief supplies was the most powerful deterrent to any trans-blockade relief scheme. According to Sol Bloom, attempts to send $50,-000,000 in supplies to Greece and other Nazi-held lands in 1941–1942 had failed, with the Germans taking most of the goods.[46] Even Long had to admit that this was something of an overstatement. The U.S. continued to ship 18,000 tons of wheat and vegetables to Greece each month in 1943, but only because Greece was beyond the limits of the Atlantic blockade and the

Germans had granted safe conduct to the eight Swedish cargo vessels carrying this produce.[47]

Although these supplies continued to flow into German-controlled ports in the Aegean, the Allies would not trust the Germans elsewhere in Europe. "If you send food to Antwerp," Long told Representative John Vorys of Ohio, "the Germans will take it and you contribute to the welfare and fighting strength of the German Army." [48] Long did not explain why the Germans in Belgium or Poland would be more inclined to steal medicine and food from the sick and underfed populations of those countries than their comrades in Greece.

In fact, before Long even testified, the U.S. had sent twenty million units of insulin for distribution in France. Countless ragtag garments had also been passed to the persecuted through neutral intermediaries. The American Red Cross through its international affiliate had spent more than $340,000 on drugs and pharmaceuticals for Belgians since the United States became embroiled in the war.[49] Many thousands more dollars had been spent by the Joint Relief Commission of the International Red Cross and the Swedish Relief Commission to feed and clothe refugees in Poland, Yugoslavia, Norway, the Netherlands, and even in some of the worst "detention camps" like Terezin, Gurs, and Vittel.[50] Doubtless some of this relief was confiscated by the Nazis, but Jewish leaders like Wise, Goldmann, and Hecht felt that the risks involved were justified on the theory that eventually some Jewish lives might be preserved. The State Department, regarding the matter much more impersonally, could not agree.

Perhaps that part of Long's testimony which was most unacceptable to Jews, however, was that on the availability of shipping. After telling Bloom's committee of efforts to secure neutral vessels for the transport of refugees to places of relative safety, Long lamented that no transportation was available. Long claimed that fewer than 200 persons a month could be accommodated on available shipping.[51] What had happened to the approximately forty passenger vessels belonging to neutrals which had been the subject of serious discussions at Bermuda several months before Long did not specify.[52] Nor did he explain how it was that the Swedes, Spanish, Portuguese, and Turks, eager to profit from what Jews in this country estimated in August 1943 to be a potential traffic of 50,000 persons a month, were no longer interested in such fares by the next November. He also did not elaborate on the conditions which existed aboard those vessels which continued to ply the Atlantic trade through 1943. On June 22, 1943 the *Serpo Pinto,* out of Lisbon, arrived at Philadelphia carrying thirty passengers. Its capacity was 600. Other steamers from neutral nations, the *Yasa,* the *Magallenes,* and the *Gripsholm,* came to the United States in 1943 carrying less than 10 percent of their potential passenger loads.[53]

The failure to obtain neutral shipping resulted from the American government's reluctance to subject these vessels and their passengers to the "insuperable" hazards of German U-boats.[54] Jews could reply that by the spring of 1943 the Mediterranean was open to Allied shipping at Gibraltar and Suez, and that the U-boat menace in the Atlantic, which had accounted for nearly one million deadweight tons of Allied shipping sunk each month in 1942, was virtually nonexistent by the summer of 1943. During the first half of 1942, 220,000 tons of shipping had been lost for every U-boat sunk. But by May 1943 that ratio had dropped to 5,500 for every German submarine sunk, the equivalent of one ship lost for every U-boat lost. The improvement was based on improved radar, a wider range of Allied aircraft operating out of Newfoundland, Reykjavik, and Londonderry, and the presence of escort carriers in convoys.[55]

On May 20, 1943, Winston Churchill was telling Congress that the submarine menace in the Atlantic was dead. Although his evaluation may have seemed headstrong at the time, subsequent tallies proved him correct.[56] In June 1943 the Nazis lost twenty-one U-boats in return for sinking twenty Allied vessels. The next month thirty-three German submarines were destroyed, while the Allies lost only forty-five surface vessels. Thereafter, the German High Command considered it fortunate if it sank 100,000 tons of shipping in any month. Short on fuel, forced to stay underwater for great lengths of time and then to battle convoys supported by air power, the average U-boat lasted for only two or three sorties. Vice-Admiral Friedrich Ruge concluded, "Admiral Doenitz thus had no option but to give up the main theatre of operations in the Atlantic. Those that remained were of little use." [57] The Germans lost 725 submarines during World War II, including 237 in 1943 and 241 in 1944 (up from thirty-five sinkings in 1941 and eighty-five in 1942), but to VE-Day, the Allies remained fixated by the fear of a mythological "U-boat offensive." [58]

If the American government was unwilling to risk the sinking of neutral vessels in the face of this alleged U-boat menace, were there any American vessels available? Both the navy and the army operated their own transport services during the war, amphibious transport ships, luxury liners, converted Liberty ships, which carried eight million Americans overseas between December 1941 and December 1945. Allegedly these ships were returning empty. Then there were the American merchant vessels, bound for Europe with tons of supplies, returning with what many believed to be empty bottoms. Jewish leaders like Emanuel Celler and Stephen Wise clamored for these vessels to be placed under the flags of the Red Cross to ferry refugees back across the Atlantic. [59]

The office of Naval Operations rejected the idea of using military craft for such an operation in February 1943. Apart from the obvious slowdown in making such vessels available for new troop shipments (American staging areas were chaotic enough at the time), the proposal raised questions concerning reception, quartering, and surveillance of refugees. [60] The matter of passengers on cargo ships presented even greater problems. Most of the Liberty Ships were of the C-1 (cargo only) class, with accommodations for fewer than fifty persons, including the crews. Criticized for their lack of speed, with only a top range of eleven knots, these vessels had been streamlined down to the substitution of a steel bell in place of the heavier, standard brass bell to give them an added fragment of maneuverability on the high seas. [61] To load them down with refugees, either housed in inhuman cargo holds or in compartments requiring repeated conversions of the vessels, would have been, in the words of

Harold Willis Dodds, "unthinkable, absolutely impossible." [62] As a result, the subject of transporting civilian passengers on cargo vessels was dropped in the summer of 1943 when the navy, army, and War Shipping Administration, unable to agree on a policy since the subject was broached in midsummer 1942, failed to receive the necessary presidential go ahead.[63]

None of these objections—availability of transports, safety of passengers, availability of decent accommodations, compatibility with the war effort—had interfered when the Americans shoe-horned their soldiers into four tiers of bunks, two to a bunk if bunks were available, on every conceivable type of vessel (including the squalid Liberty ships) for the journey across the Atlantic.[64] None of these objections had been raised when the British undertook to transport thousands of Muslim pilgrims from the Indian Ocean to the Red Sea to make the *Hajj* to Mecca in the spring of 1943.[65] None of these objections had been raised when Great Britain transported 100,000 prisoners of war to Jamaica, Kenya, Tanganyika, and the British Isles in 1943.[66] Nor had anyone objected when the U.S. transported 146,246 civilians, government officials, dependents, contractors and their employees, and Axis POWs, who constituted 41 percent of that figure, back to the United States in September 1944.[67]

In 1943, when fewer than 25,000 immigrants were admitted to the United States and when fewer than 5,000 of these were Jews, more than 200,000 German and Italian prisoners of war were ferried across the ocean. At a time when military planners and the State Department fretted over the cost of setting up camps for refugees from Hitlerism in this country, the War Department was busily constructing 155 base camps and 500 branch camps in forty-five states, which would ultimately hold 371,000 German, 50,000 Italian, and 5,400 Japanese POWs by the end of May 1945.[68]

There were, then, few empty bottoms among the vessels returning to the United States, as available shipping was used for the transport of prisoners, as well as sick or wounded soldiers or soldiers returning on leave. Such movement of prisoners was defended on the grounds that it relieved theater commanders of the burden of housing, feeding, and guarding the captured enemy near the frontlines, where they might escape in a counterattack to fight again.[69] It was, however, difficult to explain to some Americans how it was that some Nazi POWs rode in Pullmans on the way to their detention camps in this country while American troops leaving for San Francisco or New York used coaches.[70] The Jewish Agency in Palestine summed up the attitude of most free Jews who would have advocated feeding the Nazis nothing and transporting them in the same type cattle car used to expedite the slaughter of the Jews in Poland when it noted acidly that the Allies seemed more concerned about the well-being of the enemy than the persecuted peoples of Europe.[71]

Actually, the question of shipping should have been academic in 1943. Apart from Palestine, which undeniably was accessible to Jews fleeing the Balkans on foot, aboard leaky tankers, or via the much-debated Turkish railroad system, another sanctuary lay within a few hours ferry service of the European mainland. This was French North Africa. Since Roosevelt announced the invasion of North Africa on November 8, 1942, allegedly to prevent "the systematic plunder of the French by Italians and Germans," [72] the British had constantly pressed for its use as a refugee haven, perhaps as much to relieve them of pressure for the opening of Palestine to Jews as anything else.[73] The Spanish also desired to be relieved of the congestion of displaced persons fleeing France after the Germans had completely occupied that nation on November 11, 1942.[74] Portuguese vessels were available for transport.[75] And already in January 1943, General Dwight D. Eisenhower and his civilian adviser Robert Murphy had given their assent to a scheme to remove 4,000 refugees, who might be useful to the Allied war effort, from Spain to North Africa.

That last statement was especially significant, for it indicated that from the beginning Herbert Lehman's Office of Foreign Relief and Rehabilitation Operations (OFRRO), created by the president on November 18, 1942 to develop relief policies in territories occupied by U.S. forces, was subordinated to military control.[76] At best, the military high command was committed to a policy of highly selective immigration to Algeria and Morocco. The War Department backtracked on April 22, 1943 from its earlier offer to rescue some of the refugees in Spain and listed several objections to the presence of refugees, principally the Jews. Such persons, the department argued, would only complicate military operations in a war zone not yet secured from the Nazis. Their presence would divert personnel, material, and shelter at a time when every man was needed for combat and when many American soldiers themselves were without adequate supplies or shelter. The War Department cautioned the State Department against making any commitments to the British, Spanish, or Portuguese without first consulting "the French," who, nominally at least, controlled North Africa.[77] And finally, Major General George Strong, author of this memorandum which reached Long's desk during the Bermuda deliberations, emphasized that "the Transport of Jewish refugees into the Moslem country of North Africa is of such military concern to the War Department that it should preclude any further consideration of the matter." [78]

By the time Strong submitted his résumé to Long the Allies were walking a diplomatic tightrope between Charles de Gaulle in Algeria and Henri Giraud in Morocco, representing various divisive factions in the Free French government. To spare either man the onus of refusing to help refugees Hull had issued instructions to the American delegation at Bermuda to strike North Africa from consideration as a haven and to substitute instead Madagascar or French Equatorial Africa.[79]

However, the Axis war effort in Africa had collapsed by early May 1943. General Giraud had notified Eisenhower that he would be amenable to admitting most of the 20,000 refugees now in Spain to areas under his control. Giraud made no specific mention of Jews, but he underlined the fact that he would welcome any emigrant from Central Europe who might aid the Allied war effort.[80] Hull, so fastidious in shunning the word "Jew" in official parlance until now, sought the opinions of the Joint Chiefs and Eisenhower on introducing Jewish refugees to the area.[81] Neither the Joint Chiefs nor Eisenhower shared Giraud's optimism. Like Hull, they believed that refugees, particularly Jewish refugees, would have a disruptive influence on North Africa.[82]

The principal rationalization used against the movement of Jews to this region was that their very presence would incite their age-old enemies, the Muslims, to riot and revolution, a detriment to the Allied war effort. On November 14, 1942 the Adjutant General of the War Department received a troubled cable from Allied headquarters in London warning that "any further trouble in Morocco will stir up tribes with disastrous effect." [83] Although journalist Walter Lippmann three days later reported to Hull that Eisenhower had questioned the reliability of intelligence reports on North Africa, military and diplomatic planners in Washington were still concerned about the earlier report which had also warned that "a huge army of occupation" might be needed in the area.[84]

In February 1943 another civilian adviser, Thomas Lamont, warned Hull that the surest way to stir up the Arab tribes was to introduce more Jews to North Africa and repeal anti-Jewish laws instituted by the Vichy government. He wrote that the Muslims were heirs to an anti-Jewish tradition that went back centuries and that any attempt to aid the Jews "would provoke a grave crisis which would interfere with the speedy outcome of the military campaign." [85]

On March 20, Lt. Col. Harold Hoskins of army intelligence concurred with Lamont's analysis when he also warned that a huge army of occupation would be required to secure North Africa if Jews were introduced there. Hoskins linked Arab hatred of the Jews with the problem of Palestine and the holy shrines of the three major faiths. Zionism purportedly aroused the entire Arab world, including the natives of North Africa, who recognized that Jews would only temporarily be detained in this region before going on to Palestine, where they would threaten other Arabs and the sacred shrines as well. As a solution, Hoskins recommended de-Zionizing the Middle East situation by creating a Jewish haven in the desolate and virtually uninhabited Jebel Achdar region of Cyrenaica.[86] His recommendations received the most favorable attention from Hull and also from Rosenman, who was at this time laboring in conferences with Jewish leaders and government officials to defuse the Palestine situation.[87]

These were the reasons the American delegates at Bermuda were instructed to strike North Africa from discussions as a potential haven and work instead for Cyrenaica, Angola, or some other remote spot in Africa. The American government, Hull noted, was concerned about "any matter which might disturb the political situation" in North Africa and would be unwilling to discuss the subject of refugee transfers to that area, even when military considerations permitted.[88]

For such reasons, also, the American military authorities permitted discriminatory legislation against the Jews, drawn up by the Vichy government in Algeria and Morocco, to remain in force months after the Allied invasion. Moroccan Jews, declassed as citizens, were permitted no sugar, butter, soap, cereals, potatoes, or fresh milk, and little clothing, in the rations established by the Allies.[89] To appease French authorities the Americans made no protest when the Free French banned Jewish officers and noncommissioned officers from combat units, when they denied Jewish soldiers reinstatement in the Free French army unless they had been previously wounded or decorated for valor, and when the Free French established quotas for Jewish physicians and other professionals in North Africa.[90]

As late as January 1944 the Joint Chiefs were cautioning against opening North Africa to additional refugees (Jews) because of the danger of flooding the area with unpopular immigrants. Undersecretary Stettinius, however, objected most strenuously to this policy of sacrificing the Jews for the sake of expedience. Writing to Hull on January 8, he said, "If that is a true expression of military policy, and I question if it can represent the considered opinion of high military leaders, we might as well 'shut up shop' on trying to get additional refugees out of occupied Europe." Stettinius urged Hull to have Roosevelt suggest to the military that the rescue of refugees was "extremely important and something which should not be brushed aside." [91]

Stettinius might not have written the above memorandum if he had seen Roosevelt's earlier letter to Hull on North Africa. The president, who had found the region sufficiently safe to visit for discussions with the British and Free French at Casablanca in January 1943, was convinced that the introduction of "large" numbers of Jews could not fail but be disruptive. He wrote Hull on May 14, 1943:

> I agree that North Africa may be used as a depot for these refugees from Spain, but not a permanent residence without full approval of all authorities. I know, in fact, that there is plenty of room for them in North Africa, but I raise the question of sending large numbers of Jews there. That would be extremely unwise.[92]

The people of North Africa traditionally had prided themselves on their tolerance of Jewish *dhimmi*. One of Algeria's best governors, Maurice Viollette, once told the French senate, "If there is anti-Semitism in Algeria, be sure that it is Europeans who fan it." [93] As recently as 1962, French historian Harvey Goldberg was telling American audiences that the Algerian rebels harbored no antipathy toward the Jews or Zionists.[94] Today the phrase that Jews have always lived in peace among their Arab cousins has almost become a bromide.[95]

To assume then that the totally disorganized tribes of North Africa, still a generation removed from the contagion of nationalism that would lead to their own independence, would have risen in revolt because of the appearance of a few thousand more Jews in detention camps of the *Magheb* or as far away as Palestine is questionable. Likewise, those who attempt to telescope events of recent years into the 1940s and impute strong anti-Zionist feelings to the Moroccans and Algerians then also err, for such feelings were probably minimal twenty-five years ago.

What eliminated North Africa as a haven for the Jews was the same military callousness and foreign office timidity that had ruled out Palestine. Fear, deception, and insensitivity to the suffering of the Jews characterized the practices of the

201

British and American governments in 1943. Such themes, evident in the testimony of Breckinridge Long, were sufficient to
convince Congress that it should drop the idea of creating a
special commission for rescue of Jews. Instead the Seventy-Sixth
Congress passed two resolutions (H.R. 203 and S.R. 100) applauding Allied actions taken to date on behalf of the Jews.

9. New Agencies: Old Rationalizations

There were twenty-eight nations fighting Hitler by the end of 1943, and yet not one, including Great Britain and the United States, said, "We will undertake the rescue of the Jews." In the eighteen months which had elapsed since Nazi genocide was confirmed to the time that Congress passed limp resolutions praising Allied efforts on behalf of the refugees in December 1943 an additional two million persons had been gassed in the new death factory of Birkenau-Auschwitz.[1]

To the long list of stated reasons barring effective rescue operations were now added the cost of such operations and accessibility of refugees. The expense associated with any venture, including the bribing of Nazis, transport, food, clothes, and housing were always of great concern to Cordell Hull. On May 7, 1943 he wrote Roosevelt: "The unknown cost of moving an undetermined number of persons from an undisclosed place to an unknown destination, a scheme advocated by certain pressure groups, is, of course, out of the question."[2]

Even if such funds could be raised, the State Department was committed to the view that the Allies could not negotiate with the Nazis over one particular group of people to the exclusion of other captive nationalities in Europe, that they could not negotiate with the Nazis over the release of civilian internees, in short, that they could not negotiate with the Nazis at all.[3] In his special résumé on refugees prepared for Stettinius in the fall of 1943, R. Borden Reams argued that the unconditional surrender formula agreed upon at Casablanca precluded any deal with the Germans over refugees.[4] While Reams worried about the prospect that the Nazis might unload three to five million Jews on the Allies and thereby transfer "the onus for their continued persecution from the German Government to the United Nations," Assistant Secretary Breckinridge Long and IGCR Vice-Director Patrick Malin wrote off the fate of the Jews, charging that there was nothing the Allies could do to get refugees out of Europe in large numbers, as the Germans seemed bent on eradicating, rather than exporting, Jews.[5]

Hull later summarized these objections to ransom negotiations with the enemy when he wrote:

> The inescapable fact was, however, that Jews could not leave German-occupied Europe unless they escaped across borders into neutral Spain, Switzerland, or Sweden, or unless the German authorities permitted them to leave and the Germans permitted Jews to leave only when they were amply paid to do so. We were reluctant to deposit sums of money to the credit of the Nazis even though the deposits were to be made in Switzerland, were to be liquidated only after the end of the war, and apparently could not be used by the Nazi leaders. Moreover, the State Department did not have the large amounts of money and the personnel needed to carry out a plan of reaching and bribing the German officers in charge of the extermination program.[6]

Even allowing that the expenses of the war were astronomical (by the spring of 1943, it was costing the United States more than $40 million a day), the cost involved in transporting and maintaining what refugees might be ferreted out of Europe were, in Long's words, "not so large . . . perhaps $2,000 to $5,000 per person per year." [7] The government was spending at least that, or more, in the care and feeding of prisoners of war.[8]

But even allowing that the American government did not have the funds to underwrite mammoth rescue operations, there were other sources available which were eager and willing to help. Apart from the Joint Distribution Committee, the American Friends Service Committee, or the American Jewish Conference, all of which would have gladly supplied needed millions, the Danish ambassador to the United States, Henrik de Kauffmann, wrote Hull in the fall of 1943 offering to support any measure the American government might attempt on behalf of Danish refugees, particularly 8,500 Jewish refugees in Sweden. Kauffmann wrote:

> As far as financial responsibilities may be involved, I undertake the guaranty towards your government or any other government that may incur expenses in the effort to bring help to Danish Jews or other Danish nationals persecuted by the Nazis, to reimburse such expenses out of the Danish public funds under my control in this country.[9]

Though Kauffmann had more than $20,000,000 credited to the Danish National Bank at his disposal at the time, the State Department suppressed the contents of his letter, since it was felt publication "would work to the disadvantage of the Jews."

Officially, then, the Allies felt it would be unwise to involve themselves in ransom projects. But unofficially the British and Americans did negotiate, frequently and poorly, first with Nazi collaborators like King Boris in Bulgaria, Antonescu in Rumania, Laval in France, and eventually with the Nazi warlords themselves.

The 170,000 Jews in France had been of some concern to the Allies since the collapse of the Third Republic in 1940. Until the invasion of North Africa, representatives of ORT, JDC, OSE, HICEM, and the American Friends continued to function in the unoccupied southern regions of France, continued to describe the horrors of detention camps and of Drancy, the deportation center for Jews from France. They told of mass suicides among Jews, of monthly fines of as much as six million francs which were levied against the Jewish community, of the deportation of large numbers of Jews to slave camps in the East. They also told of thousands of Jewish refugee children from Poland, Germany, and Czechoslovakia who were being loaded sixty to a cattle car, without adult supervision, and without the most primitive sanitary facilities, and sent to certain death in the death camps of Eastern Europe.[10]

On August 13, 1942, James McDonald, Paul Baerwald, and George Warren of the President's Advisory Committee pleaded with Welles to intervene with Vichy to halt the deportation of the rachitic and emaciated children.[11] A month went by before Hull, reacting to what he called "this revolting and fiendish persecution of children" cabled consuls in Marseilles, Lyons, and Nice to prepare visas for 1,000 children.[12] Breckinridge Long also was touched by the plight of these youngsters as he noted in his diary, "The appeal for asylum is irresistible to any human instinct." But Long added, "We cannot receive into our own midst all, or even a large fraction, of the oppressed." [13]

Long and Welles tried to convince Roosevelt to limit the number of child immigrants (all of whom were to fall within the confines of their respective national quotas) to 1,000, but the president indicated that he favored the number of 5,000 recommended by his Advisory Committee.[14] Any fewer might embarrass the U.S., especially since the Dominican Foreign Minister Arturo Despradel had announced the willingness of the Trujillo regime to accept 3,500 children.[15] Roosevelt was also under heavy pressure from the National Coordinating Committee, HIAS, the Joint, and the Committee for the Care of European Children, whose one effort to rescue British children in 1940 had been scuttled by government dilettantism, but which still packed a powerful punch in the form of cochairman Eleanor Roosevelt.

On November 7, 1942, the Portuguese liner S.S. *Mouzinho* left Baltimore, bound for Europe with doctors, nurses, and child care experts. In a matter of weeks the volunteer relief organizations had collected $908,000 for the initial wave of 1,000 children. One hour after the *Mouzinho* set sail, however, French Premier Laval canceled the exit visas of the children.[16] The official American view was that the Nazis had vetoed the scheme for Laval with an announcement through the German Transoceanic News Agency that "Vichy may not allow these children to leave unless inimical propaganda against France and Germany ceases in America." [17] The United States certainly could not abide by such an instruction. Here supposedly was positive proof that the Nazis would not permit any rational negotiations, even through their underlings. As a result, only thirty-two of the projected 5,000 children ever made their way to the United States by the spring of 1943.[18]

Such an evaluation of the facts, however, may have been inaccurate. Abbé Glasberg, a Catholic priest active in the

Oeuvre de Secours aux Enfants, later told Arthur Morse that more enthusiasm, more visas, more money, could have saved the lives of all the 60,000 Jewish children in France who were exterminated by the Nazis.[19] While this estimate may have been overly optimistic, it is true that four months of precious time were lost before the United States finally got around to clearing the *Mouzinho* for passage. Six weeks before the vessel sailed for Europe, Roosevelt had already written the children off, telling Celler, "Unfortunately, we have to face the disagreeable fact that most of the damage has already been done." The sole palliative the president could offer distressed persons in this country was the news that for the time being the American Red Cross would be distributing free milk among needy children of all races and religions in unoccupied France.[20]

Negotiations with the Rumanians in 1943 were also hesitant and unfruitful. Apart from the major rescue operation to save 70,000 Trans-Dnistrian Jews, the British and Americans at Bermuda discussed another Rumanian enterprise. This called for the transport of 4,500 Jewish children from Constanza to Palestine aboard two vessels chartered by the Allies. The British government was willing to accept the children in Palestine under terms of the White Paper. The Antonescu regime was willing to usher them out of Rumania. Yet the scheme fell through, and Long blamed the Nazis. "The Germans got wind of it and stopped it," he told Congress in November.[21]

What Long did not relate was that the State Department's procrastination of several months had delayed the project long enough to permit the Gestapo to intervene and veto the project. The American share of expenses was to be no more than $150,000.[22] The Bureau of the Budget had notified Assistant Secretary of State G. Howland Shaw that such monies could readily be obtained from the President's Emergency Fund (containing more than $500,000 in April 1943).[23] And the State Department also misled the British for weeks, saying that funds necessary for the project would have to be allocated by Congress before any guarantees could be made.[24]

At the same time Long, Reams, and Brandt squelched a Swedish offer to negotiate with the Germans for the release of

20,000 Jewish children from the continent. Under this proposal the children would have been detained in Sweden until the end of the war, with Great Britain and the United States sharing the costs of food, shelter, medicine, and supervision. On May 19, 1943 the British Foreign Office cabled its acceptance of this scheme and awaited American confirmation, but it was not forthcoming. Long and his associates in the European Division sat on the proposal for six months, arguing that while Jewish philanthropists were prepared to underwrite the full cost of the operation, it was wrong to limit the plan to Jewish children alone. The State Department, invoking an old rationalization, added that singling out the Jews for special treatment might well boomerang against this oppressed people, and the Nazis might only intensify their persecution. When the British suggested broadening the rescue operation to include Norwegian children as well, the Americans finally agreed. By that time, however, it was December 1943 and more precious time had been lost and neither the Swedes nor the Germans expressed much interest in the scheme anymore.[25]

One man who grew increasingly horrified by the indifference of the State Department was Treasury Secretary Henry Morgenthau, Jr. A longtime associate of the president, who jokingly commented that Morgenthau was trying to overcompensate for the militant anti-Zionist attitudes of his father, Morgenthau was privy to all refugee negotiations in 1942 and 1943. He knew that the official State Department line ruling out the possibility of direct talks with the Nazis was constantly violated. Since October 1943, the Allies had maintained a regular exchange with the Axis of civilian internees, merchant seamen, medical personnel, disabled prisoners, and sisters of the German Red Cross. Between October 1943 and January 1945 ten such exchanges took place at Gothenburg, Barcelona, Oran, and Kreuzlingen.[26] Morgenthau knew also that the State Department made no special effort to honor Breckinridge Long's pledge of $4 million in aid to the International Red Cross for relief purposes.[27] Morgenthau knew of the negotiations for the Jewish children in France, the Jewish children in Rumania, and the Jewish children in Poland (bound for Sweden). He had issued the necessary licenses for funds in each of these cases and had been inevitably frustrated when these rescue schemes went awry because of the State Department's fumbling. When Cordell Hull informed him that the British had vetoed the long-delayed proposal for the rescue of the Trans-Dnistrian Jews on December 20, Morgenthau had had enough.

On January 16, 1944, Morgenthau, accompanied by the Treasury's General Counsel Randolph Paul and Foreign Funds Division Chief John Pehle, went to the White House to protest the State Department's inaction. Morgenthau presented Roosevelt with an eighteen-page memorandum entitled "Report to the Secretary on the Acquiescence of This Government in the Murder of the Jews." The product of the labors of Paul, Pehle, and Josiah Dubois, Jr., this report charged that unnamed State Department officials had: "utterly failed to prevent the extermination of Jews in German-controlled Europe"; "hidden their gross procrastination behind such window dressing as intergovernmental organizations to survey the whole refugee problem"; and "suppressed reports to the State Department on German atrocities after publication of similar reports had intensified public pressure for action." [28] In demanding immediate action on behalf of the Jews, the report charged:

> There are a growing number of responsible people and organizations today who have ceased to view our failure as the product of simple incompetence on the part of those officials in the State Department charged with handling this problem. They see plain anti-Semitism motivating the actions of these State Department officials and, rightly or wrongly, it will require little more in the way of proof for their suspicion to explode into a nasty scandal.[29]

Roosevelt must have been stung by criticism that his administration was actually using its machinery to prevent the rescue of Jews. He could argue that much had been done, specifically at his instance, to aid refugees of all faiths. Apart from Evian or Bermuda, there was the Office of Foreign Relief and Rehabilitation Operations, chartered in November 1942 under Governor Herbert Lehman, a Jew. There was the Foreign Economic Administration, again chaired by Lehman, which in

September 1943 had absorbed the offices of Lend-Lease, OFRRO, Economic Warfare, and Foreign Economic Coordination. There was FEA's successor, the United Nations Relief and Rehabilitation Agency, again the direct product of Roosevelt's thinking, again with Lehman as director-general, which had been chartered in November 1943 with the express purpose "to plan, coordinate, administer, or arrange for the administration of measures for the relief of victims of war in any area under the control of the United Nations, through the provision of food, fuel, clothing, shelter, and other basic necessities, medical and other essential services." [30]

Like so many other steps that Roosevelt took in the area of human planning, those actions were not concerted, popular, or particularly effective. Rather, they were tardy, visceral reactions to spontaneous crises which could not compensate for the government's lack of foresight. Since the middle of 1941, even before America's entry into the war, the British had pressed for the establishment of a joint board between the Allies, empowered to handle problems of economics and relief. OFRRO was not born until the end of 1942, and even then the idea of extending relief to refugees while some in this country still went hungry was criticized strongly by Claire Hoffman (R.-Mich.), Arthur Vandenberg (R.-Mich.), and Tom Connally (D.-Tex.) in Congress and Cissy Patterson's *Washington Times-Herald*, which lambasted "world planning, WPA-ing, and World Spending of U.S. Money." [31]

Lehman was never popular with Hull, and Hull was given no prior notification of the appointment. The OFRRO director did not receive clarification of his duties from the State Department until March 1943, five months after Roosevelt dropped his announcement about the creation of a purely American relief agency among comments about problems in South and Central America. Lehman fought "the Battle of the Potomac," the battle for priorities among the War Department, Office of Lend Lease, State Department, Shipping Adjustment Board, Food Board, etc., and lost. He went to plead with Admiral William D. Leahy, Roosevelt's chief military adviser, and was told:

Now look here, young man, I want you to know just one thing. I've no doubt you need the supplies, and I'm very sorry that people are suffering. But I'm here to look after the Army, and I'm going to see that the Army gets everything they want. No use your coming and arguing with me any more, because that's my position, and I'm going to stick to it.[32]

Lehman labored in vain for another six months, hampered by a lack of supplies for the few miserable refugee camps which were set up in North Africa. He was subordinated to the demands of the military (who, he grumbled, oversubscribed everything for their own use), stymied by the official view that trans-blockade feeding was impossible, and undermined by Hull's favorite, Dean Acheson, who continued to work toward an international body to supplant OFRRO. It was, therefore, no surprise when the totally inadequate OFRRO gave way to FEA in September 1943 and still less a surprise when this organization demonstrated a greater zeal for preemptive purchases of the world's supply of tungsten, corundum, cinchona bark, rubber, chromium, ball bearings, and nickel than the saving of human lives.[33]

But it was the much-ballyhooed UNRRA, with 44 nations as adherents, representing 80 percent of the human race, by Roosevelt's calculations,[34] that raised the most doubt about the effectiveness of government relief measures for refugees in 1943–1944. Like the Inter-Governmental Committee on Refugees, whose work it was not to duplicate but which it could not help but duplicate, UNRRA was to have authority to deal only with "displaced persons" (a new euphemism coined to describe the twenty-one million Europeans who had been uprooted and enslaved by the Nazis), but only in "liberated areas." [35] Once more there was to be no attempt at negotiations with either the Nazis or their lackeys, no attempt to rescue displaced persons in concentration camps. In fact, UNRRA's charter provided that in liberated areas the cost of caring for the victims of Nazi oppression was to be borne by the enemy itself, however this might be accomplished before the war was won.[36]

Once more, ultimate victory was the principle which determined all UNRRA policy. From the beginning the officials at Supreme Allied Command Headquarters in London who were charged with planning the invasion of Europe were committed to the view that the Nazis would use refugees as a shield, much as they had done in 1940, to disrupt Allied lines with masses of terrified civilians or to infiltrate saboteurs.[37] UNRRA officials thus would have to be extra meticulous, extra hesitant in extending aid even to those persons who fled to the Allied lines. According to the United Kingdom's John Llewellin, "We have unanimously decided that war needs come first and that it would be wrong to do anything to impede the quickest liberation of all countries overrun by the Axis." [38]

Like the IGCR, UNRRA did not envision any mass movement of refugees during or after the war. Like the IGCR, UNRRA could not foresee the outbursts of anti-Semitism in Central and Eastern Europe and the many pogroms and individual assaults on Jews from Kielce to Frankfurt after the war was over. Like the IGCR, UNRRA was committed to the return of displaced persons to their lands of birth, regardless of the traumatic effect that such a return might have.

Far from complementing the work of the IGCR, UNRRA actively competed with Emerson's committee for available funds and material resources. For 1944, the United States authorized $1 million for the IGCR and $2,150,000 for UNRRA.[39] But UNRRA did not receive a cent of its congressionally-approved credit until March 28, 1944. Since the United States contributed 82.36 percent of UNRRA's funds between 1944 and 1947, the international relief organization was still inoperative five months after its charter had been signed at the White House.[40] Great Britain, which operated its own Middle East Relief and Refugee Administration (for Gentiles only) from July 1942, did not merge MERRA with UNRRA until April 1944.[41] Even then UNRRA was hard-pressed to claim any accomplishments until the spring of 1945 when the European war was all but won. Lehman noted the hapless condition of the body when he wrote in his diary on December 3, 1944, that unless something spectacular were done to help the refugees, "UNRRA is going to suffer very greatly in prestige." [42]

Thus, while Roosevelt contented himself in January 1944 that he had done everything possible to help the refugees through the establishment of a legion of anagrammatic agencies, he could not take pride in the results. By this time the elements which had consistently clamored for a more vigorous refugee policy through 1943 were already consolidating their forces to establish an extra-governmental commission to aid the Jews in Europe.[43] With the initiative slipping from him and with his extreme sensitivity to the specter of anti-Semitism in his government, Roosevelt responded to Morgenthau's memorandum by violating another of his sacred precepts of government—that barring duplication of agencies. By Executive Order 9417, issued on January 21, 1944, he authorized the establishment of the War Refugee Board, yet another commission empowered to deal with refugee problems.

Hull insisted that if the president went through with his plans for such a commission, "I want this out of the State Department. I want it outside."[44] The secretary had his wish fulfilled, as responsibility for saving the victims of Hitlerism was now transferred to a board consisting of the secretaries of Treasury, War, and State, along with an executive director appointed by FDR. Roosevelt originally wanted some well known personality to fill the directorship, and Morgenthau suggested Wendell Willkie. However, the popular and cooperative Republican was dismissed in an early planning conference as someone who already had had a sufficiently big public buildup. Because the secretaries could not agree upon any prominent figure, the manifold tasks of the War Refugee Board fell to Acting Director John Pehle. A more fortunate choice could not have been made.

What Pehle may have lacked in charisma he made up in vigor and sincerity. A deceptively quiet, compassionate man, Pehle had gone directly from Yale Law School to the Treasury Department in 1934. He was a brilliant and dedicated worker and had demonstrated a deep interest in the plight of the refugees while he had administered the department's Foreign

Funds Division. As director of the WRB, he was in a position to make good the basic instruction of the board "to take all measures within its power to rescue the victims of enemy oppression who are in imminent danger of death and otherwise to afford such victims all possible relief and assistance consistent with the successful prosecution of the war." [45]

The statement might seem to be little more than a repetition of the mandates of the IGCR and UNRRA. Pehle's instructions about consulting with other government agencies for information on supplies and shipping, about accepting financial aid from all interested volunteer relief agencies, and about reporting and making recommendations to the members of the board and the president might be read as duplicates of the principles of the Intergovernmental Committee and UNRRA. However, Pehle was exempted from the provisions of the Trading with the Enemy Act, was empowered to appoint special attachés with diplomatic status, was allowed to go wherever assistance to refugees might be rendered, was permitted to negotiate with any foreign power for the rescue of these people.

Pehle began by assigning able assistants to vital posts in Europe and the Middle East. Department store executive Ira Hirschmann, who had served as the financial guarantor of hundreds of Austrian Jews during the prewar period and who would subsequently become chief of the State Department's Refugee Division, was assigned to Turkey.[46] Robert C. Dexter of the Unitarian Services Committee was sent to Lisbon; Ivor C. Olsen to Stockholm; Leonard Ackermann to Egypt; and Roswell McClelland, a thirty-year-old Quaker from the American Friends Service Committee, to Switzerland.[47]

These WRB operatives readily merged their activities with those of Joint Distribution Committee representatives like retired lace manufacturer Saly Mayer in St. Gall, Switzerland; the unassuming economist Moses Amzalak in Lisbon; the Kadoorie brothers in China; and Joseph J. Schwartz, the Russian-born rabbi who had served as director general of the JDC since 1942.[48] It is no coincidence that of $20 million spent by the War Refugee Board during its brief existence, more than

$16 million came from the Joint and associated Jewish groups in the United States.[49]

Because of the energy and capability of his professionals, Pehle could report to Morgenthau five weeks after his appointment that:

(1) The Balkan bottleneck had been broken. Because of American guarantees of maintenance made to the Turkish government, rail transports carrying 150 children every ten days were crossing through Bulgaria and Turkey bound for Palestine. Within twenty-four hours after Hirschmann learned that Rumania would permit 1,000 Jews to leave Constanza if the Allies supplied the necessary vessels, Hirschmann destroyed the myth of a shipping shortage by obtaining the necessary commitments from Myron Black, field director of the War Shipping Administration, and Admiral Land of the Mediterranean Fleet Command.

(2) The Spanish-North African bottleneck had also been broken. As in the case of Turkey, the French government had been persuaded to keep its borders open to transient refugees passing through to Camp Marechal Lyautey near Casablanca.

(3) Neutral intermediaries, including the Vatican, had been drawn in to refugee work to press Nazi puppets in Bulgaria, Hungary, Rumania, and Slovakia to halt the deportation of Jews to death camps. The International Red Cross was cooperating with the board in bringing persons from Poland and Slovakia, where they faced certain death, to places of relative safety, like Hungary and Rumania, or to Switzerland.

(4) At the same time the WRB was successful in getting the Office of War Information to step up its propaganda to Germany and satellite countries, emphasizing the pending retribution that the Allies would seek for the heinous crime of genocide.[50]

The most important contribution of the War Refugee Board, however, could not adequately be expressed in the formal language of diplomatic reports. It was the hope that this organization gave to the unfortunates in Europe. Ira Hirschmann noted that all the refugees coming through Turkey knew of FDR's order creating a war refugee board and knew that a representative of that commission was in Turkey to aid them. "Some of it was embarrassing to me," he wrote Isador Lubin in the spring of 1944," as they tried to thank me, and I was only a privileged instrument of the President's board. Apparently it has become a symbol for salvation to these lost people." For Hirschmann, the time was "five minutes to twelve . . . the witches' sabbath that spells doom for European Jewry," but the Jews in Europe could not see that. For people who, in Hirschmann's words, had become "so demoralized and desperate that they stopped trying for themselves," the WRB offered "a new hope to fight on for themselves." [51]

This jubilation of the refugees was matched by their brethren in the United States. The Roosevelt files bulge with congratulatory messages from twenty-five Jewish organizations, claiming to represent nearly one million members, all of them praising his message of January 22, which established the War Refugee Board. Like the enthusiasm of the refugees, however, such rejoicing was premature.[52]

The board was harassed from the start by the State Department, whose attitude was basically unhelpful. Rumors prevalent in Washington contended that the principal figures on the board's staff, including Pehle, Dubois, McClelland, and others who had no trace of Hebrew lineage, were in fact Jews. Ruth Shipley, head of the State Department's Passport Division, once called Pehle to inquire if the board employed any "Americans," because its cables "just aren't worded like our cables." When the board attempted to have the International Red Cross upgrade the status of Jews in concentration camps from persons in protective custody to internees to gain equal treatment with citizens of belligerent nations in the distribution of Red Cross parcels, the State Department vetoed the idea and implied once more that such supplies might be confiscated by the Nazis.[53] And when public pressure in the United States to force the British to extend the cutoff date of Jewish immigration to Palestine beyond May 1944 began to mount, the State Department, which had consistently regarded Palestine as primarily an internal question for the British cheered Secretary of

War Stimson's statement of March 17 to the House Committee on Foreign Affairs, which read: "Without reference to the merits of these resolutions, further action on them at this time would be prejudicial to the successful prosecution of the War." [54]

Sol Bloom's committee heeded this stern advice and promptly tabled the Palestine resolutions. Official Jewish immigration to the Holy Land was to be halted that spring, despite the fact that there were still more than 22,000 visas available under the original terms of the White Paper. [55] Although the State Department continued to affirm that the Palestine and refugee questions were unrelated, the closing of Palestine to Jewish refugees necessarily would have repercussions on the total refugee picture.

The Latin American states once more were demonstrating their indifference to the fate of the European Jews, refusing or canceling visas even when deportation and certain death awaited refugees applying for or possessing such papers. [56] This made Palestine all the more crucial to the operations of the War Refugee Board. Lacking that haven, the board would have difficulty convincing Turkish authorities to keep their borders open to Jews who had no place to go. In turn, this would create a backup of refugees, not only in the Balkans, where there were ominous rumblings of plans for massive deportations under S.S. Colonel Eichmann, but also in North Africa, which depended upon Palestine to siphon off its Jewish refugees, in Italy where 1,800 arrivals each week from Yugoslavia were glutting existing UNRRA facilities, and in Spain, where the WRB was having difficulty in convincing U.S. Ambassador Carleton Hayes of the urgency of the situation. [57]

Pehle, searching desperately for some stopgap solution, latched on to an amazing scheme first suggested by the American Jewish Conference in September 1943. This "free port" proposal called for adapting to human beings the practice of letting merchandise lie duty free in certain ports while awaiting transshipment. The new "human cargo" would be permitted to enter the United States without complying with the formalities of American immigration laws. Nativist sensitivities would not be offended, however, since such "cargo" would be shipped for the duration to abandoned army posts along the Eastern seaboard or to camps recently vacated by the Japanese in the West. At the end of the war they would be repatriated to their native lands, if possible.[58]

This scheme caught the interest of several congressmen who introduced twelve bills in the House and Senate in the winter of 1943–1944 calling for the establishment of free ports in this country.[59] Pehle's associate Josiah Dubois argued that this was the least the U.S. could do, unless this country wanted to supply Hitler with an excuse for exterminating the Jews by failing to give them shelter. Pehle also found Undersecretary of State Stettinius to be receptive to the plan. As a result, he formally proposed the free ports to Hull, Morgenthau, and Stimson on May 8, 1944.[60]

The secretaries agreed that something had to be done to relieve the congestion of refugees in liberated zones. But now the principal objection to bringing these people to the U.S. was not that the nation might be flooded with potential saboteurs. Rather, the secretaries feared the people's and Congress's reac-actions to this obvious flouting of immigration laws. When attorney General Francis Biddle guaranteed that such a scheme was constitutional and emphasized it would be temporary, the executive board of the WRB reluctantly approved the creation of free ports. Stimson cautioned, however, against "inundation by foreign racial stock out of proportion to what exists here." [61]

Roosevelt discussed the matter with Pehle and the secretaries on May 18 but did not give his assent until June 1. He then directed Morgenthau to locate an appropriate camp within twenty-four hours. FDR finally on June 9 announced that he had instructed Robert Murphy in Algiers to arrange for the shipment of a number of "mixed European refugees" to Camp Ontario at Oswego, New York. Perhaps as many as 2,000 persons could be accommodated in the eighty acres of converted campground and barracks in the historical north woods of upperstate New York.[62]

When FDR submitted his plan to Congress three days later, public response and response in Congress was favorable.

Organized labor, leading newspapers, and Jewish groups from all points on the political spectrum indicated support. Letters praising the idea poured into the White House.[63] Even those persons most affected by this threatened "inundation," the residents of upper New York State, rallied to the defense of the refugees. The Association of New York State Canners in Rochester wired the War Refugee Board and offered to employ all of the immigrants in its food processing plants.[64] And Harry Mizen, chairman of a special Fort Ontario Citizens' Committee, wrote the president to extend "our thanks for your selection of Fort Ontario for this humanitarian objective" and to assure him of "deep appreciation of Oswegonians, and of our willingness at all times to cooperate with our government in the vast problems which confront it." [65]

This much-heralded move, like so many of Roosevelt's intermittent gestures on behalf of refugees since 1938, turned out to be more propaganda than prodigy. What had been anticipated as the beginning of a mass transfer of the unfortunates was actually the end. A mere 984 refugees, most of them Jews, representing eighteen nationalities, were selected out of 36,000 persons in Italian detention camps to come to this country. They were well-behaved, their children did well in American schools, and they proved to be good material for citizenship. The Oswego newspapers, citizens' groups, and teachers all testified to their excellent adjustment, despite the trying circumstances of their transfer to this country.[66]

From the start, however, Roosevelt was committed to "keeping faith with Congress." Through the summer of 1944 and as late as January 1945, he repeatedly confirmed that these refugees "ought definitely to go back as soon as we find places for them to go in physical safety." [67] As far as Biddle was concerned, the 984 had never legally been "in" the U.S., and thus there was no question about their returning to Europe at war's end.[68]

The first of the Oswego refugees did not arrive until August 1944. They were also the last. Apparently, Roosevelt by then no longer considered the free ports to be an especially pressing need. At a time when the U.S. was transporting

200,000 Axis POWs annually to this country, and Lehman's UNRRA organization was proving to be incapable of handling the refugee problem in Europe, Roosevelt wrote a constituent in Albany, "We do not need any more free ports at the present time because of the physical problems of transportation, and we are taking care of thousands of others in North Africa and Italy." [69]

Roosevelt called off the free port projects at the very moment 500,000 Hungarian Jews most needed help. The American Jewish Conference disclosed in May that Jews in Hungary were being herded into ghettos where they were most exposed to air raids. By mid-June the conference had formally protested a decision of the Horthy regime to place Jewish manpower at the disposal of the German Reich, an agreement which in essence meant the deportation of Jews to concentration camps in Poland and Germany.[70]

Later that summer Jewish appeals to the American government became more frantic. Sixty thousand persons gathered at Madison Square in New York City on the afternoon of July 31, to protest the shipment of 12,000 Jews daily from Hungary to their deaths in Poland.[71] About the same time Johan Smertenko, executive vice-chairman of the Emergency Conference to Save the Jewish People of Europe, appealed to Roosevelt to have the Allies blow up railroad lines carrying the Jews to their death or to bomb crematoria in the concentration camps and thereby give the inmates an opportunity to attempt mass escapes, or to threaten to use poison gas against German civilian populations unless the killings ceased.[72]

Roosevelt was hardly oblivious to developments in Hungary. Along with his presidential rival, Thomas Dewey, FDR issued a note of sympathy to the groups protesting the new massacre. FDR's serenity through this period, first approving havens for escaping Jews, then canceling the order, then issuing condolences to those persons directly involved in the Holocaust, is all the more remarkable in view of the fact that Pehle had kept the president well informed about developments in Hungary. Pehle wrote FDR on June 5, "We are reliably informed that negotiations already are being concluded for deportation to Poland of 300,000 Jews." A month later Pehle reported that Horthy would be amenable to halting the deportation of all Jewish children under age ten, provided the Red Cross could secure sufficient guarantees for their removal and maintenance.[73] This last offer was quite similar to the tantalizing one made earlier that spring by Eichmann to Joel Brand, a spokesman of the Hungarian Jewish community. Its fate was also identical.[74]

Late in 1944 Eichmann's assistant, Kurt Becher, saw a telegram from Cordell Hull which authorized the transfer of $5 million to rescue the Hungarian Jews.[75] As usual, the State Department had acted too late. Hull had known of Eichmann's initial offer to Brand since May, but instead of negotiating with the German on a cash basis, he permitted the Russians to review the proposal which originally called for the exchange of military equipment to be used on the Eastern Front. The Russians wanted no part of such a scheme.[76] This kind of diplomatic boondoggling cost the Jews another six months, during which time Roosevelt tried to soothe Stephen Wise with the comment, "We are trying to do something about it." [77] By the time something had been done, Saly Mayer of the Joint Distribution Committee had presented the bribe to Becher, more than 150,000 Hungarian Jews had been exterminated.

According to Treasury Secretary Henry Morgenthau, the War Refugee Board had compiled an impressive record in spite of tremendous difficulties.[78] This statement is indisputable. The board helped to get thousands of Jews out of the Balkans in 1944 and 1945 and somewhat impeded the flow of Jews from this region to the death camps through warnings to petty tyrants like Antonescu and King Boris. Its operatives ferried refugees across the Baltic to asylum in Sweden. It smuggled funds into France to sustain Jews in hiding there, subsidized those in camps in North Africa, Italy, and the U.S., and secured passports for many in Switzerland to travel to South America. The board dealt successfully with high-ranking Germans, among them Himmler, and was able to detour a few death trains from their destinations late in the war.[79] The WRB's final report contradicted virtually everything Hull had said, or was to say, about the feasibility of negotiating with the Germans. It stated that the board had "purchased" 50,000 Jewish lives from the Nazis before the European war ended in May 1945.[80]

Thereafter, however, the Allies did little to distinguish themselves in their actions toward the Jews who survived the Holocaust. Six million were dead, fully 90 percent of a European culture that had grown up over 2,000 years. Few of the survivors had ever heard of Evian or Rublee, Wagner or Houghteling, Bermuda or Ibn Saud, Pehle or Long. The fact that they were Jewish and had been the special target of the Nazis brought them no new liberties once the war was over. They actually became the victims of Allied discrimination because of their Jewishness.

UNRRA's mandate extended only to persons displaced from states which were members of the United Nations or former enemy nationals who faced possible persecution if they remained in their homelands. Under these guidelines UNRRA aided Volksdeutsch Germans, Germans of the Polish Corridor and East Prussia who had been dispossessed as a result of Poland's boundary shift westward, and Ukrainian POWs, many of whom had served in the S.S. Nachtigall Division in Russia (a brigade which specialized in the extermination of Jews). But many Jews were denied assistance because technically they could not qualify as "allied nationals" or as enemy persons in danger of persecution.[81]

Months after VE-Day, Jewish displaced persons were still living under guard behind barbed wire in some of the most notorious concentration camps of Germany, Austria, and Poland. Within two months of liberation 18,000 Jews died of starvation and disease in Bergen-Belsen. Throughout 1945 the death rate at Dachau was sixty to a hundred a day. As late as December 1945, Jews at Landsberg were packed twenty-five to a room fifteen feet by twenty-five feet and slept on wooden tiers in unheated cells. In Austria the daily ration was 1,200 calories a day. The walking dead received no fresh fruits, vegetables, or meats. The sight of these people still wearing the striped pajama uniforms issued by the Nazis to concentration camp inmates, festering in idleness, disease, and starvation, so outraged Earl Harrison, President Truman's special delegate to the camps in the summer of 1945, that he, along with Joseph Schwartz of the Joint and Herbert Katzski of the WRB, issued a scathing denunciation of UNRRA efforts in August 1945. Harrison charged that "we appear to be treating the Jews as the Nazis treated them, except that we do not exterminate them. Beyond knowing that they are no longer in danger of gas chambers, torture, and other forms of violent death, they see—and there is—little change." [82]

Truman received this report on August 1, 1945, but it was not until September 30 that he instructed General Eisenhower, who had seen a summary of the Harrison report as early as August 3, to make some sort of special accommodation for the Jews. As a result, twelve separate detention camps for Jews, supervised by the Joint, ORT, the Jewish Agency, HIAS, and other interested relief groups, were established that fall.[83] These proved incapable of handling the hundreds of Jews who fled westward from the death camps and postwar pogroms of Poland.

To handle the postwar exodus Truman asked the British to admit 100,000 Jews to Palestine. This was exactly what the British did not want. The British treated the flight of Jews from Polish pogromschiks as a well-financed Zionist plot to relax restrictions on immigration to Palestine.[84] On December 5, 1945 they prohibited further movement of Jews into or through their zone via Berlin and subsequently ruled that persons who did infiltrate would not be admitted to displaced persons centers but be required to live with the civilian German population without any special assistance from the Allied authorities.[85]

Meanwhile, Truman tried to help the refugees by ordering Hull to expedite emigration proceedings for displaced persons in Germany[86] and by having the UNRRA create the special classification of "internal displacees" for the Jews so that all European Jews might qualify for international assistance.[87] American policy in Europe, however, remained ambivalent. While the British subsequently mellowed and permitted assistance to Jews who had agreed to repatriation but then found life in their homelands unbearable, American policy was to deny assistance to any individual who had agreed to return to Poland, Rumania, Czechoslovakia but subsequently attempted to emigrate from Europe.[88]

When Congress passed the Stratton Displaced Persons Bill in 1947, it gave special priority not to Jews but to refugees from the Baltic regions east of the Curzon Line. Fully 40 percent of the total 400,000 visas was to go to persons from this region, without regard to prewar or wartime sympathies. Another 30 percent was to go to "agriculturists." The Cold War had intervened to the advantage of substantial numbers of one-time Nazi supporters.[89]

The Stratton Act stated that only those Jews for whom UNRRA camps had records as of December 22, 1945 were eligible for admission to the United States. But it was not until December 23 that Truman made his special appeal to the State Department on behalf of the Jewish refugees. Also, it was not until that month that UNRRA formally extended its coverage to all Jews. During that month, also, the British tried to cut off Jewish emigration through their zone. In December 1945 only 18,000 of the 700,000 persons in UNRRA camps in Germany and Austria were Jews. Nine months later, however, on the heels of the Kielce pogrom in Poland, that number had swelled to more than 130,000.[90] These arrived too late to profit from America's modification of its immigration laws, and only 2,499 of the 220,000 persons admitted to the United States under the Stratton Immigration Law were Jews.[91] Victims of hypocrisy in 1938 and through the war years, the Jews were to be ignored even in time of peace, and this came at a time when the sufferings of the Jewish people under Hitler were fully substantiated.

10. The Yoke of Shame

*W*hen *you are* in a dirty war, some will suffer more than others." Onetime Presidential Adviser Benjamin Cohen summarized the refugee policy of the Roosevelt administration between 1938 and 1945 in this manner. It was a policy based at first on fear—fear of complicating the domestic employment situation, fear of arousing nativists and neo-Nazis, fear of allowing foreign agents intent on wrecking the industrial capacity of America to filter into the country. After the U.S. entered World War II, the policy was based completely on military expedience. "The question was whether you could reduce the suffering without a sacrifice on your part," Cohen said. "Things ought to have been different, but war is different, and we live in an imperfect world." [1]

Could it have been any different? Could Secretary of State Cordell Hull, described by Sol Bloom as "the most wonderful fellow God ever put on earth," [2] have overcome what many persons believed to be the anti-Semitic biases of a few officials in the State Department and established policies helpful to the Jews? Cohen implied that he might have "if Hull had been more eager," but quickly added, "of course, he was up in years." Hull aged terribly during the war and became "harassed and weary," as Henry Morgenthau noted.[3] Moreover, Morgenthau wrote, "Hull did not seem to be well-informed as to what was going on." [4] By his own admission, Hull had been distracted by a thousand worldwide exigencies other than refugee problems between 1938 and 1945.[5] Also, he was married to a Jewess, was extremely sensitive to any charge of favoritism on behalf of the Jews, and, according to Breckinridge Long, even declined to run for the vice presidency in 1940 because he feared he and his wife might suffer abuse in the campaign.[6]

If Hull were incapable of supplying the leadership necessary to effect some kind of accommodation toward the Jews, then what of Franklin Roosevelt? No man in the twentieth century was more idolized by Jews throughout the world than Roosevelt. The files of Hyde Park are filled with letters of praise from the doomed, the saved, the hopeful. The president received kosher calendars and bogus checks guaranteeing him "365 days of happiness." The spastic children of the Jewish Sanitorium for Chronic Diseases in Brooklyn notified him that a section of trees had been planted in his name in Eretz, Israel. A seventy-five-year-old Jew sent him a cabalistic amulet to protect him from harm. Rabbi Stephen Wise "blessed" the president. The usually shy Albert Einstein was moved to write poetry about FDR. And Charles Schwager, publicity director of the magazine *Jewish Forum,* wrote to Roosevelt, "I will predict that you were chosen by God to be the Saviour for America and the rest of the world."[7] The name Roosevelt was a magic talisman to millions of Jews in ghettos and concentration camps. The starving and the strangled believed that if only the United States and Roosevelt knew about the murders, then something would be done to stop the Nazis.[8]

Roosevelt was troubled by the plight of the Jews in Europe, but consistently avoided acknowledging their singular persecution between 1933 and 1945. He declined to issue such a statement for the Emergency Conference to save the Jews in September 1943. He turned down a request from the Independent Jewish Press Service to commemorate the heroism of Jews in the Warsaw Ghetto in the spring of 1944. He did not issue a statement on the Jewish situation for Senator Guy Gillette, who was hosting a special banquet for Albert Einstein in August 1944. He refused to meet with representatives of Jewish parochial schools in New York who had come to Washington to protest Nazi genocide in December 1944. On the advice of Charles Bohlen of the division of European Affairs, and Assistant Secretary of State Berle, all such requests were answered with form letters which indicated that: (1) the president was either out of town or could not be reached and (2) Roosevelt had already given tangible evidence of his determination to give all possible assistance to Jewish victims of Nazi oppression.[9]

There was no mention of the Jewish tragedy in the declaration signed by Roosevelt, Churchill, and Stalin on November 1, 1943, which promised retribution for Nazi atrocities perpetrated against the French, Poles, Dutch, Belgians, Norwegians, and Italians. Morgenthau, Stimson, and Stettinius later recommended that the president issue a specific condemnation of the Jewish massacres in hopes that this might save "many hundreds of thousands of lives." [10] They sent a one-page draft of such a statement to FDR. It began, "One of the blackest crimes in history, the systematic murder of the Jews of Europe, continues unabated." [11] When the final draft was delivered that summer, after the Hungarian deportations began, it spoke first of the sufferings of Warsaw, Lidice, Kharkov, Nanking, the Chinese, Filipinos, Poles, Czechs, Norwegians, Dutch, Danes, Greeks, Russians, and U.S. servicemen. The Jews were not mentioned until the middle of the second page, and even then the deterrent effect the message was supposed to have upon Balkan fascists was diluted when Roosevelt concluded with another generalized appeal to free people everywhere to welcome "all victims of oppression." [12]

Cohen defends FDR by saying, "To imagine that Roosevelt could come up with a magic wand to solve the Jewish problem might be expecting too much." However, Roosevelt was "boss" of the largest democracy in the world. After the United States' entry in the war, FDR got action whenever he wanted it.[13] Roosevelt could have ordered reprisals of some sort against German-Americans (as least against those who had belonged to the Nazi Bund), but this was the only group of Axis nationals in the United States which was spared the indignities of restrictions. As Johan Smertenke has suggested, FDR could have warned the Nazis that unless the gassing of Jews stopped, the Allies would retaliate against the civilian populace of Germany with poison gas.[14] This action was rejected on humanitarian grounds, and instead the civilian populations of Dresden, Cologne, and Berlin were attacked with conventional bombs.

The president could have ordered the bombardment of railway lines to the death camps or against the crematoria in the camps themselves. This idea had been suggested to the Allied High Command early in 1944 by Chaim Weizmann of the Jewish Agency. It also had the approval of Roswell McClelland in Switzerland and John Pehle in Washington. Since May 1943, when the Warsaw Ghetto was in its death throes, Russian bombers were striking at Warsaw, Malkin, Brest, and Lublin in nighttime raids. At the same time American bombers based in North Africa were passing daily over the very railroad lines leading from South Central Europe to the camps in the north The American planes came to attack the Ploesti oil fields in Rumania, and then they continued on to Russian airfields, where they took on additional bombs for the return flight. In this circuit, the prime targets were the oilfields, but in operational scratches, sometimes resulting from poor visibility, the aviators were permitted to dump their bombloads on targets of opportunity, with first preference going to the railroad lines.[15] Despite this policy, the tracks from Hungary and Rumania to Poland's death camps remained relatively unscathed and their traffic in human lives uninterrupted.

The camps were within easy reach of American and British squadrons based in Western Europe, Italy, or Greece by 1944 and 1945. The Luftwaffe had been destroyed. The Allies were dropping weapons, explosives, and money into Poland for the rightist, anti-Semitic Polish Home Army. The British were parachuting teams of Jewish suicide commandos behind enemy lines in Eastern Europe.[16] But even with complete control of the skies, the Allies made no attempt to raid the camps. Weizmann was told that his request was "technically unfeasible." [17] And Assistant Secretary of War John McCloy informed Pehle that it could be executed "only by the diversion of considerable air support essential to the success of our forces . . . and would in any case be of such very doubtful efficacy that it would not amount to a practicable project." [18]

Except for several revolts staged by concentration camp inmates which disrupted the operations of Treblinka or Sobibor, the Nazi death furnaces continued to be stoked with human flesh until the last weeks of the war when Himmler gave the order to stop. The Allies perhaps did not wish to endanger the lives of the concentration camp inmates, but it is doubtful that the prisoners would have cared, for they were doomed already. There might have been satisfaction, however, in knowing that through one's death the camps would cease to function.

Roosevelt could have pressed Congress for some practical relief to the Jews before the war, including a lowering of immigration barriers, but he did not. He could have given more consistent support to the Intergovernmental Committee on Refugees, but by 1939 it was difficult to assess where FDR stood from month to month on the continued existence of this hapless body. He could have spoken up on behalf of the Wagner Bill or the measures favoring the admission of Polish, Jewish, or British children in 1940, but did not. During the war he could have pressed the British on Palestine. Instead he equivocated. He could have opened North Africa to Jewish refugees, but he balked. He could have increased the number of free ports, but he limited the number to one at a time when Hungarian Jewry was being decimated. Some time during this seven year period, this man, so idolized by the Jewish people, might have issued a statement which said to them, "We know and we will avenge you!" But he failed to do so.

Roosevelt may have been an idol with clay feet, but he was no hypocrite. *Rather,* he was an astute politician with an ability to mesmerize personal acquaintances. Repeatedly through this period, he reacted to crises rather than acted. The measures of refugee relief which were endorsed were generally hastily drawn and soon rejected. Often they represented the thinking of Jewish advisers such as Rosenman, Niles, Frankfurter, Baruch, Bloom, and Berle, who felt a need to prove their 100 percent Americanism.[19] Even if such measures did not win the univeral consent of the American Jewish community, FDR had the ability to manipulate the Jewish factions against one another.

FDR's failure to live up to the Jews' expectations lies not so much with the man but with the people who deified him. American Jews also bore some responsibility for mistakes made and measures not attempted to save their European brethren. Examples are Wise's actions in suppressing the news of Nazi genocide and in belittling the efforts of the Emergency Conference to expedite the rescue of the Trans-Dnistrian Jews. It can be seen in the actions of Congressman Bloom at Bermuda, in the statement to FDR by Representative Celler upon hearing of the foundation of the War Refugee Board that "the nation's security must not be imperiled by the admission of spies and espionage agents under the guise of refugees,"[20] in the servility of Jews close to the president, including both government officials and those like Wise and Silver who fancied themselves to be influential confidants of the man in the White House, in the timidity of the American Jewish population, rent with internal bickering, which in large measure itself opposed the mass transfer of European Jews or the lowering of immigration barriers for fear of intensifying anti-Semitism in this country.[21]

Ultimately, however, the blame for inaction lies with the faceless mass of American citizens. Some people of all faiths and nationalities responded positively to the prewar crises of European Jewry and to the more terrible massacres during the war. Catholic bishops, presidential hopefuls, labor leaders, newspaper editors, and even black children in New York City, who contributed their pennies to a wartime fund designed to help feed the Jewish children of Europe, expressed their disapproval of Nazi policies. But such expressions were never translated into a mandate for Congress to alter existing immigration laws and welcome the Jews, nor the president to issue executive decrees to aid these people.

Americans were too preoccupied with jobs in 1938, with the Japanese menace in 1942, and with their own biases against Zoot Suiters and Negroes in 1943 and 1944 to care about Jews. Many still clung to the medieval view that persecution of Jews was fit retribution for the Jewish sin of deicide. To untold numbers, therefore, the Nazis were merely the unwitting allies of God.[22] But most tragic, and most reprehensible of all, some

Americans took a masochistic delight in the eradication of European Jewry. They told themselves that the beatings, the starvation, and the gassings were horrible, but such brutalities nevertheless possessed an appeal to the atavistic instincts of man. Civilized men gaped, with a twisted kind of envy, at the ability of the Nazis to flaunt the restraints of morality. They then dismissed the plight of the Jews as something unreal, or at least nothing that they could do anything about. As the editors of the *New Republic* so aptly wrote in 1938:

> There is a masochistic type of pity which merely enjoys feeling the woes of the unfortunate but actually is reluctant to do anything effective to ameliorate the plight of the victims— since that would end the possibility of luxuriating in the sorrows of others. We have all known people who feel this way in their personal relationships; it is sometimes expressed in social terms by the type of philanthropy which wants to keep the poor in their place so that the more fortunate may enjoy the privilege of giving. Another aspect of false pity, more germane to the present instance, is that which is used mainly to express anger at the oppressor. We have to sympathize with the victim in order to maintain our rage at the common enemy, but we are really far more interested in punishing the guilty than in succoring his victim.[23]

A passage from the Dead Sea Scrolls begins: "Lo, I am stricken dumb, for naught comes out of men's mouths but swearing and lying." That ancient sage thus might have lamented the dismal record of the United States toward Jewish refugees between 1938 and 1945. It was a record blemished by fear, hesitance, insincerity, and deceit. It was not merely the product of the machinations of a small clique of anti-Semitic functionaries in the State Department. Literally hundreds of persons, many of them Jews or philo-Semites, participated in the decision making process during this critical era. The yoke of shame weighs heavy upon every Jew and Gentile in the United States.

Twenty-five years have passed, and World War II has begun to fade in man's memory, its atrocities as meaningful to a generation spared the necessity of sustaining life with Karo syrup sandwiches or thin lentil soup as the horror stories of the catacombs of Rome or the skull pyramids of Tamerlane. An entire generation has grown up knowing little of the anguish and fear of those terrible years of depression and war, but this has not deterred its members from expropriating the verbal legacy of those times. The world, they argue, has entered a new age, one in which men will never again passively accept the debasement of his fellow man, one in which "ghettos," "genocide," "the Wall," "Nazis," and "racial purity" will not exist. From the black saviors in the U.S. who cry that they will never be led to the slaughter like the Jews, to the white anarchists in Germany, who refuse to participate in "immoral wars," the world is alive with a feeling of commitment and concern, of uniqueness, newness, and reproach for the old system.

Some things have indeed changed. There is at present no worldwide depression to offer a convenient excuse for people's inadequacies, fears, or prejudices. Economists say that this country will never undergo an economic dislocation comparable to that of the 1930s, when the United States government, not merely with the public's consent but at its insistence, denied immigration to the doomed Jews of Europe. This most prosperous nation in history is enjoying its most prosperous times, and yet the Anti-Defamation League of B'nai B'rith reported, in an April 19, 1969 statement that a four-year survey revealed 37 percent of the American people still having negative images of Jews based on "old canards that Jews control international banking, engage in shady business practices, are too powerful, clannish or ambitious." The Coughlins, Reynoldses, and Pelleys are gone, but more than 50 percent of the Americans interviewed by ADL indicated they would vote for an anti-Semitic candidate in times of economic crisis.[24] Seemingly, this may be threatening only for Jews in the event of the depression which economists believe impossible, but there are fearsome echoes of the past in the opposition to Cuban immigration into Florida. Just as many American nativists of the 1930s opposed German-Jewish immigration because they feared that these skilled or professional persons would aggravate the employment situation for the unskilled, so Negro militants in the South are

232

voicing discontent over the arrival of desperate Cuban refugees, allegedly because these new arrivals, many of them skilled craftsmen, may deprive American blacks of menial jobs.

There is no world war looming in the background of all government decisions and shunting the refugee question to the back pages of the newspapers or the lower echelons of the State Department. But the old sense of priorities persists as the world attempts to adjust to a permanent state of nonpeace. Very little has been done to diminish the sufferings of 100,000 Tibetan, 900,000 Vietnamese, 1,000,000 Arab, 4,000,000 Korean, 4,000,000 Chinese, or 4,000,000 German stateless wanderers,[25] and nothing has been done by the civilized states to prevent the racial eradication of millions of people in Biafra, Pakistan, the Sudan, and Uganda.

The lower echelon personnel at the State Department who evidently disliked Jews and who during the war treated the refugee question as an irritant are gone. The U.S. government no longer considers it barbaric or medieval to ransom political prisoners or individuals persecuted in foreign concentration camps, as the negotiations with Castro for the release of the survivors of the Bay of Pigs incident illustrates. The government has moved rapidly to accommodate freedom fighters and other refugees from Communist oppression—the Hungarians in 1956–1957 and the Cubans since 1959. And on July 1, 1968 the old discriminatory provisions of the Johnson-Reed Immigration Act were eliminated by a new law instituted which provides for a common reservoir of 170,000 immigration certificates on a "first-come, first-serve" basis.

This last act, lauded as one of the finest achievements of the Kennedy-Johnson era, was supposed to help peoples of Southern and Eastern Europe, India, and the Philippines. Instead, it perpetuates discrimination in another form. No nation can use more than 20,000 of the certificates. If another racial or religious minority encounters large-scale persecution, again the law would provide sanctuary for only 20,000, unless Congress passed another special act, as in 1938 and 1945. For the first time the United States has an immigration quota for the

Western Hemisphere, 120,000 in all, and special priorities for Cuban refugees within that number threaten to wipe out the entire allotment. Some persons may have hoped that the sentiments of Breckinridge Long or Malcolm MacDonald who wanted to save the best of the refugees by giving priority to those who might benefit a particular nation belonged to another era. However, the new bill establishes a system of six priorities, the top being 17,000 permits reserved for professional or specially skilled persons whose admission has been judged beneficial to the U.S. At the bottom are 17,000 certificates for unskilled persons with no close relatives in the U.S.[26] Such a law would have helped few, if any, Polish or Hungarian Jews between 1938 and 1945.

Jews, blacks, and other minority groups claim to have learned something from this tragic story. They have seen how improper organization, incompatible programs, and conservative leadership make pressure groups ineffective in crisis situations. They have also witnessed, through the examples of Rabbi Wise, Representative Bloom, and others how, as a corollary to Lord Acton's famous principle on power, proximity to power may compromise. And yet with the lesson of "no-man's land," Evian, Auschwitz, and Bermuda behind them, dissident Jewish groups in the United States were at odds among themselves during times of peace in the Middle East and found they were powerless to rally Gentile support or influence the government when Israel needed aid in 1967.

If the various religious and political segments that constitute American Jewry were unable to come to the assistance of their brethren in those anxious moments of May and June 1967, how much greater must be the responsibility of the Western powers, who, in a moment of conscience had accorded diplomatic recognition to the survivors of the Holocaust and then stood by transfixed as this remnant faced extinction? In 1967, no less than in 1938, national self-interest, the primal instinct of biological self-preservation, compromised the leaders of the democracies. What Arthur Miller wrote of the Holocaust is no less applicable today:

Part of knowing who we are is knowing we are not someone else. And Jew is only the name we give to that stranger,
that agony we cannot feel, that death we look at like a cold
abstraction. Each man has his Jew; it is the other. And the
Jews have their Jews. And now, now above all, you must see
that you have yours—the man whose death leaves you relieved
that you are not him, despite your decency. And that is why
there is nothing and will be nothing—until you face your own
complicity with this . . . your own humanity.[27]

Notes

List of Organizations Cited in the Text, with Abbreviations

Agudath Israel. Hebrew for "Union of Israel," it is the World Organization of Orthodox Jews. It was founded in 1912 and numbered perhaps 500,000 members, chiefly from Chisidic elements in many countries by World War II.

American Council for Judaism. Splinter organization of assimilationist American Jews established in opposition to Zionist Biltmore Program in 1943. Insisting that Judaism is merely a religion and not a nationality, the council has no more than 25,000 adherents today.

American Friends Service Committee. Long-standing humanitarian organization of American Quakers based in Philadelphia. It was chaired by Clarence Pickett during the Holocaust period.

American Jewish Committee. Founded in 1906 in response to Russian pogroms, its leaders included Louis Marshall, Oscar Straus, Jacob Schiff, Julius Rosenwald, and Mayer Sulzberger. Prestigious, with important political connections in both major parties, it numbers 43,000 members.

American Jewish Conference. Umbrella organization championed by Stephen Wise and including members of the American Jewish Committee, American Jewish Congress, Synagogue Council of America, B'nai B'rith, and the Jewish Labor Committee. From 1943 through 1949 it attempted to rescue Jews from Europe and aid Jewish migration to Palestine.

American Jewish Congress. Organized in 1915 in response to pogroms on Eastern Front during World War I, it continued to function at Versailles. It was reorganized in 1922 under Stephen Wise as a more activist body than the conservative American Jewish Committee. It was affiliated with the World Jewish Congress in 1936, and its strength can be measured by the 698,993 ballots cast in the June 1938, Congress election.

B'nai B'rith. The oldest (founded 1843) and largest (130,000) of American Jewish organizations, it has operated hospitals, orphanages, libraries, vocational training programs, and Hillel facilities across the nation. It founded the Anti-Defamation League, which serves as America's principal watchdog against anti-Semitism, in 1913.

Committee for an Army of Stateless and Palestinian Jews. Activist front organized by *Irgun Zvai Leumi* in the United States after 1939, nominally headed by Colorado Senator Edwin Johnson but actually directed by Peter Bergson (Kook) and Ben Hecht. It was opposed by Rabbi Wise as a troublemaker.

Emergency Committee to Save the Children of Europe. Founded at FDR's urging in the spring of 1940, its purpose was to use $5,000,000 to underwrite expenses for admission of 70,000 children (Jewish and non-Jewish) to the U.S. Headed by Frank Kingdom and supported by Eleanor Roosevelt, Marshall Field III, Raymond Clapper, and Joseph Alsop, it never reached its goals.

Emergency Conference to Save the Jewish People of Europe. Distinct from the Commission of Rescue of the American Jewish Conference, this conference, like the Committee for a Jewish Army, was organized by Peter Bergson and included among its leaders Ben Hecht, Max Lerner, Emil Lengyel, Louis Bromfield, Pierre Van Paassen, and Will Rogers.

General Jewish Conference. Abortive proposal of Pittsburgh philanthropist Edgar Kaufmann which sought to unite the American Jewish Committee, American Jewish Congress, B'nai B'rith, and Jewish Labor Committee between 1938 and 1941. It foundered amidst disputes over leadership and funds.

German-Jewish Children's Aid Committee. Proposed by Max Kohler to Labor Secretary Frances Perkins in 1934, it succeeded in relocating several hundred such children through the Department of Naturalization and Immigration before 1939. It was created primarily by Jewish social workers in the U.S.

HIAS. Hebrew Sheltering and Immigrant Aid Society. Established in New York City in 1909, its purpose was to assist immigrants enroute to the U.S. After the war it merged with the United Service for New Americans and the Overseas Migration Services of the Joint Distribution Committee.

HICEM. Established in 1927 as a combination of the services of HIAS, ICA, and Emig-Direct for the purpose of securing emigration permits and refuge for Jewish refugees, it was dissolved after 1945.

Hilfsverein der Deutschen Juden. This German Jewish Aid Society, founded in 1901 to aid the persecuted Jews of Eastern Europe, functioned until 1941. In its last ten years it concentrated on the problems of German Jewry and the securing of exit visas for 90,000 persons.

ICA. A Jewish colonization association established in 1891 by Baron Maurice de Hirsch. Its purpose was to secure land where Jews could, after centuries of legal barriers, once more become agriculturists. Initially it focused on South America.

IRO. International Refugee Organization which existed from 1947, when it supplanted UNRRA, to 1951.

IGCR. The Intergovernmental Committee on Refugees. This was established at Evian in 1938 and revived from a near-dormant state at Bermuda in 1943. It was allegedly chartered to assist all refugees who were forced to leave Germany and Austria because of political opinions, religious beliefs, or racial origin. It proved hapless, inconsequential, and frustrating for its directors, who included George Rublee and Herbert Emerson.

Irgun. This was the "National Military Organization," which was a dissident faction headed by Vladimir Jabotinsky in Palestine in 1937. It rejected the concept of self-restraint championed by regular Zionists in Palestine for a much more activist approach to self-determination. It had no more than 3,000 to 5,000 members by 1946, but its strength lay with the many nonmember Jews who sympathized with its programs.

Jewish Agency. This was created in 1919 in response to Article IV of the British Mandate over Palestine, which called for "an appropriate Jewish agency" to advise and cooperate with the British administration in reviving a Jewish National Home in Palestine. After 1929 the World Zionist Organization was recognized as the Jewish Agency. It continues to function in Israel, sponsoring youth aliyah and underwriting the United Jewish Appeal.

Jewish Labor Committee. Established in 1934, it claims to represent 756 labor groups and 500,000 workers. It was originally headed by Baruch Vladeck, but since 1938, Adolph Held has served as chairman.

Joint Distribution Committee or Joint. Autonomous creation of the American Jewish Committee and several Orthodox groups, the Joint was founded in 1914 for the purpose of giving aid to Jews around the world. By 1967 its relief and rescue operations had amounted to more than $872,000,000.

JNF. Jewish National Fund or "Keren Kayemet le-Yisrael." A perpetual fund for the Jewish state of Israel founded by the World Zionist Organization to redeem land for Jewish colonization in Galilee, Samaria, and the Negev. By 1948 the JNF had purchased 235,523 acres of land in Palestine at bloated prices.

MERRA. Middle East Relief and Refugee Administration. Between July 1942 and April 1944, when it merged with UNRRA, this British operation permitted 45,000 non-Jewish Yugoslavs, Greeks, and Poles to gain refuge in the Egyptian Delta, Sinai, and Cyprus.

Nansen Office. This was known as the Nansen Organization for Help to Refugees when it was chartered by the League of Nations in 1921. From 1930 to December 1938 it was called after its chairman, a well-known Norwegian explorer. It was empowered to issue "international passports" to the stateless which were supposed to be good in fifty-two nations.

NCC. National Coordinating Committee. Headed by Joseph P. Chamberlain, it was founded in October 1934 to aid refugees of all faiths coming to the U.S. from Germany. Among its adherents were the American Committee for Christian-German Refugees, American Friends Service Committee, American Jewish Committee, American Jewish Congress, B'nai B'rith, Committee for Catholic Refugees from Germany, Council of Jewish Federation and Welfare Funds, Emergency Committee in Aid of Displaced Foreign Physicians, Emergency Committee in Aid of Displaced Foreign Scholars, Federal Council of Churches of Christ in America, German-Jewish Children's Aid, HIAS, HICEM, Intercollegiate Council for Refugee Students, International Migration Service, International Student Service, Jewish Agricultural Society of America, Joint Distribution Committee, Musicians' Emergency Fund, National Board of the YWCA, National Council of Jewish Women, and Zionist Organization of America.

NRS. This was organized in 1939 to facilitate the adjustment of refugees from Nazism in the U.S. It assisted more than 26,000 persons before it became the United Service for New Americans in 1946 and eventually merged with HIAS in 1954.

NZO. New Zionist Organization known as "Ha-Tzohar." Founded in 1925 by Vladimir Jabotinsky, it existed as a separate Zionist international from 1935 to 1946 when it again rejoined the WZO. It was activist, revisionist, and eventually became the gestation of Herut or the Freedom party in Israel today.

NSC. Special Non-Sectarian Committee for German Refugee Children, an adjunct of the NCC. Headed by Clarence Pickett, its purpose was to lobby for passage of the Wagner Bill, which would have admitted 20,000 German-Jewish refugee children to the U.S. in 1938.

Office of High Commissioner for Refugees from Germany. This office complemented the work of the Nansen Office after its creation in 1933. Until the Evian conference this hapless office was charged with the principal task of assisting refugees from Nazism. Ultimately in the summer of 1939, Herbert Emerson, League commissioner since September 1938, took on responsibility for IGCR functions as well.

OFFRO. Office of Foreign Relief and Rehabilitation Operations. Founded by FDR in November 1942, it was to develop relief policies in territories under U.S. control. In September 1943, OFFRO, which was headed by Herbert Lehman, became the Foreign Economic Administration. Two months later it became UNRRA.

ORT. Society for Propagation of Artisanal and Agricultural Work among Jews. Founded in Russia in 1880 by Baron Horace de Gunzburg, ORT has had its central offices in Geneva since 1943 and continues to promote retraining in agriculture and workshops in twenty-three countries.

OSE. Russian "Oshtchestvo Zdravookhranyenie Evreyev" for Jewish Health Society. Founded at St. Petersburg in 1912, it grew into an international federation by 1923.

President's Advisory Committee on Political Refugees. Called into being after the Anschluss in March 1938, it was chaired by former League Commissioner for Refugees James McDonald. Others who assisted the State Department in matters pertaining to refugees included Samuel McCrea Cavert of the Federal Council of Churches in America, Paul Baerwald of the American Jewish Committee, Bernard Baruch, Hamilton Fish Armstrong, Joseph Chamberlain, the most Reverend Joseph F. Rummel, Basil Harris, James Spears, and Louis Kennedy. It was reorganized in 1940 with the title of National Coordinating Committee for Aid to Refugees.

REC. Refugee Economic Corporation organized in 1939 by Felix Warburg and other latecomers to appreciate the threat of Hitler. It labored to seek admission of Jews to Australia and Argentina during the war. All twenty of its directors were Jews.

Synagogue Council of America. This was established in 1926 for the purpose of serving as the umbrella religious organ of orthodox, conservative, and reform Jews in the U.S.

UNRRA. Chartered in November 1943 to deal with twenty-one million "displaced persons in liberated areas," UNRRA existed until 1947 under the frustrated leadership of Lehman and Fiorello La Guardia. Jews were especially victimized by UNRRA's preference shown to nationals of states which were members of the U.N. or "enemy nationals" who might face persecution upon return to their homes. Jews fell into neither classification.

WRB. This group created by executive order and at the urging of Treasury Secretary Henry Morgenthau in January 1944, when it was evident that UNRRA could not or would not assist Jews outside the liberated areas. Composed of the secretaries of Treasury, War, and State, its Director was John Pehle, who did not hesitate to spend $20 million wherever possible to rescue Jews and other victims of Nazism.

World Jewish Congress. This was organized in 1936 among Jewish bodies in sixty-five countries to replace outmoded Comité des Delegations Juives. Stephen Wise served as president until his death in 1949, when he was succeeded by Nahum Goldmann.

WZO. World Zionist Organization, chartered by Theodor Herzl and representatives from two dozen states at Basle in 1897. Since then the WZO has functioned through its adjuncts in individual countries and as the Jewish Agency in Israel.

YIVO. Yiddish Institute for Scientific Research established in Vilna in 1925 but transferred to New York City with the outbreak of World War II. It operates branches in thirty countries.

ZOA. Zionist Organization of America, which was formally chartered in 1917 after a diffused start among "Lovers of Zion" in the U.S. since the 1880s. Among its chairmen have been Louis Brandeis, Stephen Wise and Abba Hillel Silver. During the war the ZOA's membership peaked at about 50,000. In recent years it has become the haven of the elderly.

Introduction

1. Chomski, "Children in Exile," *Contemporary Jewish Record,* 4 (Oct. 1941): 522–28.

2. Zerach Warhaftig, *Uprooted: Jewish Refugees and Displaced Persons after Liberation* (New York: Institute of Jewish Affairs of the American Jewish Congress and the World Jewish Congress, 1946), p. 118.

3. (New York: Random House, 1968).

4. Trans. Richard and Clara Winston (New York: Grove Press, 1964). For the controversy this book aroused, see also *Storm Over the Deputy,* ed. Eric Bentley (New York: Dell, 1964).

5. (New York: Coward McCann, 1966).

6. Trans. Helen Weaver (New York: Simon and Schuster, 1967).

7. There have been several general surveys of American immigration policies published in recent years, including William S. Bernard, *American Immigration Policy* (New York: Harper and Bros., 1950); Marion T. Bennett, *American Immigration Policies: A History* (Washington: Public Affairs Press, 1967); John Higham, *Strangers in the Land: Patterns of American Nativism, 1860–1925* (New York: Atheneum, 1966); and Robert A. Divine, *American Immigration Policy, 1924–1952* (New Haven: Yale University Press, 1957). The only one which gives more than passing attention to the Jewish refugee question under Hitler is Divine's work, and there the discussion covers a mere twenty pages.

8. Studies of the individual refugee include Donald P. Kent, *The Refugee Intellectual: The Americanization of Immigrants, 1933–1941* (New York: Columbia University Press, 1953); Harold Fields, *The Refugee in the United States* (New York: Oxford University Press, 1938); Laura Fermi, *Illustrious Immigrants: The Intellectual Migration from Europe, 1930–1941* (Chicago: University of Chicago Press, 1968); Sophia Robinson, *Refugees at Work* (New York: Columbia University Press, 1942); and Maurice Davie and Samuel Koenig, *Refugees in America* (New York: Harper and Bros., 1947). The best studies of Jewish refugee problems are Oscar and Mary Handlin, *A Century of Jewish Immigration to the United States* (New York: American Jewish Committee, 1949); Allen Lesser, *Jewish Immigration 1654–1880, 1881–1924* (New York: Bureau for Intercultural Education, 1939); and Arieh Tartakower and Kurt Grossmann, *The Jewish Refugee* (New York: Institute of Jewish Affairs of the World Jewish Congress and the American Jewish Congress, 1944).

9. "America's Moment of Failure," *Midstream,* 14 (May 1968): 66–72. Adler also criticized Morse's improper techniques of citation, his failure to explore congressional reports, his absolute reliance on the editorial columns of the *New York Times* as demonstrative of the will of the American people during this period, and his failure to explore additional library holdings. Letter from Adler to Saul S. Friedman, Feb. 15, 1967.

10. Personal interview with Szajkowski, Dec. 30, 1968.

11. Henry Feingold, rev. of *While Six Million Died: A Chronicle of American Apathy* by Arthur D. Morse, *American Jewish Historical Quarterly,* 58 (Sept. 1968): 150–55. Feingold later published his own comprehensive study, *The Politics of Rescue: The Roosevelt Administration and the Holocaust* (New Brunswick: Rutgers University Press, 1970). Like Morse's work, Feingold's book fails to analyze the anomie of the Jewish community and leadership during the crisis. Feingold also makes omissions relative to congressional, "patriotic," and labor pressures on Roosevelt before 1939. He also does not consult Harold Willis Dodds, chief delegate to the Bermuda conference, who emerges in Feingold's book as a one dimensional functionary, and he does not probe the feasibility of North Africa as a haven for refugees beyond the statements of minor army intelligence officials. Even less satisfactory because of its circumscribed nature is David S. Wyman's *Paper Walls: America and the Refugee Crisis, 1938–1941* (Amherst: University of Massachusetts Press, 1968).

Chapter 1

1. George Washington established this precedent when he said in New York on Dec. 2, 1783: "The bosom of America is open to receive not only the Opulent and respectable Stranger, but the oppressed and persecuted of all Nations and Religions; whom we shall wellcome (sic) to a participation of our rights and previleges (sic), if by decency and propriety of conduct they appear to merit the enjoyment." *The Writings of George Washington: from the Original Manuscript Sources, 1745–1799,* ed. John C. Fitzpatrick (Washington, 1938), pp. 27, 254. For virtually identical statements from Thomas Jefferson, Andrew Jackson, James Polk, Zachary Taylor, Franklin Pierce, and U. S. Grant, see Robert Ernst, "Asylum of the Oppressed," *South Atlantic Quarterly,* 40 (Jan. 1941): 1–10. See also *National Party Platforms, 1840–1956,* comp. Kirk H.

Porter and Donald Bruce Johnson (Urbana: University of Illinois Press, 1956).

2. Quoted in Earl G. Harrison, "Immigration Policy of the United States," *Foreign Policy Reports, 23* (Apr. 1947): 14.

3. U.S., *Statutes at Law,* 22, 216 (Aug. 3, 1882).

4. In the winter of 1896–1897, Lodge made the error calling for such a test in the language of the immigrant's native or resident country. Because this would have prejudiced the entrance possibilities of Russian Jews, whose native language was Yiddish, and because American sympathies at the time were still in favor of succoring the victims of Tsarist persecution, the measure failed. For the heated debate on this subject, see U.S., Congress, House, *Congressional Record,* 54th Cong., 2d Sess., 1897, 29, pt. 2:1219–22.

5. A lonely, embittered person, Grant contended in *The Passing of the Great Race* (New York: Charles Scribner's Sons, 1916) that the Civil War had destroyed the best "unalloyed" stock of Americans and that, since 1865, their place in the population had been taken by diseased and mentally deficient aliens and Negroes. The work, which predicted doom to Western civilization at the hands of atavist races, went through four editions, including one edited during wartime in which Grant hastily attempted a distinction between Alpine Teutons, who were corrupt barbarians, and pure Nordics, the backbone of Western civilization. Stoddard railed against what he termed the "underman" in *The Rising Tide of Color* (New York: Scribner's, 1920); *The Revolt Against Civilization* (New York: Scribner's, 1922); and *Racial Realities in Europe* (New York: Scribner's, 1924). As late as 1940, he was warning that civilization was being suffocated by masses of inferior, colored, and Asiatic peoples, among whom he included the Jews. For works by the other eugenicists, see Charles Conant Josey, *Race and National Solidarity* (New York: Scribner's, 1923); Harry Laughlin, *Eugenical Sterilization in the United States* (Chicago: Municipal Court Reference Library, 1922); *Historical, Legal and Statistical Review of Eugenic Sterilization in the United States* (Chicago: Municipal Court Reference Library, 1922); *Report of the First Twenty-Seven Months Work of the Eugenics Record Office* (Washington: Eugenics Record Office, 1913); and William Z. Ripley, *Races of Europe: A Sociological Study* (New York: Appleton, 1899). The damage done by Hendrick and Jordan stemmed not so much from their monographs (generally innocuous pieces dealing with important American figures like Walter Hines Page) as it did from the prestige they lent to the entire restrictionist movement in speeches or testimony before congressional hearings.

6. Quoted in Donald S. Strong, *Organized Anti-Semitism in America: The Rise of Group Prejudice During the Decade 1930–1940* (Washington: American Council on Public Affairs, 1941), p. 61. For a better appreciation of Ross, see *Russia in Upheaval* (New York: The Century Co., 1919), *Sin and Society* (Boston: Houghton Mifflin, 1907), *Social Control: A Survey of the Foundations of Order* (New York: Macmillan, 1932), and *Social Psychology* (New York: Macmillan, 1917).

7. Samuel Joseph, "Survey of Jewish Immigration to the United States," *Jewish Social Service Quarterly, 15* (Mar. 1939): 301–302.

8. Higham, *Strangers in the Land,* pp. 203–204.

9. P. 301. See also Louis L. Jaffe, "The Philosophy of Our Immigration Law," *Law and Contemporary Problems, 21* (Spring 1956): 358–75.

10. "The Integration of American Immigrants," *Law and Contemporary Problems, 21* (Spring 1956): 269.

11. All immigration statistics used in this paper refer to fiscal years ending June 30 and are taken from "Table 1. Immigration to the United States: 1820–1967," a fact sheet supplied by the United States Department of Justice, Immigration and Naturalization Service.

12. Higham, pp. 312–18.

13. Bennett, *American Immigration Policies,* p. 50.

14. Emanuel Celler, *You Never Leave Brooklyn* (New York: John Day Co., 1953), p. 98.

15. The law continued nonquota exemptions for Western Hemisphere Caucasians. At the same time, however, it excluded all Orientals, thereby abrogating the Gentlemen's Agreements of 1907–1908 and touching the sensitivities of the Japanese, who proclaimed a day of national mourning when the law went into effect.

16. *Whom Shall We Welcome: Report of the President's Commission on Immigration and Naturalization* (Washington, 1952), p. 88.

17. Read Lewis and Marian Schibsby, "Status of the Refugee Under American Immigration Laws," *Annals of the American Academy of Political and Social Science, 203* (May 1939): 76.

18. Only 41 percent of the small Polish quota, 40 percent of the Czech quota, and 37.7 percent of the German quota were ever used in this period. These statistics can only be accounted for by difficulties faced by refugees in leaving Europe and in breaking through the consular barriers to the United States. See Bernard, *American Immigration Policy,* p. 304. Only Spain, Greece, and Portugal annually filled their respective quotas of 252, 307, and 440. "Immigration in the United States," *International Labor Review, 51* (Jan. 1945): 98.

19. *The Great Depression,* ed. David Shannon (Englewood Cliffs, N.J.: Prentice-Hall, 1960), pp. 6–7.

20. Quoted in Morse, *While Six Million Died,* p. 135.

21. "Hoover Statement," *Interpreter Releases, 9* (Oct. 26, 1932): 261.

22. American Federation of Labor, *Proceedings of the 53d Annual Convention* (Washington, 1933), p. 103.

23. "Aid by the United States to the European Refugees: Testimony of Breckinridge Long," *Interpreter Releases 21* (Jan. 10, 1944): 5.

24. Martin Gumpert, "Immigrants by Conviction," *Survey Graphic, 30* (Sept. 1941): 463.

25. Isabel Lundberg, "Who Are These Refugees?" *Harper's, 182* (Jan. 1941): 167. For a complete review of prewar immigration requirements, see Sidney Kansas, *U.S. Immigration Exclusion and Deportation and Citizenship of the United States of America* (Albany, N.Y.: Matthew Bender Co., 1941), pp. 42–47.

26. Fields, *The Refugee in the United States,* p. 11.

27. John Rich, "Why, Where, Who the Refugees?" *Survey Graphic, 29* (Nov. 1940): 575.

28. Memorandum of Joseph P. Chamberlain for the National Coordinating Committee, June 7, 1934, Joseph P. Chamberlain Collection, YIVO, New York. For additional complaints about the application of this clause, see the letter from Herbert Samuel to Felix Warburg, May 27, 1936, 150, 626/J208, Decimal Files, Department of State, Washington, D.C.

29. Max Gottschalk, "The Jewish Emigrant—1941," *Contemporary Jewish Record, 4* (June 1941): 262.

30. Albert Coyle to Joseph Chamberlain, June 6, 1939, Chamberlain Collection.

31. Nazi calculations of what constituted a "private fortune" were interesting. If a man, aged seventy-five, received a monthly pension of 60 DM, his annual income (720 DM) was multiplied by a special numerical unit which varied with age and life expectancy tables (in this case the multiple was seven). The result was that such a person was reckoned to possess a "private fortune" of 5,040 DM and hence owed the state 40 DM. "Nazi Property Registration Law, Apr. 26, 1938," *Contemporary Jewish Record, 1* (Sept. 1938): 45.

32. Alice Timoney, "Stepchildren of the Fatherland," *Commonweal, 30* (Oct. 6, 1939): 531.

33. No figures are available as to the precise number of applications rejected by consular officials in the period 1930–1946. All pertinent data are maintained by the Visa Division of the Department of State and are not open to researchers.

34. "Jewish Immigration and Departure," *American Jewish Yearbook, 5700,* ed. Harry Schneiderman (Philadelphia: American Jewish Committee and Jewish Publication Society of America, 1939), pp. 41, 600.

35. Pp. 329–30.

36. For a general discussion of the fear of communist power in the United States, see William E. Leuchtenberg, *Franklin D. Roosevelt and the New Deal, 1932–1940* (New York: Harper and Row, 1963), pp. 281–83.

37. Strong, pp. 176–78.

38. Writes Strong (p. 14): "Anti-Semitism in the United States may be considered as a phase of the anti-alien sentiment that has periodically manifested itself. The Jew is the perpetual alien. Since he is frequently identified as a member of a separate group, he is invariably a victim of any anti-alien movement."

39. U.S., Congress, House, *Investigation of Un-American Activities,* 76th Cong., 1st Sess., 1939, H. Rept. 2, p. 117.

40. The best studies of these groups are Gustavus Myers, *History of Bigotry in the United States* (New York: Capricorn Books, 1960); John Roy Carlson, *Under Cover: My Four Years in the Nazi Underworld in America* (New York: E. P. Dutton, 1943); Leo Lowenthal and Norbert Guterman, *Prophets of Deceit: A Study of the Techniques of the American Agitator* (New York: Harper and Bros., 1949); Ralph Lord Roy, *Apostles of Discord: A Study of Organized Bigotry and Discrimination on the Fringes of Protestantism* (Boston: Beacon Press, 1953).

41. U.S., Congress, House, *Investigation of Un-American Activities in the United States,* 76th Cong., 3d Sess., 1938, H. Rept. 1476, p. 16.

42. Myers, pp. 319–42; Carlson, pp. 27–30, 108–20; and Strong, pp. 21–40.

43. Such was the estimate of Louis Bean, statistical analyst of the U.S. Department of Agriculture, in a special report on the influence of nationality groups upon election returns done for Roosevelt in 1941. See Louis L. Gerson, *The Hyphenate in Recent American Politics and Diplomacy* (Lawrence: University of Kansas Press, 1964), pp. 120–21.

44. Long before Samuel Lubell made his analysis of the constituency of American isolationists in the pre-World War II period (see Lubell's *Future of American Politics* [New York: Harper and Row, Colophon Edition, 1965] pp. 132–51), Bean had attributed the growth of this sentiment to propaganda

among German-Americans and Russian-Americans in the Midwest. The result was a much more intensified effort on the part of the Nationalities Division of the Democratic party to placate these groups even between election campaigns. Gerson, pp. 30–32.

45. Once a highly successful Hollywood movie script writer, Pelley underwent an eerie transformation in 1928. At that time, he "died and went to heaven." Reborn, he was guided by an unseen oracle, which gave him instructions. The most important was to found the Silver Shirts on Jan. 31, 1933, the day after Hitler took power in Germany. Pelley promised salvation of the United States by 1962, when he again would be transfigured. Harold Lavine, *Fifth Column in America* (New York: Doubleday, Doran and Co., 1940), pp. 171–80.

46. Myers, pp. 343–59.

47. H. Rept. 1476, pp. 19, 22.

48. The best contemporary analyses are *Father Coughlin: His 'Facts' and Arguments* (New York: General Jewish Council, 1939); *The Fine Art of Propaganda: A Study of Father Coughlin's Speeches*, ed. Alfred M. and Elizabeth B. Lee (New York: Harcourt, Brace and Co., 1939); and Charles Tull, *Father Coughlin and the New Deal* (Syracuse: Syracuse University Press, 1965).

49. Coughlin continued to denounce Jews, aliens, and reds and to praise Nazi Germany in the pages of *Social Justice* until Pearl Harbor, when his paper ceased publication and he went into semi-retirement. On Feb. 23, 1959, his secretary, H. Thomas, responding to an inquiry from this author regarding Coughlin's views of Jews, Roosevelt, and the depression era, wrote the following cryptic reply: "At this time, Father Coughlin finds it not proper to inscribe any remarks relative to his activities or to his career. This seems a very curt answer to a serious young man. However, I know that he understands that there are hidden activities in personnel who oftentimes interfere with the course and determination of events."

50. Gary T. Marx, *The Social Basis of the Support of a Depression Era Extremist* (Berkeley: Survey Research Center, 1962), pp. 16, 111.

51. H. Rept. 1476, p. 25.

52. For details of McWilliams's checkered background from inventor to communist to fascist, see Carlson, pp. 75–84, and Lavine, pp. 90–99.

53. Strong, pp. 133–37.

54. There were infrequent "marriages" between organizations. In Aug. 1939, 7,000 persons (many of them Bundists) crowded Innisfail Park in the Bronx to cheer Joe McWilliams. The Bund and Christian Mobilizers subsequently pledged themselves to a united front in a closed session at Ebling's Casion (Carlson, pp. 77–80). Edward James Smythe of the Ku Klux Klan also promised that organization's cooperation with the Bund at Camp Nordland, N.J., in Aug. 1940 (Myers, p. 339). For evidence of connections between the Bund and Silver Shirts, see August Raymond Ogden, *The Dies Committee: A Study of the Special House Committee for the Investigation of Un-American Activities, 1938–1944* (Washington: Catholic University Press, 1945). Efforts of George Deatherage to consolidate seventy-two fascist groups ended in failure at Los Angeles in Aug. 1938 (Myers, p. 362).

55. Lavine, pp. 54–55, and George Seldes, *You Can't Do That* (New York: Modern Age Books, 1938), pp. 154–55.

56. Seldes, p. 156.

57. Carlson, pp. 457–60.

58. Col. McCormick presents a particularly fascinating image. A vigilant anti-communist, anti-alien (they meant the same for McCormick), he filled the columns of his journal with spurious assaults on Bolshevism, claiming, among other things, that the comintern was actively seeking Roosevelt's reelection in 1936 and that the proposed polar air route from the U.S.S.R. to the U.S. was a communist plot. He also supplied Mrs. Dilling with a front-cover endorsement for *The Red Network* (Chicago: publ. by the author, 1935 and 1936). He was actively associated with the Sentinels and supplied Harry Jung, whom he considered an authority on communism, with offices in the Tribune Towers Building. See Carlson, pp. 196–97, 396; Seldes, *You Can't Do That*, pp. 148–58; Roy, pp. 40–42; and George Seldes, *Lords of the Press* (New York: Julian Messner, 1939), pp. 54–57.

59. Seldes, *You Can't Do That*, pp. 138–43.

60. Blasted by Sen. Lewis Schwellenbach (D.-Wash.) as a bunch of "leeches, rascals, crooks and bloodsucking lawyers," the Liberty League was also linked to the Black Legion, according to Gov. Earle of Pennsylvania, and charged by Robert Harris of *Common Sense* with a desire to maintain the liberty of starvation, unemployment, and death. Seldes, *You Can't Do That*, pp. 102–107. For a less empassioned treatment of the league, see Arthur M. Schlesinger, Jr., *The Coming of the New Deal, The Age of Roosevelt* (New York: Houghton Mifflin, 1958), 2:486–88.

61. Included in this collective noun were the major chains across the country, including Scripps-Howard, the Chandler and Hearst newspapers on the West Coast, and the *New York Herald Tribune,* which editorialized on May 22, 1932: "The hour has struck for a fascist party to be born in the United States." Holland, however, intended to direct his remark against McCormick and the *Chicago Tribune* and the colonel's relatives, Joseph Medill Patterson of the *New York Daily News* and Eleanor "Sissy" Patterson of the *Washington Times-Herald,* journals accounting for 5 percent of the country's daily readership (Seldes, *Lords of the Press*, pp. 20–86). Of these papers, which published exposés of "Jewish power" in Washington, which turned over their columns to defenses of Pelley when he was charged with sedition, and which editorialized as late as Aug. 30, 1942 (*Daily News*) that "Hitler was not wholly to blame" for the war and that "a big bloodletting might help matters," William L. Shirer commented, "Hardly a day goes by that they are not cited by Goebbels to prove one of his points" (Quoted in Carlson, p. 399).

62. On the resurgence of the right in this period, see Schlesinger, pp. 423–511, in which the author attributes this phenomenon to an abiding fear among conservatives that communism genuinely menaced the American form of government.

63. Leading Wall Street bankers were implicated in several plots to "save the republic" in the 1930s. The first, exposed by the McCormack Committee in 1935, involved the cooperation of ex-Marine Gen. Smedley Butler, who testified he had been approached with money ($3,000,000) and manpower (500,000 men) to lead a Mussolini-type march on Washington in Aug. 1934 (Seldes, *You Can't Do That*, pp. 173–84). A less cooperative witness, ex-Maj. Gen. George Van Horn Moseley, told the Dies Committee in May 1939 that he was to prevent the takeover by 150,000 Spanish Republican mercenaries in the employ of Jewish Bolsheviks by directing a spontaneous uprising in the summer of 1939. Walter Goodman, *The Committee: The Extraordinary*

Career of the House Committee on Un-American Activities (New York: Farrar, Straus, and Giroux, 1968), pp. 60–61. In the same year other leading bankers were implicated in an unsuccessful coup to be directed by German Consul Manfred von Killinger in San Francisco (Carlson, pp. 137–39).

64. The American Legion's 1937 convention in New York City endorsed vigilantism ("but not in uniforms") and opposed any attempt to alter existing immigration laws. A year later in Los Angeles, National Commander Stephen Chadwick and the executive committee forced the passage of a resolution calling for a ten-year suspension of immigration. About the same time the legion was linked with the Black Legion, the northern group which specialized in flogging, arson, and murder. See Carlson, pp. 285–86; Seldes, *You Can't Do That*, pp. 114–25; and Leuchtenberg, pp. 276–77.

65. Trevor's connections with Walter S. Steele, William Pelley, and John Snow were well documented, and he would later be cited in connection with the wartime sedition trial of American Nazis. Still, he was considered an authority on immigration problems after the publication of *An Analysis of the Immigration Act of 1924* (New York: Carnegie Endowment for International Peace, 1924).

66. Olin West, secretary of the AMA, and *Medical Economics Magazine* attacked government policy in permitting a "flood" of inferior alien doctors into this country before the war. For a refutation of their charges that aliens were practicing cutrate medicine, see Lucille Milner and David Dempsey, "The Alien Myth," *Harper's, 181* (Sept. 1940): 376. For details of BPOE and the Chambers' actions, consult Seldes, *You Can't Do That*, pp. 73–83, 137.

67. Divine, pp. 77–109.

68. Mark Starr, "Labor Looks at Migration," *Current History, 5* (Dec. 1943): 299.

69. "Fortune Survey XX," *Fortune, 19* (Apr. 1939): 102.

70. *Public Opinion, 1935–1946*, ed. Hadley Cantril (Princeton: Princeton University Press, 1951), pp. 384, 1081.

71. "Fortune Survey XX," p. 102.

72. Carlson gives a complete record of the connections of congressmen and Nazi agents.

73. Efforts were made to link Dies, no friend of foreigners, with fascism through forged letters from Pelley in 1940. Nothing more substantial could be uncovered. Although he was a friend of Winrod and a recipient of neo-Nazi praise for his Red hunts, Dies did assist the government in uncovering underground fascist activities in 1940–1941. See U.S., Congress, House, *A Preliminary Digest and Report on Un-American Activities of Various Nazi Organizations and Individuals in the United States, Including Diplomatic and Consular Agents of the German Government*, 1940.

74. Only the Smith Act was ever voted into law. Effective June 28, 1940, this bill required the fingerprinting of aliens over age fourteen and detailed penalties for aliens who engaged in subversive activities. Approximately 4,000,000 aliens registered in the first year. See Kansas, pp. 141–43, 147–48.

75. "Feather in Hat," *Time Magazine, 33* (Feb. 13, 1939): 16.

76. Reynolds opposed the administration on only 14 percent of the roll call votes to 1939, a record in direct contrast with that compiled by his fellow North Carolinian, Josiah Bailey. In fact, thirty-one Democratic senators opposed the administration more often than Reynolds, who was not an intimate

of the leading conservative insurgents like Glass, Tydings, or George. See James T. Patterson, *Congressional Conservatism and the New Deal: The Growth of the Conservative Coalition in Congress, 1933–1939* (Lexington: University of Kentucky Press, 1967), p. 352.

77. U.S., Congress, Senate, *Congressional Record*, 76th Cong., 1st Sess., 1939, *84*, pt. 4:3624.

78. Fields, pp. 202–203. Such statistics obviously are inaccurate, since fewer than 5,000,000 aliens registered under the Smith Act and not all were employed or employable. See Earl G. Harrison, "Axis Aliens in an Emergency," *Survey Graphic, 30* (Sept. 1941): 466.

79. U.S., Congress, Senate, *Congressional Record*, 76th Cong., 1st Sess., 1939, *84*, pt. 1:370.

80. In the same discussion Reynolds took a *Washington Herald* report of the passage of a handful of illegal immigrants across the Canadian border into the U.S. and transmuted it into a gigantic smuggling operation involving "thousands" of persons. Two months later, quoting from Coughlin's *Social Justice*, he set the figure of illegals at 25,000. U.S., Congress, Senate, *Congressional Record*, 76th Cong., 1st Sess., 1939, *84*, pt. 4:3627, 3629.

81. Again, Reynolds apparently took a *New York Times* report of Apr. 9, 1939, that stated that 10,975 men on WPA projects in the city had been dismissed during the previous week and inflated it to a figure of 30,000 men being laid off weekly. *Congressional Record, 84*, pt. 4:4546. His remarks on sharecroppers are from pt. 2:1011. Lurid examples came readily to Reynolds, who bewailed the abnormally high arrest rate among Americans under twenty-one. He was especially perturbed by the number of young white and Negro girls who stood on the street corners of major Eastern cities and offered themselves as prostitutes for fifteen or twenty cents. Reynolds also told of an eighteen-year-old girl in Washington who wanted to sell her eyes for $1,500 to help her family, which included six siblings.

82. Higham, pp. ix–x.

Chapter 2

1. Gordon Brook-Shepherd, *The Anschluss* (Philadelphia: J. B. Lippincott, 1963). A more charitable view of Hitler and his program can be found in A. J. P. Taylor, *The Origins of the Second World War* (New York: Atheneum, 1961). For America's role in this, see Arnold A. Offner, *American Appeasement: United States Foreign Policy and Germany, 1933–1938* (Cambridge: Harvard University Press, 1969).

2. Brook-Shepherd, pp. 198–99.

3. Ibid., pp. 210–11.

4. "Sack of Austria," *National Jewish Monthly*, 52 (Apr. 1938): 266.

5. "2,000 Jews Commit Suicide in Austria," *National Jewish Monthly*, 52 (June 1938): 539.

6. More than 99 percent of the 4,500,000 voters who ultimately participated in this referendum approved the Nazi takeover.

7. The Vienna State Opera, rejuvenated by Bruno Walter, also suffered, as Walter, Artur Rodzinski, Pierre Monteux, Ignaz Friedman, Rudolph Serkin, Fritz Kreisler, Yehudi Menuhin, Richard Tauber, Alexander Kipnis, and Emanuel List were barred from performing with Aryans. "The Locust Strikes Again," *National Jewish Monthly*, 52 (Apr. 1938): 281 ff.

8. "Human Punishment," *National Jewish Monthly*, 52 (May 1938): 308.

9. Joseph Hyman, *Twenty-five Years of American Aid to Jews Overseas: A Record of the Joint Distribution Committee* (New York: Joint Distribution Committee, 1938), p. 176.

10. Albert Viton, "The Exile of the 16,000," *National Jewish Monthly*, 53 (Feb. 1939): 213.

11. Viewing these camps a year afer the expulsions, Max Brod noted bitterly that the democracies had done little to help these unfortunates. "Democratic solidarity is the solidarity of do-nothing," he noted. "Rivals in Misfortune," *National Jewish Monthly*, 53 (Mar. 1939): 227.

12. Germany was not a signatory to such treaties, but on May 29, 1919, the Weimar government pledged: "Germany is resolved on her part to treat the national minorities living on her territory according to the same rules, that is to say, according to the principles laid down in the minorities treaties." Joseph Roucek, "Minorities—Basis of the Refugee Problem," *Annals of the American Academy of Political and Social Science*, 203 (May 1939): 6.

13. Nathan Caro Belth, "The Refugee Problem," in *American Jewish Yearbook*, 1939, p. 378.

14. Norman Angell, *You and the Refugee: The Morals and Economics of the Problem* (Harmondsworth, England: Penguin Books, 1939), p. 60.

15. At Brussels in 1936 the Institute of International Law agreed that the term "refugee" would apply to persons who were forced to leave their homeland for political reasons, who were deprived of diplomatic protection, or who had acquired no diplomatic protection in another state. John Hope Simpson later suggested that the term more properly should apply to those who were "deprived of legal protection, mutual support, access to employment, and the measure of freedom of movement which happier mortals take as a matter of course." *The Refugee Problem: Report of a Survey* (London: Oxford University Press, 1939), p. 3. This meant that anyone stripped of de jure national status, and even those who had not yet managed to flee a country, should be considered a refugee. Tartakower and Grossmann, *The Jewish Refugee*, concur with Simpson's view (p. 2).

16. *American Jewish Yearbook*, 1939, pp. 310–14.

17. U.S., *Foreign Relations of the United States* (Washington, 1938), *1*: 778–80.

18. *American Jewish Yearbook*, 1938, p. 299. One way by which the Polish government attempted to outdo Germany was the issuance of a decree in Oct. 1938 which required Polish citizens living abroad to renew their passports by Oct. 29. The time factor prevented many in Germany from meeting the requirement, thereby depriving them of Polish citizenship and making them the responsibility of Germany. This precipitated Germany's hasty roundup and dumping of nearly 18,000 persons on Oct. 29. See Belth, p. 378.

19. Wilson to Hull, Mar. 24, 1938, Correspondence File, Cordell Hull Papers, Library of Congress, Washington, D.C.

20. Brook-Shepherd, p. 391.

21. Henry Levy, "Goodwill to Men," *National Jewish Monthly*, 53 (Dec. 1938): 28–30.

22. U.S., Congress, House, *Congressional Record*, 75th Cong., 3d Sess., 1938, *83*, pt. 3:3358.

23. Fermi, *Illustrious Immigrants*.

24. The Jewish alliance with the Democratic party in this country is at-

tributable to Roosevelt, who consistently earned 90 percent of the Jewish vote. See Lawrence Fuchs, *The Political Behavior of American Jews* (Glencoe, Ill.: The Free Press, 1956), pp. 99–101.

25. "The Morgenthau Diaries: VI, The Refugee Runaround," *Colliers, 120* (Nov. 1, 1947): 63. For Roosevelt's concern that the country should remain a haven for the oppressed, witness his comment three years later: "For centuries this country has always been the traditional haven of refuge for countless victims of religious and political persecution in other lands. These immigrants have made outstanding contributions to American music, art, literature, business, finance, philanthropy, and many other phases of our cultural, political, industrial, and commercial life. It was quite fitting, therefore, that the United States Government should follow its traditional role and take the lead in calling and conducting the Evian meeting." *Public Papers and Addresses of Franklin D. Roosevelt,* comp. Samuel I. Rosenman, (New York: Macmillan, 1941), 7:170. Hereafter cited as *Public Papers of FDR.*

26. U.S., Congress, House, *Congressional Record,* 76th Cong., 1st. Sess., 1939, *84,* Appendix A:841.

27. Roosevelt's efforts to remove the obstreperous Carter Glass (Va.), "Cotton Ed" Smith (S.C.), Millard Tydings (Md.), Pat McCarran (Nev.), and Walter George (Ga.), among others, was a total failure. In addition, the Republicans gained eight seats in the Senate, eighty-one in the House, and even captured eleven governorships. See William L. Langer and S. Everett Gleason, *The Challenge to Isolation, 1937–1940* (New York: Harper and Bros., 1952), p. 39.

28. James MacGregor Burns, *Roosevelt: The Lion and the Fox* (New York: Harcourt, Brace & Co., 1956), pp. 337, 339.

29. Divine, *American Immigration Policy,* p. 94.

30. "The Fortune Quarterly Survey," *Fortune, 18* (July 1938): 80.

31. On the overriding importance of the depression, see "American Institute of Public Opinion Surveys, 1938–1939," *Public Opinion Quarterly, 3* (1939): 595. In *Fortune's* July 1938 survey, nearly one-third of those interviewed indicated they were most disturbed by Japan's invasion of China. Austria, Spain, and Russia's purge trials elicited the next most interest, in that order. "The Fortune Quarterly Survey," p. 80.

32. Polls conducted by the AIPO and ORC in Mar., Apr., and May 1938 consistently showed that 10 to 12 percent of those surveyed blamed such persecutions entirely on the Jews, while another 48 to 50 percent indicated that it was "partly" the Jews' own fault. See "Jewish Question," in Cantril, p. 381, and Charles Stember et al., *Jews in the Mind of America* (New York: Basic Books, 1966), pp. 138–39.

33. There were four distinct clusters of criticism: (1) Jews were overly concerned about money, unscrupulous in getting it, and dishonest in business; (2) Jews were pushy, domineering, aggressive, obstinate, and lacking in respect for the rights of others; (3) Jews were clannish, discriminated against non-Jews, and covered up for one another; (4) Jews were unrefined, ill-mannered, unclean, and generally repellent. Stember et al., pp. 54–69. The editors of *Fortune* published a good analysis of the Jews, *The Jews in America* (New York: Random House, 1936), and there were other studies which probed the origins of anti-Semitism in totalitarian thought or analyzed Christian responsibility for hatred of Jews with a purpose of demonstrating the absurdity

of pinning specific traits upon certain peoples. See Johann Smertenko, "Hitlerism Comes to America," *Harper's, 187* (Nov. 1935): 66–70; Frank Eakin, "What Christians Teach About Jews: Church Lesson Materials," *Christian Century, 52* (Sept. 18, 1935): 1173–76; Lyford Edwards, "Religious Sectarianism and Race Prejudice," *American Journal of Sociology, 41* (Sept. 1935): 167–79; Marjorie van de Walter, "Racial Psychology," *Science, 88* (Dec. 30, 1938): 7–8; May Sukov and E. G. Williamson, "Comparison between Jews and Non-Jews with Respect to Several Traits of Personality," *Journal of Applied Psychology, 22* (Oct. 1938): 487–92; K. Sward and M. B. Friedman, "Jewish Temperament," *Journal of Applied Psychology, 19* (Feb. 1935): 70–84; and Ethel Beer, "Americanization of Manhattan's Lower East Side," *Social Forces, 15* (Mar. 1937): 411–16.

34. As late as 1946 only a handful of Americans could even approximate the number of Jews in this country. One in four estimated that there were more than 20,000,000 Jews in America. And 10 percent of those polled put the figure at more than 40,000,000. Stember et al., p. 77.

35. Quoted in "Editorial Comment," *Contemporary Jewish Record, 1* (July 1938): 54–55.

36. The AIPO figure in polls conducted in Apr. 1938, Mar. 1939, and May 1939 was 12 percent every time. "American Institute of Public Opinion Surveys," p. 595.

37. Only in 1942 did another group displace the Jews in this category. In that year, with the disastrous news from the Pacific fresh in Americans' minds, the Japanese were regarded with greater dread than were the Jews. Invariably, however, the Jews placed ahead of the Germans. See Stember et al., p. 128. All kinds of explanations have been advanced for this, ranging from Talcott Parsons's suggestion that the Jews have been blamed for the anomie resulting from the rapid development of an impersonalized, industrial society ("Some Sociological Aspects of the Fascist Movement," *Social Forces, 31* [Nov. 1942]: 138–47) to Richard Hofstadter's claim that "there has been a curiously persistent linkage between anti-Semitism and money and credit obsessions." *The Age of Reform* (New York: Alfred A. Knopf, 1955), p. 81. Whatever the cause, there is no doubt that these anti-Jewish sentiments were shared by large segments of the population in every area of the country. See Stember et al., p. 224, and Arthur Schlesinger, Jr., *The Politics of Upheaval* (Boston: Houghton Mifflin, 1957), pp. 67–69.

38. Burns, p. 355.

39. Basil Rauch, *Roosevelt from Munich to Pearl Harbor: A Study in the Creation of a Foreign Policy* (New York: Creative Age Press, 1950), pp. 47–55, chronicles the ineptitude and naïveté of American foreign policy late in 1937.

40. *New York Times,* Oct. 6, 1937, p. 1.

41. Some historians hostile to Roosevelt hold that he decided at this point to plunge the United States into war because he had been unable to resolve the problems of the depression in peacetime. See Frederick A. Sanborn, *Design for War: A Study of Secret Power Politics, 1937–1941* (New York: Devin-Adair, 1951), pp. 21–48, and *Perpetual War for Perpetual Peace,* ed. Harry Elmer Barnes (Caldwell, Idaho: Caxton Printers, 1953).

42. *Working with Roosevelt* (New York: Harper and Bros., 1952), p. 167.

43. Langer and Gleason, p. 139.

44. Memorandum of Wise to Louis Lipsky, June 7, 1938, American Jewish

Congress File, Stephen Wise Papers, Brandeis University Library, Waltham, Mass. Exactly such an attitude of disbelief in "atrocities" on the part of American Jewish Committee President Louis Marshall had led to a schism within the committee in World War I and the eventual founding of the Congress. See *To the Jews of America: The Jewish Congress versus the American Jewish Committee* (New York: Jewish Congress Organizing Committee, 1915), pp. 5–8.

45. According to the Committee and B'nai B'rith, such actions would oversimplify the danger of Nazism to democratic institutions by merely identifying the movement with anti-Semitism. It was also argued that such boycott could only lead to reprisals against the Jews in Germany. By the fall of 1933, however, both organizations had come around to the position of the Congress. "American Jewish Congress," *Universal Jewish Encyclopedia*, 1940, 1:250.

46. Memorandum of Wise to the Governing Council of the American Jewish Congress, Jan. 19, 1937, Wise Papers.

47. See the scathing letter from Lillie Shultz to Sol Stock, chairman of the executive committee of the American Jewish Committee, Nov. 6, 1939, Wise Papers.

48. Lipsky to Wise, Apr. 10, 1941, Wise Papers.

49. Tartakower and Grossmann, p. 496. William Haber of the NRS finally negotiated a plan acceptable to all by July 26, 1940. The Joint was to handle matters in Greater Germany, and the HIAS-HICEM in all matters in other countries. HIAS would receive all unattached men or men with families when they arrived in the U.S. and handle all appeals before the Department of Naturalization and Immigration. The National Council of Jewish Women would greet all unattached women. All of these agencies would act as referrals to the NRS, whose duty was to assist the refugee in resettling in the U.S., and to give him vocational and educational training. See Albert Phiebig and Frederick Grubel, *HIAS Survey 1940–1941*, special report prepared for HIAS, New York, 1942, YIVO, pp. 11, 99.

50. This was a common fear which was also expressed by Henry Pratt Fairchild in "Should the Jews Come In?" *New Republic, 94* (Jan. 25, 1939): 344.

51. The upshot of this was the creation by Rosenwald and other leading assimilated American Jews of the American Council for Judaism. Founded in 1943, it was responsible for forcing the Department of Immigration and Naturalization to drop the category "Hebrew" from its annual statistics on immigration by "race." Since that time, the council (numbering 20,000 members, including Stanley Marcus of Neiman-Marcus, Donald Klopfer of Random House, Walter Rothschild of Abraham and Strauss, and John Mosler, president of the Urban League of Greater New York) has consistently spoken out against Zionism. James Yaffe, *The American Jews: Portrait of a Split Personality* (New York: Random House, 1968), pp. 185–86, and *New York Times*, July 16, 1967, p. 48.

52. The historical fact that people simply did not come to the U.S. during such economic crises was thoroughly examined in Bernard Ostrolenk, "The Economics of an Imprisoned World—A Brief for the Removal of Immigration Restrictions," *Annals of the American Academy of Political and Social Science, 203* (May 1939): 194–201. Such findings were later borne out by John Thomas, "The Economic Aspect," in *The Positive Contribution by Immigrants:*

A *Symposium Prepared by UNESCO, The International Sociolog-Association and the International Economic Association,* General Rapporteur Oscar Handlin (Paris: UNESCO, 1955), pp. 165–85, and S. Kuznets, *National Production Since 1869* (New York: National Board of Economic Research, 1946), p. 118.

Between 1935 and 1939 only 28.6 percent of those persons entering the U.S. listed unskilled occupations, and most of these were servants, an occupation ever in great demand (Bernard, p. 46). Among the new arrivals were some 1,500 physicians, far less than the tidal wave feared by the AMA. See Memorandum for Joseph Chamberlain, undated, Chamberlain Collection. At the time the U.S. was graduating only 5,000 physicians a year, had even fallen behind the doctor-patient ratio in the country in 1886, and the deans of Bellevue, Harvard, Tufts, Johns Hopkins, and Yale medical schools all were calling for assistance to emigrant physicians who were badly needed here. See Henry Smith Leiper, "Those German Refugees," *Current History,* 50 (May 1939): 20–21.

Finally, in 1942, a team of social workers headed by Sophia Robinson reported that some 800 "refugee" enterprises had been located in the U.S. More than half of these had introduced something to the American market which had never previously been produced in this country, including harmonicas and Lebkuchen. More significant, it was estimated that each refugee entrepreneur had created jobs for approximately seven American workers. See Sophia Robinson, *Refugees at Work.* See also Oscar and Mary Handlin, "The United States," in *Positive Contributions by Immigrants,* p. 33; Abe Revusky, "Refugees in America, "*National Jewish Monthly,* 53 (Apr. 1939): 260–61; Memorandum of Joseph Chamberlain, undated, 1938, and letter from Joseph Hyman of the Joint Distribution Committee to Chamberlain, Chamberlain Collection.

53. Bernard W. Levmore, "A Stimulus for American Industry: Non-Professional Refugees," *Annals of the American Academy of Political and Social Science,* 203 (May 1939): 166.

54. Ibid.

55. British citizens were employed in the production of surgical adhesives, gelatin products, patent fasteners, canes, wristwatch straps, leather bags, furniture fabrics, bottlecaps, and furs as a result of the exodus from Germany after 1933. *Refugee Facts: A Study of the German Refugee in America,* report prepared for the American Friends Service Committee, Philadelphia, 1939, American Friends Service Committee Library, p. 19. When the war broke out these same refugees would win high praise from the British for their assistance in the manufacture of searchlights, prismatic reflectors, hardened glass ball bearings (substitutes for steel bearings), special torches, and other engineering work hitherto unknown in Britain. Julius Isaacs, "Jewish Refugees in Great Britain," in *Positive Contributions by Immigrants,* p. 69.

56. Bernard, p. 27.

57. Levmore, p. 163.

58. Gerhart Saenger, "The Refugees Here: In the United States," *Survey Graphic,* 29 (Nov. 1940): 576.

59. Throughout the prewar period, restrictionists circulated rumors that an influx of refugees, particularly Jewish refugees, would result in wealthy Jews who were already in this country laying off as much as 2 percent of their

work force, particularly Negroes, to accommodate their kinsmen. This charge was leveled against the New York department stores, where it was said one eventually would need a German dictionary to transact any business. The charge was vehemently denied by Delos Walker of Macy's, Walter Hoving of Lord and Taylor, Kenneth Collins of Gimbel's, and executives of Stern Bros., Bloomingdale's, and Abraham and Strauss. See Leiper, p. 20, and also a report issued to the *New York Times* by the National Coordinating Committee, Nov. 25, 1938, Chamberlain Collection.

As for radicalism and criminality among immigrants, the Department of Immigration and Naturalization deported an average of forty persons a year for radicalism between 1907 and 1939. During that same period more than 14,000,000 persons came to the United States (Milner and Dempsey, "The Alien Myth," p. 378). The Wickersham Committee testified in 1931 that "in proportion to their respective numbers, the foreign-born commit considerably fewer crimes than the native-born of the same age and sex" (Bernard, p. 122). A decade later the U.S. Census Bureau noted that the foreign-born constituted 4.1 percent of the institutionalized population of the U.S., while simultaneously accounting for 8.6 percent of the total civilian population. These figures are confirmed by a special survey done by the National Coordinating Committee in the summer of 1937. See report of New York City Commissioner A. H. McCormick, Department of Corrections, to NCC Secretary Cecilia Razovsky, June 25, 1937, Chamberlain Collection.

As for the threat of welfare dependency, no aliens were permitted on federal relief rolls in 1939. Only 4 percent of the total number of families on WPA rolls in 1936 were headed by men who were not citizens (Bernard, pp. 89–90). The states recording the highest per capita income were those with the greatest alien populations. A greater percentage of the foreign-born owned their homes (51.8 percent) than native-born (48.9 percent) (Milner and Dempsey, p. 377). And those foreign-born who did rent paid a higher average monthly rent than the native-born (Bernard, p. 73). Such indices reveal that the foreign-born were boosts to the economy.

60. Chamberlain of the NCC issued a memorandum in July which spoke glowingly of "more food, shoes, hospitals, churches, beauty parlors" if this country welcomed the refugees. See Memorandum Regarding Emigration from Germany and Austria, July 7, 1938, Chamberlain Collection.

61. U.S., Congress, House, Committee on Immigration and Naturalization, *Hearings on Admission of German Refugee Children,* H. J. Res. 165 and H. J. Res. 168, 76th Cong., 1st Sess., 1939, p. 7.

62. Tartakower and Grossmann, p. 461.

63. "Adjustment of the Professional Refugee," *Annals of the American Academy of Political and Social Science 203* (May 1939): 155.

64. Zosa Szajkowski, "Private and Organized American Jewish Overseas Relief and Immigration, 1914–1938," *American Jewish Historical Quarterly,* 57 (Dec. 1967): 242–43.

65. Personal interview with Benjamin Cohen, June 5, 1968.

66. Among successful or influential Jews this feeling of ambivalence toward one's Jewish background is especially pronounced. Termed "Jüdische Selbsthäss" by Lessing in 1930, it explains the reluctance of powerful Jewish figures to champion the cause of their brethren in times of stress. See Kurt Lewin, "Self-Hatred Among Jews," *Contemporary Jewish Record,* 4 (June

1941): 228–29. The idea that "semitophobia can lead to induced social neuroses in Jews, namely social-climbing or egomania" is also put forward in Read Bain, "Sociopathy of Anti-Semitism," *Sociometry, 6* (Nov. 1943): 460–64.

67. A good example of this reluctance to identify oneself as a Jew, even to help a relative, can be seen in a letter from Frankfurter to Roosevelt, dated Oct. 24, 1941. Frankfurter informed the president of the death of an aged uncle, Solomon Frank, onetime director of the library of the University of Vienna, in a Nazi concentration camp where he had been detained since the Anschluss. "Precisely because I wanted to avoid the criticism even of the evil-minded and hardhearted against any charge of favoritism by your administration, I did *not* invoke the good offices of the State Department," Frankfurter wrote. *Roosevelt and Frankfurter: Their Correspondence, 1928–1945,* an. Max Freedman (Boston: Little, Brown & Co., 1967), p. 619.

68. Eleanor Roosevelt, *This I Remember* (New York: Harper and Bros., 1949), p. 162.

69. Walter Adams, "Extent and Nature of the World Refugee Problem," *Annals of the American Academy of Political and Social Science, 203* (May 1939): 27–30.

70. Louis W. Holborn, "The League of Nations and the Refugee Problem," *Annals of the American Academy of Political and Social Science, 203* (May 1939): 126. It is interesting to note that during World War II, Nansen's son Otto, presently active in U.N. refugee work, was placed in a concentration camp for aiding Jews in Norway. He was required to wear a yellow Star of David inscribed "I am a Jewish slave."

71. Tartakower and Grossmann, pp. 405–406.

72. League of Nations, International Bureaux, *Nansen International Office for Refugees: Report of the Governing Board for the Year Ending June 30th, 1938* (XII.B,1–3), 1938, p. 3.

73. Most of the money was contributed by Jewish relief groups, which, though disagreeing among themselves, were unstintingly generous toward refugees of all faiths (Fields, pp. 189–92).

74. James McDonald, "Text of Resignation as High Commissioner for Refugees Coming from Germany," *Christian Century, 53* (Jan. 15, 1936): 101–21.

75. Holborn, p. 135.

76. League of Nations, International Bureaux, *International Assistance to Refugees* (XII.B,1–3), 1938, p. 5.

77. *Public Papers of FDR,* 7:170.

78. Ibid., p. 169.

79. Arthur Sweetser, U.S. observer at the League of Nations refugee conference in Geneva, informed James McDonald that the U.S. now had "the center stage" and that the various nations were looking in this direction for constructive leadership. "What seems to be hoped for from us is that we will present a program which will make it possible to approach the refugee problem in a big rather than the purely individual way," Sweetser wrote. May 17, 1938, President's Advisory Committee on Political Refugees File, Wise Papers.

80. John Hope Simpson, *Refugees: A Review of the Situation Since September, 1938* (London: Royal Institute of International Affairs and Oxford University Press, 1939), pp. 5–6, 52–59, 114.

81. Adams, p. 32. Identical opinions were offered by Vera Dean, research

director of the Foreign Policy Association of New York, "European Power Politics and the Refugee Problem," *Annals of the American Academy of Political and Social Science*, 203 (May 1939): 18–25, and Frances Reinhold, professor at Swarthmore College, "Exiles and Refugees in American History," *Annals of the American Academy of Political and Social Science*, 203 (May 1939): 65. Refer also to Houghteling to Frances Perkins, Jan. 5, 1940, Immigration File, Roosevelt Library, Hyde Park, N.Y. and Dodds interview, June 2, 1968.

82. *Public Papers of FDR*, 7:172.

83. *Foreign Relations of the U.S.*, 1:743. Italy also explained that it could not participate if Germany was unrepresented. This prompted *The New Republic* to comment: "One could as reasonably refuse to attend a funeral because the murderer had not been asked." "Doors Close Against the Refugees," 85 (July 13, 1938): 263.

84. *Foreign Relations of the U.S.*, 1:742, 743, 753.

85. *New York Times*, Mar. 26, 1938, p. 2.

86. Such letters and telegrams came from persons calling themselves "patriotic Democratic Americans" and a spurious Democratic Hollywood Movie Association. They were more than matched, perhaps as much as ten to one, by congratulatory messages from private citizens in this country and abroad. Especially pathetic were the pleas of a young Jewish girl in Czechoslovakia praising the president for his efforts and asking admission to the United States. In another an American Jew asked help for his relatives abroad. In a third an aged woman in this country spelled out in block letters her gratitude for all that the president had done for her people (Roosevelt Library).

87. Virtually every American newspaper played up the positive contributions of refugees to American culture and argued that admission of Jewish refugees would be a signal act of Christian charity. The Fort Worth *Star-Telegraph* went so far as to suggest swapping Nazi-minded Americans for German Jews. See "The Evian Conference: Editorial Comment," *Contemporary Jewish Record*, 1 (Sept. 1938): 47–56.

Chapter 3

1. Tartakower and Grossmann, *The Jewish Refugee*, p. 140.

2. Simpson, *The Refugee Problem: Report of a Survey*, pp. 248, 251, 261, 397.

3. Foreign Relations of the U.S., 1:743–45.

4. The list includes the Central Bureau for the Settlement of German Jews, Jewish Colonization Association, German-Jewish Aid Committee, Comité d'aide et d'assistance aux victimes d'antisémitisme en Allemagne, Comite voor Bijzondere Joodsche Belangen, Joint Foreign Committee of the Board of Deputies of British Jews and the Anglo-Jewish Association, Agudath Israel World Organization, American Joint Distribution Committee, Council for German Jewry, HICEM, World Jewish Congress, New Zionist Organization, Alliance Israelite Universelle, Comité pour le développement de la grande colonisation juive Freeland League, ORT, Centre de recherches de solutions au problème juif, Jewish Agency for Palestine, Comité pour la défense des droits des Israelites en Europe centrale et orientale, Union des Sociétés OSE, and Société d'émigration et de colonisation juive EMCOL.

5. This was the statement of British deputy Sir Michael Pailaret to Taylor in Rome. Taylor to Hull, July 1, 1938, State Department Files, 840.48/442. For the memorandum of the Jewish Agency, see Tartakower and Grossmann, pp. 538–45.

6. Nora Levin, *The Holocaust: The Destruction of European Jewry, 1933–1945* (New York: Thomas Y. Crowell, 1968), pp. 92–93.

7. Speech by Wise, Jan. 7, 1936, American Jewish Congress File, Wise Papers.

8. The memorandum also directed the conference to acknowledge the special position of Jewish refugees and to permit 100,000 Jews to emigrate to Palestine annually. For the complete statement of the World Jewish Congress, see Tartakower and Grossmann, pp. 529–37.

9. These groups were especially concerned about the possible repercussions in Poland, Hungary, and Rumania if Germany succeeded in becoming *judenrein* by force. "Memorandum of Miscellaneous Jewish Organizations," in Tartakower and Grossmann, pp. 545–55.

10. Two petitions, bearing the signatures of more than 300,000 persons, were presented to the White House. Presidential Secretary Marvin McIntyre accepted them with pro forma courtesy, and nothing more was ever done. See Petition of Jewish People's Committee, June 7, 1938, Political Refugees File, Roosevelt Library.

11. The other members were James McDonald, former League commissioner, who was lured back into refugee work as chairman of the advisory committee; Samuel McCrea Cavert of the Federal Council of Churches in America; Paul Baerwald of the American Jewish Committee; Bernard Baruch, Hamilton Fish Armstrong, Joseph Chamberlain, the Most Rev. Joseph F. Rummel, Basil Harris, James Spears, and Louis Kennedy.

12. Minutes of the 1st Meeting, May 16, 1938, President's Advisory Committee on Political Refugees File, Wise Papers.

13. Ibid. See also Memorandum of Messersmith to Hull, State Department Records, 150.01/34, in which the assistant secretary disclosed the same basic ideas to six Jewish congressmen.

14. These remarks may be found in *Proceedings of the Intergovernmental Committee, Evian, July 6 to 15, 1938. Verbatim Record of the Plenary Meetings of the Committee, Resolutions, and Reports* (July 1938), pp. 12–13, 16, 20. Hereafter cited as *Proceedings, Evian Committee.*

15. Australia, with a population of 6,000,000, had more than 500,000 square miles of land which was readily available. It was estimated that the continent could sustain a population of perhaps 25,000,000. However, the government was committed to a narrowly construed, all-white restrictionist immigration policy which did not exclude Jews but worked against them. See Dorothy Thompson, *Refugees: Anarchy or Organization* (New York: Random House, 1938): p. 84; Marie Clements, "Australia: A Haven?" *National Jewish Monthly*, 53 (Jan. 1939): 163; and Ludwig Lore, "Watchman: What of the Refugees?" *National Jewish Monthly*, 52 (Aug.–Sept. 1938): 4–5.

16. *Proceedings, Evian Committee*, p. 20.

17. By the end of Dec. 1937, Great Britain actually had given asylum to just 5,500 German refugees. Even then immigration procedures were highly selective and discriminatory against children, the aged, the disabled, the unskilled, and those without transit visas. Isaac, in *Positive Contributions by Refugees*, p. 54.

18. *Proceedings, Evian Committee,* pp. 21–25. These statements can be challenged. While arguments may be made on either side as to whether the British actually pledged themselves to create a Jewish state, there is no question that British colonial officers did little to promote the flow of Jews into Palestine. What emigration did take place was conducted by Jewish agencies and against the will of the mandatory. Proof of Britain's uncooperative action can be seen in the censure measure taken by the Permanent Mandates Commission of the League of Nations against His Majesty's Government in June 1939. For a copy of this statement, see Oscar I. Janowsky, *Foundations of Israel* (Princeton, N.J.: Anvil Press, 1959), p. 142.

19. The best description of the schemes and counter-schemes may be found in Habe's novel, *The Mission.* See also Arnold Levin, "Are Colonies the Solution?" *National Jewish Monthly, 53* (Apr. 1939): 258–59 and "Evian and Palestine," *Spectator, 161* (July 15, 1938): 92–93.

20. Representatives of these countries spoke with pride of the 40,000 refugees welcomed to Latin America since 1933. More impressive were the 171,000 immigrants accepted by Brazil between 1900 and 1939 and the six million accepted by Argentina since 1864. Delegates also could hardly be faulted for misinterpreting Mexico's pledge to remain "an asylum to foreigners who were afraid for their lives." "Evian Conference on Political Refugees," *Social Service Review, 12* (Sept. 1938): 516.

21. George Warren noted this regretful situation in his daily communiqués to Chamberlain during July. See letters of July 8, 9, 11, 1938, President's Advisory Committee on Political Refugees File, Wise Papers.

22. *Proceedings, Evian Committee,* p. 21.

23. Tartakower and Grossmann, p. 344.

24. *Proceedings, Evian Committee,* p. 25.

25. According to Samuel Inman, "Various plans for Jewish immigrants have been wrecked in recent months by exaggerated publicity which led the native population to protest at what mistakenly appeared as an overwhelming invasion of their economic security." "Refugee Settlement in Latin America," *Annals of the American Academy of Political and Social Science, 203* (May 1939): 193.

26. Mann and Estorick, "Private and Governmental Aid of Refugees," pp. 151–53.

27. Cited in Mark Wischnitzer, *The Historical Background of the Settlement of Jewish Refugees in Santo Domingo* (New York, 1942), p. 46. The Evian record does not specifically quote this offer from Trujillo.

28. In a letter to James Rosenberg, president of the Dominican Settlement Association, Roosevelt called the project "a turning point" in relief work on behalf of the Jews. Roosevelt to Rosenberg, Dec. 12, 1939, Church Matters: Jewish File, Roosevelt Library. See also Joseph Rosen, "New Neighbors in Sousa," *Survey Graphic, 30* (Sept. 1941): 474–78.

29. The *Report Covering Field Investigations of Settlement Possibilities Existent on Selected Lands in the Dominican Republic* (New York, 1939), prepared by Henry D. Barker, principal pathologist, Bureau of Plant Industry; William P. Kramer, chief of operations, Forestry Service; and A. F. Kocher, Bureau of Chemistry of Soils, Soil Conservation Service, painted a bleak picture of the Dominican's capacity to accommodate even a fraction of the proposed 100,000 immigrants.

NOTES

30. Wischnitzer, p. 47.

31. Karl Pelzer, *Settlement Possibilities in British Guiana and Surinam* (Baltimore: Institute for Pacific Relations, 1939). Another Anglo-American team, headed by Joseph Rosen, explored Guiana in the spring of 1939 and concluded that "trial settlement" was possible, even though "British Guiana is not an ideal place for refugees from Mid-European countries." Belth, "Refugee Problem," p. 382.

32. *Quest for Settlement: Summaries of Selected Economic and Geographic Reports on Settlement Possibilities for European Immigrants* (New York: Refugee Economic Corporation and Johns Hopkins University, 1948). Despite the late publication date, these manuscripts were available from the REC before World War II. Specifically, they included McBride and McBride, *Possible Central American Zones for Settlement of Refugees* (Los Angeles, 1939); Waibel, *Costa Rica: The Natural and Historic Conditions of Settlement and Possibilities for Further White Colonization* (New York, 1939); *Guatemala* (New York, 1940); *Salvador* (New York, 1940); *Report on British Honduras* (New York, 1941); Roberts, *The Republic of Panama* (Panama City, 1933); Cox, *Lower California and Its Natural Resources* (Berkeley, 1939); Strausz-Hupe, *Settlement in Venezuela* (Washington, 1945); Platt, *Settlement Possibilities in the Drought Region of Northeastern Brazil* (New York, 1939); and Golodetz and Henriques, *Report on the Possibilities of Jewish Settlement in Ecuador* (New York, 1940).

33. *Foreign Relations of the U.S.,* 1:755–57.

34. On Aug. 31, 1938, FDR sent a memo to Hull informing him that earlier that spring Hitler had told Mussolini, Henlein, and Esterhazy of Hungary that he would present the Czechs with an ultimatum about the Sudetenland in ten weeks—by Sept. 1938. He did. Roosevelt to Hull, Aug. 31, 1939, Correspondence File, Hull Papers.

35. *Foreign Relations of the U.S.,* 1:756.

36. "Who Wants Refugees?" *95* (July 20, 1938): 291.

37. Many Jews were cheered to note that they were not deemed "a superfluous part of a country's population" as a result of the consultations at Evian. See Jonah Wise, "Impressions of Evian," *Contemporary Jewish Record, 1* (Sept. 1938): 40–42. For editorial comments, see "The Evian Conference: Editorial Comment," *Contemporary Jewish Record, 1* (Sept. 1938): 47–50.

38. *Public Papers of FDR,* 7:171.

39. *Foreign Relations of the U.S.,* 1:763.

40. Ibid., p. 768. There is some question whether Hull even desired this much success. A month later he wired Biddle in Poland: "Our efforts on behalf of German refugees must not, if it can possibly be avoided, encourage persecution by other governments aimed at forcing out unwanted sections of their populations and the dumping of these people onto the hands of international charity" (p. 783).

41. Minutes of the 6th Meeting, Aug. 8, 1938, President's Advisory Committee on Political Refugees File, Wise Papers.

42. These events are reported in *Foreign Relations of the U.S.,* 1:772, 780.

43. Ibid., p. 753.

44. Ibid., p. 821.

45. In the note, delivered by Ambassador Joseph Kennedy to Chamberlain on Oct. 6, the president suggested that "it would seem reasonable to

NOTES

anticipate that the German Government will assist the other Governments . . .
to permit the arrangement of orderly emigration . . . and [to permit the
refugees] to take with them a reasonable percentage of their property." *Public
Papers of FDR*, 7:172–73.

46. Rublee's remarks are recorded in *Foreign Relations of the U.S.*, 1:796,
798, 802.

47. This special concern for Sudetenland Aryans was evident in the efforts
of the British to whisk a Czech theater group to Canada in Oct. 1938. See
letter of Lord Winterton to Myron Taylor, Correspondence File, Hull Papers.

48. *Foreign Relations of the U.S.*, 1:806.

49. Ibid., p. 829.

50. Ibid., p. 865.

51. Warren to Chamberlain, July 19, 1938, President's Advisory Committee on Political Refugees File, Wise Papers.

52. *Foreign Relations of the U.S.*, 1:825. On Dec. 13, Lord Winterton,
chairman of the IGCR, indicated that in all conflicts between his organization
and the High Commission, he was bound to support the League Commission
(p. 868).

53. Ibid., p. 822.

54. Quoted in *The American Jewish Yearbook*, 1939–1940, p. 262, this
comment originally appeared in the *Beobachter* on Nov. 13, 1938.

55. On Sept. 1, 1941, Grynszpan, who had been retried by victorious
Nazis in France, was tortured to death.

56. *The Jewish Religion in Axis Europe* (New York: Institute of Jewish
Affairs, 1942), pp. 5–9.

57. "Latest Nazi Wave of Terror," *Contemporary Jewish Record*, special
supplement, *1* (Nov. 1938): 56a–56h. The most complete study of these events
is Lionel Kochan, *Pogrom: 10 November 1938* (London: A. Deutsch, 1957).

58. *American Jewish Yearbook*, 1939–1940, p. 261.

59. Ibid., p. 263.

60. Morse, *While Six Million Died*, p. 228.

61. Minutes of the 20th Meeting, Feb. 24, 1939, President's Advisory
Committee on Political Refugees File, Wise Papers.

62. Memorandum from Nicholas Murray Butler to Hull, Correspondence
File, Hull Papers. Such information is supported by the analyses of Nora Levin,
pp. 69–94; C. E. Black and E. C. Helmreich, *Twentieth Century Europe: A
History* (New York: Alfred A. Knopf, 1966), pp. 457–58; and Alan Bullock,
Hitler: A Study in Tyranny (New York: Bantam Books, 1961), pp. 311–12.

63. *Foreign Relations of the U.S.*, 1:864.

64. N. Levin, p. 125.

65. *New York Times*, Nov. 23, 1928, p. 8.

66. Countries like France and England, with limited numbers of "good
Jews," could not comprehend the strong feeling against the Jews in Germany,
von Ribbentrop said. Rublee to Hull, Dec. 8, 1938, *Foreign Relations of the
U.S.*, 1:862–63, 872.

67. Ibid., p. 874.

68. Tartakower and Grossmann, p. 443.

69. *Foreign Relations of the U.S.*, 1:775.

70. *Public Papers of FDR*, 7:174.

71. *Foreign Relations of the U.S.*, 1:809–13.

72. Hull also remarked that the Treasury Department was concerned that the dollar would be the currency used to underwrite the entire scheme. Ibid., p. 812.

73. Ibid., p. 775.

74. *Public Papers of FDR*, 7:174.

75. *Foreign Relations of the U.S.*, 1:876.

76. Rublee to Hull, Dec. 16, 1938, ibid., p. 875.

77. Rublee to Hull, Dec. 18, 1938, ibid., p. 876.

78. Welles to Rublee, Dec. 21, 1938, ibid., pp. 878–79.

79. *New York Times*, Feb. 12, 1939, p. 1.

80. Ibid., Feb. 15, 1939, p. 1.

81. Minutes of the 21st Meeting, Mar. 6, 1939, President's Advisory Committee on Political Refugees File, Wise Papers.

82. See cable of Anthony Rothschild to George Warren, May 26, 1939, ibid.

83. The White Paper also stated that no further Jewish immigration would be permitted after 1944, that the British government would be under no obligation to create a Jewish state, and that an independent Arab state of Palestine would be proclaimed within ten years. In every essential aspect, it was a violation of the original League mandate. See H. C. Allen, *Great Britain and the United States: A History of Anglo-American Relations* (New York: St. Martin's Press, 1955), p. 916.

84. Long before the issuance of the White Paper, Rabbi Abba Silver of the ZOA and Solomon Goldman of the WZO exchanged telegrams warning that any closing of Palestine to Jewish immigration would mark the total failure of the IGCR. See Goldman to Silver, Oct. 11, 1938, Zionist Organization of America File, 1938–1939, Abba Silver Papers, the Temple Library, Cleveland.

85. *Foreign Relations of the U.S., General, British Commonwealth and Europe*, 2:39. A good example of this was Wise's rejection of any settlement plan for the Jews in Africa in lieu of Palestine. Apart from the indignity of asking refined Europeans to settle in the backward former German colonies of East Africa, Wise objected that "there will be an element of reprisal if Jews were to occupy the once German territories. The destruction of these Jewishly-occupied territories would become one of the supreme objectives of the German Reich." Wise to Taylor, Nov. 23, 1938, FDR File, Wise Papers.

86. "The German police will not dictate what the Committee can or cannot do," Winterton commented. *Foreign Relations of the U.S.*, 2:110–14.

87. Pell wrote to Hull, "To ask the general public and its representatives in Congress, most of whom have no direct interest in the problem other than a remote humanitarian one, to approve expenditures for this purpose would be utopian." Ibid., pp. 135–36.

88. Belth, p. 390.

89. *Public Papers of FDR*, 8:360–61.

90. Ibid., p. 361.

91. Ibid., pp. 546–47.

92. Memorandum of George Warren for President's Advisory Committee, Nov. 6, 1939, President's Advisory Committee on Political Refugees File, Wise Papers.

93. Minutes of the Co-Ordinating Foundation of the IGCR, Oct. 30, 1939,

Refugee File, Wise Papers. Van Zeeland did little but visit Latin America and the U.S. during the first years of the war, mainly to generate interest in the foundation. After 1944 it was absorbed by UNRRA. See Report of Van Zeeland, Dec. 29, 1943, Refugee File, Wise Papers.

94. Report of Emerson to John Winant, Aug. 1942, Correspondence File, Hull Papers.

95. *Public Papers of FDR*, 8:364.

96. Emerson repeated his comments to the 20th Ordinary Session of the League of Nations on Aug. 18, 1939. His dreary, ten-page report held out little hope of solution of the refugee problem. League of Nations, International Bureaux, *International Assistance to Refugees* (XII.B,1–4) (Geneva, 1939).

97. N. Levin, p. 127.

Chapter 4

1. *Foreign Relations of the U.S.*, 2:396–98.

2. "Americans Protest Pogrom," *National Jewish Monthly*, 53 (Dec. 1938): 131.

3. "German Crisis Arouses the World," *National Jewish Monthly*, 53 (Dec. 1938): 124–25.

4. Hans Thompson, German chargé d'affaires in Washington, issued a protest to Welles several days later. The undersecretary rejected it, saying that Ickes was entitled to his own opinion and adding that it was ironic that Germany should protest in view of Nazi vituperations against Roosevelt. See *The Secret Diary of Harold L. Ickes: The Inside Struggle* (New York: Simon & Schuster, 1954), 2:503–504.

5. "German Crisis," p. 125.

6. National Executive of the American Legion to Roosevelt, Nov. 19, 1938, Germany 1933–1945 File, Roosevelt Library.

7. "German Crisis," p. 150.

8. "Statement of Henry Ford," *National Jewish Monthly*, 53 (Jan. 1939): 156.

9. This last figure was more a reaction to the Germans' confiscation of property belonging to American nationals (who, coincidentally, were Jewish) than to abuses of Jews per se. See "American Institute of Public Opinion: Surveys, 1938–1939," *Public Opinion Quarterly*, 3 (1939): 581–607.

10. *New York Times*, Dec. 23, 1938, p. 4.

11. *Public Papers of FDR*, 7:597.

12. Ibid., p. 598.

13. The editors of *Commonweal* even demanded the suspension of all financial guarantees for the refugees. See "No Room at the Inn," *Commonweal*, 29 (Nov. 18, 1939): 86; "Editorial Comment," *Commonweal*, 29 (Nov. 25, 1938): 113; Gregory Feige, "Shall the Jew Perish?" *Commonweal*, 29 (Dec. 9, 1938): 176–77. See also "Refugees and Economics," *The Nation*, 147 (Dec. 10, 1938): 609–11; Robert Dell, "Hope for Refugees," *The Nation*, 147 (Aug. 6, 1938): 126–28; and Freda Kirchwey, "Jews and Refugees," *The Nation*, 148 (May 20, 1939): 577–78; "Let the Jews Come In," *The New Republic*, 97 (Nov. 30, 1938): 60; "For the Refugees," *The New Republic*, 97 (Dec. 21, 1938): 189; "Refugee Children," *The New Republic*, 97 (Jan. 25, 1939): 327.

14. "The Refugee Puzzle," *The New Republic,* 97 (Nov. 30, 1938): 87.

15. Perkins informed the president that there was no public outcry to justify any change in our laws. Readings of the Gallup and Roper polls confirm her position. Morse, *While Six Million Died,* p. 236.

16. *Public Papers of FDR,* 7:602–604.

17. According to Isaiah Bowman, as many as 10,000 families might comfortably have settled in Costa Rica. Morgenthau to Roosevelt, Nov. 21, 1938, Refugee Folder, Roosevelt Library. This and similar settlement schemes had been fully debated by the President's Advisory Committee as early as Oct. 13. They had been rejected then by most experts as unrealistic and idealistic. See Minutes of Oct. 13, 1938, President's Advisory Committee on Political Refugees File, Wise Papers.

18. *Foreign Relations of the U.S.,* 1:837–55.

19. Among the more bizarre plans that crossed Hull's desk was one from Mexico which indicated that government's willingness to accept immigrants who established "mestizo" families in Mexico. Whether this meant a desire to become a naturalized citizen or to intermarry with a renunciation of the Jewish faith, no one at the State Department was able to say. In any case, prospects for mass settlement in Mexico appeared slim. For Hull's memorandum to Roosevelt, Nov. 28, 1938, see Refugee Folder, Roosevelt Library.

20. In Jan. 1939 a group of Austrian Jews bound for the Dominican Republic was stranded in the U.S. because of new laws passed after they had sailed from Europe. At the same time, thirty-seven passengers aboard the S.S. *Imperial* were denied admission to Peru because their documents were said to be invalid. Several days later Paraguay revoked the immigration permits of 300 Jewish refugees, leaving them stranded in Uruguay. Twenty-three refugees aboard the S.S. *Orinoco* were repulsed by Mexico after they had succeeded in bribing the Mexican consul in Germany for their papers. At the end of the month another eighty-three Jewish refugees aboard the S.S. *Caribia* were denied passage into Trinidad.

At first these unfortunates could find eventual havens in other Latin American nations, but these countries also tightened up their restrictions as Jews continued to pour across the Atlantic. In March, Uruguay refused to admit another group of Jews. In May, Chile suspended all immigration for a year. Twelve days later Colombia followed suit. A week later Jewish agencies in Bolivia exposed a plot to sell Jews permission to settle in that country.

The worst incident, however, took place in June, when the Cuban government of Laredo Bru revoked the landing permits of 907 passengers aboard the S.S. *St. Louis.* After considering the idea of extorting $1,000,000 from Jewish organizations in the U.S. for the passengers' safety, the Cuban government forced the *St. Louis* out to sea. For the near-happy ending of this tale see Morse, pp. 270–88. For details on the other incidents see Cecilia Razovsky, "Disorganized Panic Emigration," speech prepared for the National Coordinating Committee, Feb. 1939, Chamberlain Papers; and *New York Times,* Mar. 10, 1939, p. 5; May 5, 1939, p. 13; May 17, 1939, p. 13; May 25, 1939, p. 13.

21. Jews were no longer welcome in South Africa, Ceylon, the Philippines, or Shanghai, China, which included about 20,000 Jewish immigrants in its foreign colony by 1939. For this distressing side of the refugee problem, see David Popper, "A Homeland for Refugees," *Annals of the American Academy*

of Political and Social Science, 203 (May 1939): 168–76; and Simpson, *Refugees: A Review Since September, 1938,* pp. 107–10. For accounts of the Jews in Shanghai, see Albert Jovishoff, "A City of Refugees," *Menorah Journal, 27* (Spring 1939): 209–16; "Hitler Presents Shanghai with Another Relief Problem," *China Weekly Review, 87* (Dec. 24, 1938): 108–109; "Shanghai Receives More Victims of Anti-Semitism; Cuba Rejects 900," *China Weekly Review, 89* (June 10, 1939): 48; and "Shanghai Authorities Slam Door in Face of Refugees," *China Weekly Review, 89* (Aug. 19, 1939): 368.

22. *Foreign Relations of the U.S., 1*:858–60.

23. Several months later Goering and Hitler delighted in accusing Roosevelt of "creeping paralysis of the brain" when the president naïvely sought guarantees from Germany that it had no territorial designs on thirty-one states, including the Arabias and Liechtenstein. Despite newsreels showing Nazi deputies laughing hysterically at Hitler's reading of his note, Roosevelt followed it up with another dated Aug. 24, 1939, which began: "To the message which I sent you last April, I have received no reply." Roosevelt to Hitler, Germany 1933–1945 File, Roosevelt Library.

24. *Foreign Relations of the U.S., 1*:886.

25. Mussolini charged that if the United States opened its doors to a population comparable in density with that of Italy, this nation could accommodate at least one billion more immigrants. N. Levin, *The Holocaust,* p. 127.

26. At the same time, Rabbi M. L. Perlzweig of the British section of the World Jewish Congress rejected any proposed settlement in Djibouti. Memorandum of the World Jewish Congress to the IGCR, Jan. 16, 1939, World Jewish Congress File, Wise Papers.

27. Burns, *Roosevelt: The Lion and the Fox,* p. 337.

28. In Jan. 1939, Elmo Roper reported that 67 percent of the American people opposed any major legislative or administrative changes in government. This conservatism was also directed against Roosevelt, as only 33 percent of those polled indicated a willingness to vote for the president if he ran again in 1940, while 55 percent said no to a third term. *You and Your Leaders: Their Actions and Your Reactions, 1936–1956* (New York: William Morrow and Co., 1957), pp. 30–38.

29. Rosenman warned that any legislative debate over the problem would merely delay comprehensive international action. In view of the threatened magnitude of the Jewish refugee problem in Poland and Rumania, Rosenman argued for immediate settlement in new and undeveloped regions of Africa or South America. That leaders of Jewish organizations, especially Zionist groups, had always opposed such proposals made little impact upon Rosenman, who worried about the threat of a tidal wave of Jews, and only Jews, coming to the U.S. in this emergency. Memorandum of Rosenman to Roosevelt, Dec. 5, 1938, Personal Correspondence File, Roosevelt Library.

30. U.S., Congress, Joint Subcommittee of the Senate Committee on Immigration and the House Committee on Immigration and Naturalization, *Hearings on the Admission of German Refugee Children, S. J. R. 64 and H. J. R. 168,* 76th Cong., 1st Sess., 1939, p. 66.

31. The first group did not arrive until Feb. 15, 1935, over the opposition of John Trevor's American Coalition, which exhorted Americans "to be on guard" against this subversion of their immigration laws. See German-Jewish Children's Aid File, Chamberlain Collection.

32. According to a lengthy study done by the German-Jewish Children's Aid, none of the children admitted in the previous four years had encountered significant difficulties in social, educational, or vocational adjustment. Thirty-two thus admitted had already achieved self-support. Memorandum of German-Jewish Children's Aid, Jan. 1, 1939, ibid. Spewack wanted to bring in *all* refugee children from Germany and Austria who were under age ten. Memorandum of Rosenwald to Chamberlain, Dec. 2, 1938, ibid.

33. Minutes of the 14th Meeting, Dec. 23, 1938, President's Advisory Committee on Political Refugees File, Wise Papers.

34. According to Rosenwald, Isidor Lubin had said that Perkins was trying to instigate legislation in Congress to enable German Jewish children to come over as immigrants, but not under the quota system. Precisely the same idea was embodied in the Wagner-Rogers Bill. Memorandum of Rosenwald to Chamberlain, Dec. 2, 1938, Chamberlain Collection.

35. *Hearings on German Refugee Children*, p. 9.

36. *American Jewish Yearbook*, 1939–1940, p. 380.

37. Pickett vividly described the terror and insecurity felt by non-Aryan children who were spat upon, insulted, and physically degraded merely because of their Jewish lineage. *Hearings on German Refugee Children*, p. 57. Sidney Hollander, a Jewish member of the Non-Sectarian Committee, told of children who had seen their parents taken to concentration camps because they were Jewish and who subsequently had received urns containing their fathers' ashes. Hollander also told of a Jewish orphanage in Vienna which was closed down without warning in the middle of the night. The children, the eldest aged three, were carried from door to door in search of shelter (p. 91). Robert Balderston of Chicago, just back from two months' volunteer work in the soup kitchens operated by the Friends amid no-man's lands, described the plight of Jews in these purgatories (pp. 72–78). And Robert Yarnall, a Philadelphia engineer and a Quaker who had worked in Germany under the Hoover Child Welfare Administration after World War I, reported, "I am convinced there is no future for Jewish or non-Aryan children in Greater Germany now or in the near future" (p. 134).

38. See Legislative Correspondence, 1939: Child Refugees, Pro Folder, Wagner Papers, Georgetown University, Washington, D.C.

39. *New York Times*, Feb. 9, 1939, p. 5.

40. U.S., Congress, Senate, Congressional Record, 76th Cong., 1st Sess., 1939, *84*, pt. 2:2338–41, 2805; pt. 4:3865; pt. 5:4817, 5200; and pt. 11:641.

41. *Hearings on H. J. Res. 165 and H. J. Res. 168*, p. 114.

42. The Wagner file includes several hundred negative letters, including some which accused the senator of being a tool of Wall Street and one which threatened, "You are getting in too deep with some people. BEWARE. I say it again." Still, the ratio of letters ran about three to two in favor of the measure. Legislative Correspondence, 1939: Child Refugees, Con Folder, Wagner Papers.

43. *Hearings on H. J. Res. 165 and H. J. Res. 168*, p. 215.

44. *Hearings on German Refugee Children*, p. 207.

45. *Hearings on H. J. Res. 165 and H. J. Res. 168*, p. 133.

46. *Hearings on German Refugee Children*, p. 187.

47. Ibid., p. 210.

48. The most striking testimony along these lines was given by Agnes Waters, a resident of Washington, speaking as an individual, not for some

organization. She charged that 7,000,000 such alien saboteurs already were roaming the land. When the committee finally dismissed her with disgust, she continued, calling Rep. John Lesinski (D.-Mich.), who had risen to leave, "a Third Internationale." *Hearings on H. J. Res. 165 and H. J. Res. 168,* p. 256. The notion that the Jews were Nazis was also held by James Patton and James Wilmeth of the Junior Order of American Mechanics, ibid., pp. 119, 232.

49. See circular dated Feb. 20, 1939, Chamberlain Collection.

50. Rep. Noah Mason (D.-Ill.) drew applause when he challenged her by saying, "I was eight when I entered this country and I claim that I have become quite Americanized." *Hearings on German Refugee Children,* p. 225.

51. *Hearings on H. J. Res. 165 and H. J. Res. 168,* pp. 37–38.

52. *Hearings on German Refugee Children,* pp. 49, 97, 160.

53. Ibid., pp. 66–70, and *Hearings on H. J. Res. 165 and H. J. Res. 168,* pp. 25–30, 37, 62, 101.

54. Letter from Taft to Rose Frank, May 11, 1939, Immigrants and Immigration File, Jewish Archives, Hebrew Union College, Cincinnati.

55. *Hearings on H. J. Res. 165 and H. J. Res. 168,* pp. 24, 33, 43, 47, 78, 262.

56. Ibid., p. 104.

57. *Hearings on German Refugee Children,* pp. 59, 85–88.

58. *Hearings on H. J. Res. 165 and H. J. Res. 168,* p. 22.

59. *Hearings on German Refugee Children,* pp. 49, 59, 118. Such guarantees were hardly necessary, because Avra Warren of the State Department pointed out that the LPC clause had never been applied against children (p. 271).

60. *Hearings on H. J. Res. 165 and H. J. Res. 168,* p. 169.

61. Letter from Taft to Rose Frank, May 11, 1939, Immigrants and Immigration File, Jewish Archives.

62. *Hearings on German Refugee Children,* p. 224.

63. Ibid., pp. 190, 208.

64. *Hearings on H. J. Res. 165 and H. J. Res. 168,* p. 190.

65. *Hearings on German Refugee Children,* pp. 113, 125–30, 144, 150.

66. Ibid., p. 144.

67. Ibid., p. 150.

68. On Wise's attempts to win the support of Thomas Dewey, see the letters to Murray Garfein, one of Dewey's assistants, Apr. 26 and May 9, 1939, Refugee Children File, Wise Papers.

69. Auer was mollified by a letter disclaiming responsibility for the fate of the legislation which was based on suggestions made to Wise by his daughter. Auer to Wise, May 16, 1939, ibid.

70. Sen. Reynolds often recalled that Dickstein, a Jew, had said of the Johnson Act, "I believe in restriction, certainly. We cannot afford to open our doors." For Dickstein's reference to a flood of illegals, see the *New York Sun,* Mar 7, 1939, p. 1.

71. See Chamberlain's angry exchanges with Kepecs, June 16, 1939, Chamberlain Collection.

72. In the first months of 1939, Green wrote letters to Spencer Miller of the National Council of Protestant Episcopal Churches in the U.S. and to Chamberlain in which he repeatedly cautioned against "overdoing the situation" or breaking down "our quota statutes." Green to Miller, Jan. 25, 1939, and Green to Chamberlain, Feb. 22, 1939, ibid.

73. *Hearings on H. J. Res. 165 and H. J. Res. 168,* pp. 4–14.

74. The same standard was not used to impugn the testimony of Col. Thomas Taylor of the American Legion when he noted that that body had come out against the bill in May 1939. Jewish members of the legion testified that no such resolution had ever been debated in the group's convention at New York. Ibid., p. 280.

75. U.S., Congress, Senate, Subcommittee of the Committee on Immigration, *Hearings on S.407, S.408, S.409, S.410, S.411 To Restrict Immigration,* 76th Cong., 1st Sess., 1939, p. 131.

76. *Hearings on German Refugee Children,* p. 70.

77. *Hearings on H. J. Res. 165 and H. J. Res. 168,* p. 92.

78. Ibid., pp. 91–97.

79. Sen. Rufus Holman of Oregon became embroiled in a debate with Ralph Emerson of the CIO as to whether the organization was "American" or "international" in its makeup and orientation. Similar innuendoes about pro-communist activities were hurled against other witnesses supporting the bill, chief among them being Read Lewis of the International Migration Service. *Hearings on S.407, 408, 409, 410, 411,* pp. 64, 150.

80. *Hearings on H. J. Res. 165 and H. J. Res. 168,* p. 244.

81. *Hearings on S.407, 408, 409, 410, 411,* pp. 7–10, 53–55.

82. *Hearings on H. J. Res. 165 and II. J. Res. 168,* p. 71.

83. *Hearings on German Refugee Children,* p. 2.

84. *Washington Post,* Apr. 27, 1939, p. 4.

85. Cable from Eleanor Roosevelt to FDR, Feb. 22, 1939, Personal Correspondence File, Roosevelt Library.

86. *Washington Post,* Apr. 27, 1939, p. 4.

87. *Hearings on H. J. Res. 165 and H. J. Res. 168,* pp. 67, 73, 198, 226, 240, 257, 267.

88. Day to Roosevelt, June 2, 1939, Political Refugee File, Roosevelt Library.

89. *Hearings on H. J. Res. 165 and H. J. Res. 168,* pp. 229–31.

90. Ibid., p. 81.

91. Collection of Speeches Made by Wagner During the 76th Congress, July, 1938–June 22, 1940, Wagner Papers, pt.1:27.

92. *New York Times,* July 1, 1939, pp. 3, 8.

93. *New York Times,* July 3, 1939, p. 3.

94. U.S., Congress, Senate, Committee on Immigration, *Report #757 on the Temporary Prohibition of Immigration of Aliens,* 76th Cong., 1st Sess., Sec. 19.

95. "Children," in Cantril, *Public Opinion,* p. 1081.

Chapter 5

1. Fanny Adlerstein, *Special Report on Jewish Refugees,* American Joint Distribution Committee, Jan. 21, 1941, in American Friends Service Committee Library, Philadelphia.

2. This plan called for the admission to the United States of large numbers of Jewish refugees on temporary visas, transport to be supplied by neutral nations at cost to the American Jewish community. See Mark Wischnitzer,

Visas to Freedom: The History of HIAS (Cleveland: World Publishing, 1956), p. 160.

3. *National Refugee Service Information Bulletin #3*, Dec. 20, 1939, p. 2. A year later the American Jewish Congress received word that Jewish leaders in Germany had been summoned to a special meeting with Gestapo Col. "Julius" Eichmann, "a native Palestinian who speaks Hebrew fluently." Even then, after the fall of France, they were told that Europe must be free of Jews, but that the Nazis would cooperate with emigration to Palestine, Kenya, Australia, or Madagascar. Lillie Shultz to Wise, Sept. 11, 1940, American Jewish Congress File, Wise Papers.

4. The American Export Line alone accepted 10,000 bookings before the Maritime Commission in Washington ordered it to halt on Mar. 14, 1941. For a discussion of shipping possibilities between 1939 and 1941, see Tartakower and Grossmann, *The Jewish Refugee,* pp. 205–206.

5. Ibid., p. 205.

6. The American vessel *McKeesport* left Marseilles in July 1940 with scores of refugees standing on the quais and no passengers on board. The explanation offered by consular officials for their failure to expedite clearance of refugees was the need to abide by all immigration regulations, including meticulous review of the refugees' papers. Some persons argued that they were being overly scrupulous. See Jay Allen, "Refugees and American Defense," *Survey Graphic, 19* (Oct. 1940): 488.

7. The British government, concerned about its vital communication links and oil supplies in the Middle East and worried that additional Jewish immigration might lead the Arabs into the Axis camp, had 20,000 men on duty in Palestine to ward off these vessels. Winston Churchill, *The Second World War: Their Finest Hour* (Boston: Houghton-Mifflin, 1949), 2:173.

8. Tartakower and Grossmann, pp. 70–71. No accurate statistics are available, but Mark Wischnitzer chronicled the voyages of most of these ill-fated Balkan vessels in *To Dwell in Safety: The Story of Jewish Migration Since 1800* (Philadelphia: Jewish Publication Society of America, 1949), pp. 228–55, and estimated that as many as 10,000 persons died on vessels that were rebuffed from Palestine by the British.

9. Wischnitzer, *Visas to Freedom,* pp. 164–65.

10. Ultimately this group did gain admission to the United States. "Chronicles," *Contemporary Jewish Record, 4* (Oct. 1941): 543, and N. Levin, *The Holocaust,* pp. 140–41.

11. When Goldmann pointed out that Hull had permitted anti-Nazi German sailors who jumped ship to remain in the country and that the secretary could not very readily turn away the refugees if they did the same, Hull said angrily, "You are the most cynical man I have ever met." Morse, *While Six Million Died,* pp. 30–31.

12. Bruno Lasker, "An Atlas of Hope," *Survey Graphic, 19* (Nov. 1940): 586.

13. The best contemporary study of the Jews under the Nazi conquerors before the Germans implemented outright genocide is Simon Segal, *The New Order in Poland* (New York: Alfred A. Knopf, 1942). Americans also learned of this persecution in Poland through their daily newspapers. See the *New York Times,* Oct. 31, 1939, p. 3; Nov. 2, 1939, p. 10; Nov. 3, 1939, p. 9; Nov. 26, 1939, p. 34. Detailed accounts of life in a ghetto could also be found in Freda

Kirchwey, "Jews in Hitler's Poland," *The Nation, 150* (Jan. 20, 1940): 61–62; Howard Daniel, "Mass Murder in Poland," *The Nation, 150* (Jan. 27, 1940): 92–94; Bess Demaree, "Poland in Chains: German General Government, Warsaw Pattern," *Saturday Evening Post 213* (Apr. 5, 1941): 12–13 ff.; and Leib Spiesman, "In the Warsaw Ghetto," *Contemporary Jewish Record, 4* (Aug. 1941): 357–66.

14. *Bulletins* 1, 2, and 3 of the American Friends Service Committee, issued in Oct. 1941, describe the misery of 40,000 trapped refugees, most of them Jews, in camps at Rivesaltes, Vernet, Rieveres, Gurs, Rocebedou, Noe, Les Milles, Septfords, Barcares, Timinus, Levant, and Lagviche. American Friends Service Committee Library.

15. *Addresses upon the American Road, 1940–1941* (New York: Charles Scribner's Sons, 1941), p. 117.

16. *Further Addresses upon the American Road, 1938–1940* (New York: Charles Scribner's Sons, 1940), p. 244.

17. Roosevelt had nearly abandoned hope for achieving anything through the Intergovernmental Committee after the chilly response he received from Britain on expanding the role of the IGCR in Oct. 1939. The Division of European Affairs of the State Department also considered the IGCR inoperative. Memorandum to Hull, Mar. 7, 1940, Personal Correspondence, Hull Papers.

18. Houghteling to FDR, Jan. 5, 1940, Immigration File: 1933–1945, Roosevelt Library.

19. "Immigration and the Position of Aliens in the U.S.," *International Labour Review, 42* (Dec. 1940): 402.

20. Stember et al., *Jews in the Mind of America*, p. 92. This figure is consistent with the expressed level of anti-Semitism throughout the war years. Roper, for instance, indicated that 42 percent of 5,000 persons polled in Nov. 1942 would object to living next door to Jewish neighbors. Ibid., p. 96. The ORC reported that 40 to 60 percent of the Gentile Americans polled would counsel against marrying a Jew (pp. 104–105). Roughly the same percentage believed that Jews had too much power in the U.S. and questioned Jewish patriotism (pp. 116, 121).

21. "Immigration and the Position of Aliens," p. 400.

22. Francis Kalnay and R. Collins, *The New America* (New York: Greenberg Publishers, 1941).

23. State v. Carrel, 99 *Ohio Statutes* 285 (1919).

24. "Immigration and the Position of Aliens," p. 402.

25. Roosevelt to Biddle, Jan. 2, 1942, Immigration File: 1933–1945, Roosevelt Library.

26. Biddle to FDR, Nov. 6, 1941, ibid.

27. "Chronicles," *Contemporary Jewish Record, 5* (Oct. 1942): 420.

28. "Refugees and American Defense," p. 486.

29. "The Jews Are Not Alone," *The Nation, 151* (Nov. 9, 1940): 443–44. Zukerman subsequently defended his interpretation of events in Europe in defiance of the actual massacre of Jews. According to him, "Nazi anti-Semitism is generally recognized as one of the greatest political frauds of the century." Zukerman believed that the persecution of the Jews had won them more friends in Europe. "The Jewish Problem—The Greatest Bubble of the Age," *Antioch Review, 11* (Sept. 1942): 439–56.

30. On the conditions in the camps, see Simpson, *Refugees: A Review*

Since September, 1938, pp. 26–31, 33–36, 47, 63–67, 69–81; and Tartakower and Grossmann, pp. 101–20.

31. Cable of Emerson to George Warren, June 7, 1940, President's Advisory Committee on Political Refugees File, Wise Papers.

32. Minutes of the 35th Meeting, ibid.

33. *New York Times,* July 9, 1940, p. 1.

34. The government would not even consider sending surplus commodities abroad, where they might be used by starving refugees. Mordecai Ezekiel explained that the government did not actually own such surpluses and that complex procedures involving farmers, several government agencies, and retailers would have to be worked out before the use of grain or cotton could be considered. Ezekiel to Warren, Feb. 9, 1940, President's Advisory Committee on Political Refugees File, Wise Papers.

35. Disposition of these funds encountered difficulties with the British blockade. George Warren, "International Social Work," *Social Work Yearbook,* 6 (1941): 273.

36. *New York Times,* July 26, 1940, p. 7.

37. Fermi, *Illustrious Immigrants,* p. 85.

38. Welles to Attorney General Robert Jackson, Nov. 23, 1940, Political Refugees File, Roosevelt Library.

39. The State Department delayed, awaiting Vichy approval for the fictitious return of the "visitors." It never came, since it was the policy of the Laval government to wait until emigrants presented their entry permits before granting exit permits. State also possessed Johnson's list of names more than a month before it was pared and made public. As a result, by Dec. 19, 1940, only 238 visas had been issued. Minutes of the 42nd Meeting, Dec. 19, 1940, President's Advisory Committee on Political Refugees File, Wise Papers.

40. Memorandum of Breckinridge Long to Roosevelt, Jan. 6, 1941, Political Refugees File, Roosevelt Library. About this time the president pressed the Justice and State departments for special rulings to permit such visitors to go to Canada, where they could be certified as bona fide immigrants and be issued regular quota visas. Divine, *American Immigration Policy,* p. 103.

41. U.S., Congress, Hearings before the Committee on Immigration and Naturalization, *To Provide a Temporary Haven from the Dangers or Effects of War for European Children under the Age of 16,* 76th Cong., 3d Sess., 1940, p. 20.

42. Richard Titmuss, *History of the Second World War: Problems of Social Policy,* United Kingdom Civil Series, ed. W. K. Hancock (London: Longmans, Green & Co., 1950), p. 246.

43. *Hearings to Provide a Temporary Haven,* pp. 3, 14.

44. "The Evacuation of Refugee Children Our Responsibility," *Social Service Review, 14* (Sept. 1940): 544.

45. "World War 1939–1945: Refugees," in Cantril, *Public Opinion,* p. 1150.

46. Titmuss, p. 247. This compares unfavorably with the relocation of 1,400,000 children, women, aged, and sick persons in the British Isles in 1939–1940 (ibid., p. 103).

47. "The Evacuation of the Refugee Children," p. 543.

48. Morse, p. 293.

49. See Elsa Castendyck, "Refugee Children in Europe," *Social Science Review, 13* (Dec. 1939): 587–61.

50. According to Helen Eckerson, chief of the Statistical Section of the Department of Naturalization and Immigration, no sizable number of British children was ever accorded special immigration rights during the war. Personal interview with Eckerson, June 5, 1968.

51. Chamberlain to Roosevelt, June 18, 1940, President's Advisory Committee on Political Refugees File, Wise Papers.

52. Lavine, *Fifth Column in America*, p. 5.

53. "Americans vs. Fifth Columnists," *Survey Graphic, 29* (Nov. 1940): 545–50; Werner Guttmann, "What Is the Fifth Column?" *Survey Graphic, 29* (Oct. 1940): 503–508.

54. Nathaniel Weyl, *The Battle Against Disloyalty* (New York: Thomas Y. Crowell, 1951), p. 164.

55. Strasser, "Hitler on the River Plata," *Current History, 53* (May 1941): 27–28; Lubell, "War by Refugee," *Saturday Evening Post, 13* (Mar. 29, 1941): 12–13; and Keyhoe and Daly, "Hitler's Slave Spies in America," *American Magazine, 131* (Apr. 1941): 14–15.

56. *New York Times*, Aug. 28, 1940, p. 2, and Ogden, *The Dies Committee*, p. 209. Dies left little room for doubt that the real threat came from the Jewish-dominated communists. Martin Dies, *Martin Dies' Story* (New York: Bookmailer, 1963), pp. 53, 98–99.

57. *New York Times*, Aug. 21, 1940, p. 9.

58. *The War Diary of Breckinridge Long*, ed. Fred L. Israel (Lincoln: University of Nebraska Press, 1966), p. 134. Hereafter cited as *Long Diary*.

59. Feb. 11, 1941, p. 7.

60. See "Breckinridge Long," *Current Biography* (1943), pp. 454–57, and *Long Diary*, pp. 106, 150.

61. Long to Coulter, Visa Division, Aug. 30, 1940, Visa File, Long Papers, Library of Congress, Washington, D.C.

62. Long to Hull, May 1943, Refugee Movement and Nationality Groups File, Long Papers.

63. Morse, pp. 38–42.

64. On Oct. 31, 1941 the Visa Division reported that it was processing 2,000–3,000 alien applications a week. Ninety percent of these came from Europe. And of these more than 80 percent were applications of Jewish refugees. Benton to Warren, Oct. 31, 1941, Visa File, Long Papers.

65. Dec. 23, 1940, ibid.

66. On the availability of vessels, see Long to Welles, July 11, 1940, ibid. According to Admiral Emory Land of the U.S. Maritime Commission, such rescue operations were not inconceivable because several large vessels, including the *Sibboney, Manhattan*, and *Washington*, were available for such an exodus. Land to Long, Mar. 24, 1941, Special Division, Shipping File, ibid. For the second remark, see *Long Diary*, p. 119. Long derisively noted that everybody in the U.S. had somebody they wanted to bring out of Europe and predicted that enthusiasm for the rescue of the British children would soon wane (p. 109).

67. *PM*, Feb. 11, 1941, p. 7.

68. Long to Warren, June 2, 1941, Visa File, Long Papers, and Long to Travers, Dec. 16, 1943, ibid.

69. Long to Warren, June 17, 1940, Visa File, Long Papers.

70. *Long Diary*, p. 117.

71. Long to Berle, Feb. 7, 1941, Visa File, Long Papers.

72. *Long Diary,* p. 135.

73. Ibid., p. 154. For additional comments by Long on the threat of the Nazis through the manipulation of refugees, see pp. 156–57.

74. Long for Hull, Oct. 1, 1940, Visa File, Long Papers.

75. Long assented to the plan only after these officials agreed that consuls should scrutinize all applicants to sift out those who might engage in activities deemed dangerous to the interest of the U.S. See Memorandums of Long for Hull, Oct. 3 and Oct. 18, 1940, ibid.

76. Long Memorandum, Nov. 13, 1940, ibid.

77. Warren to Hackworth, Legal Division, Feb. 4, 1941, ibid.

78. Alexander to Long, Feb. 2, 1944, ibid.

79. Alexander to Long, May 7, 1943, Refugee Movement and Nationality Groups File, ibid.

80. Minutes of the Meeting of American Delegates to Bermuda Conference, Apr. 25, 1943, p. 25, ibid.

81. Long to Hull, Jan. 6, 1941, Visa File, ibid.

82. Hull to Long, Feb. 7, 1941, ibid. About the same time Hull made it clear that the U.S. would not countenance any French scheme to dump 300,000 Jews (the terms used by Premier Laval and Ambassador Gaston Henry-Haye) on the Western Hemisphere, since the U.S. would never accord preferential treatment to any ethnic or religious group and would not be a party to any international action which might be interpreted as pressuring governments to do more than already permitted by existing laws. Tartakower and Grossmann, p. 203.

83. Steinhardt to Long, May 8, 1941, Refugee Movement and Nationality Groups File, ibid.

84. Report of Long to Hull, May 1, 1941, Visa File, ibid.

85. The comments come from Long's speech to the Rotary Club of Chattanooga in the summer of 1941 but are representative of his utterances during this period. See U.S., *Department of State Bulletins, 4* (June 28, 1941): 761–64.

86. *The Shaping of American Diplomacy,* ed. William A. Williams (Chicago: Rand McNally, 1963), 2:844–86.

87. Tartakower and Grossmann, p. 473.

88. Long to Roosevelt, Aug. 20, 1941, Political Refugees File, Roosevelt Library.

89. Alexander to Long, Feb. 2, 1944, Refugee File, Long Papers. Biddle testified in the report of Nov. 1942, that the screening process had "worked well" and added, "It is my judgment, therefore, that the present procedure for control of issuance of visas is satisfactory."

90. Hull to Roosevelt, Aug. 11, 1942, Miscellaneous Immigration File, Roosevelt Library.

91. Long to Roosevelt, Aug. 20, 1941, Political Refugees File, Roosevelt Library.

92. Einstein to Eleanor Roosevelt, July 26, 1941, Roosevelt Library.

93. For the recommendations of this conference, held on Feb. 28 and Mar. 1, 1941, see Political Refugee File, Roosevelt Library.

94. Minutes of the 50th Meeting, Sept. 4, 1941, President's Advisory Committee on Political Refugees File, Wise Papers.

95. The measure had been defeated in Congress only two weeks earlier, on Nov. 20.

96. U.S., Congress, House, *Hearings Before the House Committee on Foreign Affairs on HR 350 and HR 352: Resolutions Providing for the Establishment by the Executive of a Commission to Effectuate the Rescue of the Jewish People of Europe*, 78th Cong., 1st Sess. (1943), p. 21.

97. Hull, *Memoirs* (New York: Macmillan, 1948), 2:1539.

98. U.S., Congress, House, *Hearings Before House Committee on Immigration and Naturalization on HR 2190: To Admit 400,000 Refugees into the U.S.*, 80th Cong., 1st Sess. (1947), p. 303.

99. Bernard, *American Immigration Policy*, pp. 150–51. See also Israel Cohen, "Jews in the Allied War Effort," *Contemporary Jewish Record*, 5 (Aug. 1942: 373–89.

100. John B. Gavitt, *Americans by Choice* (New York: Harper and Bros., 1922), pp. 267–68.

101. Earl G. Harrison, "Axis Aliens in an Emergency," *Survey Graphic*, 30 (Sept. 1941): 465–68.

102. Petran and Walton, p. 7.

103. U.S., Department of Justice, *Administrative Decisions under Immigration and Nationality Laws, Aug. 1940–Dec. 1943*, ed. Edwina Austin Avery (Washington, 1917), 1:390–95, 563–70.

104. "Editorial Comment," *The Nation*, 151 (Aug. 3, 1940): 83.

105. *Long Diary*, pp. 114, 135, 154.

106. Among those indicted were Gerald Winrod, William Dudley Pelley, Eugene Sanctuary, Lawrence Dennis, James True, Elizabeth Dilling, and Joe McWilliams. John Trevor's American Coalition repeatedly was referred to as a fascist front. The trial, on charges of violating the Smith Act, dragged on for nearly five years, during which time one judge died and Prosecutor Oetje John Rogge was replaced for an intemperate public outburst on the case. At the end of 1946 the Circuit Court of Appeals for the District of Columbia released the defendants because they had been denied speedy trial guaranteed them under the Constitution. For the defendants' view of this ordeal, see Lawrence Dennis and Maximilian St. George, *A Trial on Trial: The Great Sedition Trial of 1944* (New York: National Civil Rights Committee, 1946).

107. Weyl, pp. 167–79.

108. Eds. of *Look Magazine*, *The Story of the FBI* (New York: E. P. Dutton, 1947), p. 226.

109. *National Refugee Service Bulletin #6*, May 29, 1941, pp. 1–3.

110. "State Department vs. Political Refugees," *151* (Dec. 28, 1940): 649.

111. With the war going well for the Allies, visa forms were shortened, some questions pertaining to national security were deleted, and the provision requiring the applicant to show that the United States would profit from his admission in some tangible way was removed. *New York Post*, Apr. 28, 1944, p. 5.

Chapter 6

1. *Challenging Years: The Autobiography of Stephen Wise* (New York: G. P. Putnam's Sons, 1949), p. 235.

2. Personal interviews with Lillie Shultz, former special assistant to Wise at the American Jewish Congress and presently publicity director of the Weizmann Institute; Leona Duckler, former personal secretary to Wise, and Richard

Cohn, assistant executive director of the American Jewish Congress, Jan. 8, 1969. All of these people are laudatory concerning the work of Wise, whom they regard as the one legitimate U.S. Jewish hero during World War II.

3. The German attack on Russia on June 22, 1941 sealed the fate of European Jewry. In laying his plans for Operation Barbarossa, Hitler made it clear that he did not wish to be saddled with an additional 3,000,000 Jews found in Eastern Poland and the Ukraine. Starvation, brutality, and expulsion had not adequately cleared occupied Europe of its Jews. Goering thus issued a directive to Reinhard Heydrich, the handsome blond who had engineered Kristallnacht and who was currently serving as chief of the Reich Main Security Office or RHSA, "to take all preparatory measures required for final solution of the Jewish question in European territories under German influence." Through the summer and fall of 1941 special Death's Head Corps, the *Einsatzkommando* and *Sonderkommando*, performed their grisly work in league with advance units of the Wehrmacht. The massacre of 30,000 Jews at Kiev's Babi Yar Ravine dates from the early period of German genocide. On Jan. 20, 1942, Heydrich called a conference of the Gestapo heads of all occupied territories in the office of the International Criminal Police Commission in Berlin at Grossen Wannsee No. 56–58. Fifteen persons were present, including Adolf Eichmann, head of Bureau IVA, 4B of the RHSA, the office established for dealing with Jewish problems. In this Wannsee Conference, plans were confirmed to "stamp out the germ cell of a new Jewish development in Europe." The task of dealing with Jews of Eastern Europe was given to SS leader Odile Globocnik of Lublin. Under his direction, death camps were established at Belzec, Maidanek, Chelmno, Treblinka, and Sobibor in Poland. Originally the Nazis expected to execute 6,000 persons a day, using the method prescribed by Hitler—gassing. Primitive gas chambers utilizing the carbon monoxide of tank and automobile exhausts proved incapable of attaining that figure. Finally, in Mar. 1943, Lt. Gen. Heinz Kammler, the Wehrmacht engineer who designed Germany's rocket bases along the French coast, developed the now infamous system of mock shower chambers where Zyklon B gas was used. Raul Hilberg, *The Destruction of the European Jews* (Chicago: Quadrangle, 1960), pp. 177–634.

4. Morse, *While Six Million Died,* pp. 3–11.

5. Elting to Hull, Aug. 10, 1942, State Department Records, 862.4016/2234.

6. Harrison to Hull, Aug. 11, 1942, State Department Records, 862.4016/2234.

7. Memorandum of Durbrow, Aug. 11, 1942, ibid., 862.4016/2235.

8. Morse (p. 9) makes much of a memorandum addressed to "S. W. J." on Aug. 13 to lump Culbertson with those who opposed the issuance of any note to Wise. This note read: "I don't like the idea of sending this one to Wise, but if the Rabbi hears later that we had the message and didn't let him in on it, he might put up a ———. [The last word is illegible, but Morse interpolates 'kick.'] Why not send it on and add that this legation has no information to confirm the story." The signature is virtually illegible, but it appears to be initialed P. A. or P. C. It does not seem identical with Culbertson's in his letter to Wise or in any other document. See ibid., Aug. 13, 1942, 862.4016/2233.

9. Durbrow to Culbertson, Aug. 13, 1942, ibid., 862.4016/2233.

10. Welles to Harrison, Aug. 17, 1942, ibid., 862. 4016/2233.

11. Squire to State Department, Sept. 28, 1942, ibid., 862.4016/2242.

12. The original, in fractured German, reads:

Ich habe Herrn Jäger gesprochen. Er sagte mir dasser alle Angehörige der Familie Achenu ausser Frl. Eisenzweig von Warschau zu sich nach seinem Wohnsitz Kewer einladen wird. Ich bin allein hier; ich fühle mich sehr einsam . . . Jetzt wegen der Zitrus Früchte; ich hoffe, dass ich diese rechtzeitig erhalten werde. Ich weiss zwar nicht, ob ich bis dann jemand von meinen Bekannten noch antreffen werde. Ich fühle mich sehr schwach. Herrn Orlean habe ich vor 8 Tagen noch gesprochen; auch Frau Gefen telefroniert oft . . . Onkel Gerusch arbeitet auch in Warschau. Er ist ein sehr tuchtiger Arbeiter. Sein Freund Miso arbeitet jetzt mit Onkel Gerusch zusammen . . . Bitte betet fur mich.

13. See translators' commentary attached to Squire letter, Sept. 28, 1942, State Department Records, 862.4016/2242.

14. Again, the original is somewhat garbled:

Auch ich war in Trauer, denn ich bin so allein. Onkel Achenu ist verstorben. Entschuldigen Sie mir meine Ausdrucksweise. Ich nehme an, dass ich die mir avisierten Cytrus fruchte in diesen Tagen erhalte. Da der Onkel verstorben ist, weiss ich nicht, an wenn ich sie abgeben soll. Es ist mir so weh umn Herz, dass ich sie nicht nutzbrigend anwenden kann, sondern, dass sie elendiglich vertrocknen muessen. Diese schoenen Fruechte . . . Gruessen Sie auch Herrn Tschlenoff und sagen Sie ihm dass nun seine ganze Arbeit und Seine Muehe vollstaendig umsonst ist. Ich werde davon im naechsten Brief noch schreiben. Ibid.

15. The authoritative diaries of Emanuel Ringelblum bear out the September massacres. See *Notes from the Warsaw Ghetto: The Journal of Emanuel Ringelblum,* ed. and trans. Jacob Sloan (New York: McGraw-Hill, 1958), p. 312. In a ten-week action ending in September, nearly 500,000 Polish Jews, including 310,000 from the ghetto of Warsaw, were "resettled" in concentration camps. By the end of the year, more than 1,270,000 Polish Jews were dead. See *Meczenstwo Walka, Zaglada Zydow w Polsce 1939–1945* (Warsaw: Wydawnictwo Ministerstwa Obrony Narodowej, n.d.), pp. 218–21.

16. *The Black Book of Polish Jewry: An Account of the Martyrdom of Polish Jewry under the Nazi Occupation,* ed. Jacob Apenszlak (New York: American Federation for Polish Jews and the Association of Jewish Refugees and Immigrants from Poland, 1943), p. 236.

17. Morse provides an excellent chronicle of Riegner's work in this period, pp. 16–19.

18. "The Morgenthau Diaries: VI, The Refugee Run-Around," *Colliers, 120* (Nov. 1, 1947): 23.

19. Ibid., p. 23.

20. Berle to Hull, Feb. 16, 1940, and Berle to Hull, Feb. 23, 1940, State Department Records, 862.4016/2/62½ and 862.4016/2190.

21. Long to Hull, Feb. 23, 1940, ibid., 862.4016/2/198. Long's timidity may be comprehensible in view of Nazi power in 1940, but it is hardly consistent with diplomatic precedent, as the U.S. had repeatedly intervened in the "domestic questions" of the Tsarist and Ottoman empires to protest abuse

of Jews. See Cyrus Adler and Aaron Margolith, *With Firmness in the Right: American Diplomatic Action Affecting Jews, 1840–1945* (New York: American Jewish Committee, 1946).

22. "Chronicles," *Contemporary Jewish Record,* 4 (Aug. 1941): 429.

23. Goldstein to Hull, July 17, 1942, State Department Records, 862.4016/2230.

24. "Chronicles," *Contemporary Jewish Record* 5 (Aug. 1942): 426.

25. Ibid., pp. 429, 528.

26. Goldstein to Hull, July 17, 1942, State Department Records, 862.4016/2230.

27. Johnson to Hull, July 21, 1942, ibid., 862.4016/2237.

28. Molotov to Hull, July 27, 1942, ibid., 862.4016/2230.

29. *Bulletin on Refugees Abroad and at Home, #12,* Oct. 16, 1942, p. 1, American Friends Service Committee Library. Records of the American Friends Service Committee left little doubt that the deportees were being shipped eastward, not as a part of Vichy's arrangements to supply labor for the Nazis, but to their deaths. French slave laborers were not herded into cattle cars, while machine guns destroyed the stragglers. Nor were women, aged persons, or children included in the labor agreements. And finally, such slave laborers were generally not sent to concentration camps in Poland. They were used in the industrial heartland of the Rhine and Ruhr.

30. For additional data along these lines, see Morse, pp. 5–12.

31. Mendelsohn to Hull, Sept. 1, 1942, State Department Records, 862.4016/2238.

32. "The Morgenthau Diaries," pp. 22, 63.

33. See results of the AIPO poll, Jan. 1943 in Stember et al., *Jews in the Mind of America,* p. 141. For America's reactions to the Great Crusade, see Robert E. Osgood, *Ideals and Self-Interest: The Great Transformation of the Twentieth Century* (Chicago: University of Chicago Press, 1953).

34. Stember et al., p. 141. Finally, in May 1945, with pictures of Belsen and Auschwitz available to all, 84 percent of those polled conceded that perhaps more than one million Jews had been massacred.

35. The most important sources on the destruction of European Jewry are Apenszlak; N. Levin; Herman Rauschning, *The Voice of Destruction* (New York: G. P. Putnam's Sons, 1940); Leon Poliakov, *Harvest of Hate: The Nazi Program for the Destruction of the Jews of Europe* (Syracuse: Syracuse University Press, 1954); and Raul Hilberg, *The Destruction of the European Jews* (Chicago: Quadrangle Books, 1961).

36. *Foreign Relations of the United States,* 2:860.

37. This petition was presented by Maurice Wertheim, president of the American Jewish Committee; Henry Monsky, president of B'nai B'rith; Adolph Held, president of the Jewish Labor Committee; Israel Goldstein, president of the Synagogue Council of America; Rabbi Israel Rosenberg, chairman of the Union of Orthodox Rabbis; and Wise, in his capacity as president of the American Jewish Congress. Report to Roosevelt, Dec. 8, 1942, Church Affairs: Jewish, Roosevelt Library.

38. Wise to Roosevelt, Dec. 2, 1942, Correspondence Between FDR and Wise, 1929–1945, American Jewish Archives.

39. *Congress Weekly,* 9 (Aug. 14, 1942): 2.

40. See Folder #15, Polish Underground Study, Item 26, Report of the

Bund Regarding the Persecution of the Jews, in Yehuda Bauer, "When Did They Know?" *Midstream*, *14* (Apr. 1968): 57–58.

41. Ibid., p. 51.

42. "Correspondence: Reactions to News of the Holocaust," *Midstream*, *14* (May 1968): 62.

43. Ibid.

44. Ibid. Syrkin asserted that criticism of the efforts of the American Jewish community during wartime only contributed to the anti-Semitic canards of Jewish collaboration in the extermination plot, now the "familiar stock-in-trade" of neo-Nazis and Polish anti-Semites.

45. *Autobiography of Stephen Wise*, p. 274.

46. Shultz interview.

47. *Autobiography of Stephen Wise*, p. 275.

48. *The Personal Letters of Stephen Wise*, ed. Justine Wise Polier and James Waterman Wise (Boston: Beacon Press, 1956), pp. 160–61. Hereafter cited as *Wise Letters*.

49. Elie Wiesel, "Telling the Tale," *Dimensions in American Judaism*, *2* (Spring 1968): 11.

50. Shultz interview.

51. In "6,000,000 or 5,000,000," *Midstream*, *10* (Mar. 1964): 8.

52. Among other things, Washington suggested that the WJC tone down questions "loaded with dynamite" which pertained to Polish and German persecutions and that Wise shift the election day from Sunday, as this would constitute an insult to Christians in this country. Memorandum of Wise to Lipsky and Shultz, June 7, 1938, American Jewish Congress File, Wise Papers.

53. *Wise Letters*, p. 252.

54. *Wise Letters*, p. 136.

55. Wise to Bernard Richards, secretary of American Jewish Committee, Sept. 3 and Dec. 10, 1941, American Jewish Congress File, Wise Papers.

56. Carl Hermann Voss, "Let Stephen Wise Speak for Himself," *Dimensions in American Judaism*, *3* (Fall 1968): 39.

57. Henry Monsky of B'nai B'rith first suggested in Jan. 1943 that the AJ Congress, B'nai B'rith, Jewish Labor Committee, Synagogue Council of America, and AJ Committee join forces. Preliminary discussions among the various leaders took place in February, but it was not until August that the conference was actually organized. See *The American Jewish Conference: Its Organization and Proceedings, Aug. 29–Sept. 2, 1943*, ed. Alexander Kohanski (New York: American Jewish Conference, 1944).

58. *New York Times*, Oct. 25, 1943, p. 1.

59. Ben Hecht, *Perfidy* (New York: Julian Messner, Inc., 1961), p. 189. For support of this contention, see advertisements of the Committee for a Jewish Army in the *New York Times* of Feb. 16, 1943, p. 11; Apr. 13, 1943, p. 19; and May 4, 1943, p. 17.

60. *The Conference Record* (Jan. 15, 1944), 1:4, 7, 8.

61. Wise to Bloom, Dec. 30, 1943, American Jewish Congress File, Wise Papers. At the time, Chayim Greenberg expressed the same skepticism of plans to raise a Jewish army of 200,000 stateless Jews, pointing out that no such number of stateless or Palestinian males existed in the free world (Greenberg, p. 7).

62. Bergson's group had harassed the State Department since Aug. 1943.

This prompted Long to request a security clearance through Maj. Gen. George Strong. This check failed to turn up anything against the Palestinian, and he remained in the country. See Long to Brandt, Aug. 12, 1943; Strong to Long, Aug. 26, 1943; and Long to Hull, Sept. 1, 1943, Refugee File, Long Papers.

63. Long to Hull, Oct. 15, 1943, ibid.

64. Long to Hull, Oct. 6, 1943, ibid. Earlier Celler had exploded in a tirade against Bergson in a conference which originally had been designed to explore the deficiencies of the State Department in rescuing Jews. Long to Hull, Sept. 1, 1943, ibid.

65. Long to Hull, Oct. 15, 1943, ibid.

66. *New York Times,* Feb. 16, 1943, p. 11.

67. Hecht, p. 192.

68. *Wise Letters,* p. 265.

69. Hecht, p. 192.

70. "The Morgenthau Diaries," pp. 23, 62. For a complete exposition of this tragic affair, see Morse, pp. 73–86.

71. *Autobiography of Stephen Wise,* p. 278.

72. Roosevelt to Wise, Aug. 14, 1943, Church Matters: Jewish, Roosevelt Library.

73. Malcolm Hay, *Europe and the Jews* (Boston: Beacon Press, 1961), p. 303.

74. "The Morgenthau Diaries," p. 62.

75. Memorandum of Long for Hull, Oct. 28, 1943, Relief File, Long Papers.

76. Long to Riegner, Dec. 18, 1943, ibid.

77. *Autobiography of Stephen Wise,* p. 279.

78. Hecht, p. 192.

79. *Autobiography of Stephen Wise,* p. 269.

80. Personal interview with Miriam Laikind, Temple historian, the Temple, Cleveland, Oct. 15, 1968.

81. *Wise Letters,* p. 266.

82. Carl Hermann Voss, *Rabbi and Minister: The Friendship of Stephen S. Wise and John Haynes Holmes* (Cleveland: World Publishing, 1964), p. 286.

83. Chayim Greenberg lamented this preoccupation with pressing at the diplomatic level for the creation of a Jewish homeland before taking steps to ensure that there would be Jews to populate it. "A home for whom?" he asked in 1943. "For the millions of dead in their temporary cemeteries in Europe?" (Greenberg, p. 7). For the negotiations of Brandeis, Wise, and Silver with the president and secretaries Hull and Stettinius over a Jewish state in Palestine, see Documents Concerning Jewish Matters During Administration of Franklin D. Roosevelt File, American Jewish Archives.

84. Zygelboim sent his final letter to Polish President Wladyslaw Raczkiewics and Prime Minister Wladyslaw Sikorski. He wrote:

> The murderers themselves bear the primary responsibility for the crime of extermination of the whole Jewish population of Poland, but indirectly this responsibility also weighs on all humanity, on the peoples and governments of the allied nations, because they have not made any attempt to do something drastic to stall the criminal deeds. By looking on indif-

ferently while helpless millions of tortured children, women, and men were murdered, these nations have associated themselves with the criminals.

Philip Friedman, *Martyrs and Fighters: The Epic of the Warsaw Ghetto* (New York: Lancer Books, 1954), pp. 219–20.

85. William Kenney, *The Crucial Years: 1940–1945* (New York: Mac-Fadden Books, 1962), pp. 57–58.

Chapter 7

1. Zachariah Schuster, "The Passion of a People: Anno MCMXLII," *Contemporary Jewish Record, 6* (Feb. 1943): 35.

2. Ultimately, 27,208 Palestinian Jews served with the British. And 1.3 million Jews served the Allies under different national colors during the war. Frank Gervasi, *The Case for Israel* (New York: Viking Press, 1967), p. 64.

3. Indicative of this weekly agitation was the full-page advertisement in the *New York Times* of Feb. 8, 1943, which began: "ACTION NOT PITY CAN SAVE MILLIONS NOW!" The committee emphasized that the Nazis had backed down on persecution of Norwegians when the Swedes interceded, that they stopped chaining up British POWs after protests were issued through the International Red Cross, that they had not repeated the mistake of Lidice in the face of world condemnation. All the Jews were asking, the committee indicated, was a chance to defend themselves in the hope of forcing Nazis to relieve the persecution of their brethren.

4. The British had been engaged in a war with the Vichy French in Syria-Palestine until July 1942, had been startled when the nationalist regime of Rashid al-Gailani in Iraq declared war on the Allies in May 1941, and had even been compelled to join with the Russians in ousting the pro-German Shah of Iran from his throne in Aug. 1941. Between Apr. 1941 and May 1942, when the Afrika Korps of Field Marshal Erwin Rommel pushed across North Africa to within seventy miles of Alexandria, the main British naval base in the Mediterranean, none of the British-subsidized Shaykhs in the Middle East offered so much as a camel by way of assistance to the Allies. Instead, in Egypt, extremists of the Muslim Brotherhood, a fanatical anti-British terrorist group founded by Hassan al-Banna, were rioting in the streets. Onetime Premier Ali Maher and General Azia Alid Misri were preaching open sedition against the British, who, it appeared, were bound to lose. King Farouk was under virtual house arrest in his palace. And the Egyptian chief of staff was caught *flagrante delicto*, attempting to board a plane with military secrets bound for a rendezvous with the Axis High Command in Tobruk. See Sydney N. Fisher, *The Middle East: a History* (New York: Macmillan, 1959), pp. 482–83 and Pierre van Paassen, *The Forgotten Ally* (New York: Dial Press, 1943), p. 251.

5. Berle to Marvin McIntyre, Aug. 11, 1942, Church Matters: Jewish, Roosevelt Library. Eventually, in 1944, such a legion was incorporated into the British army and distinguished itself on the battlefields of Eritrea, Italy and Germany.

6. Among their complaints were: (1) the British's refusal to waive White Paper quotas in the case of 20,000 Polish and 10,000 "Balkan" Jewish chil-

dren, who were subsequently deported to Auschwitz and Maidanek; (2) the British's suspension of all Jewish immigration to Palestine between Oct. 1939 and Mar. 1940 and again between Oct. 1940 and Mar. 1941; (3) the statement accompanying these suspensions that the Jews should "save up permits for German Jews," since these were "better" types than "Balkan Jews"; (4) the British's obstreperousness in barring the way to Palestine to Jews who came in unseaworthy vessels and without proper landing credentials. See "Palestine Problem and Proposals for Its Solution; Abridged Version of a Memorandum of the Anglo-American Committee on Palestine to the General Assembly of the United Nations," *The Nation, 164* (May 17, 1947): 593.

7. British journals had not helped matters by inveighing against American negotiations with onetime fascist collaborators in North Africa during that winter. See four-page protest of Welles to Ambassador Ronald Campbell, Mar. 4, 1943, State Department Records, 548.G1/63. For a general background on American and British involvement with Vichy in North Africa, see William L. Langer, *Our Vichy Gamble* (New York: Alfred A. Knopf, 1947); Louis Gottschalk, "Our Vichy Fumble," *The Journal of Modern History, 20* (Mar. 1948): 47–56; Ann Williams, *Britain and France in the Middle East and North Africa* (New York: St. Martin's Press, 1968), pp. 78–80; and A. L. Funk, *Charles de Gaulle: The Crucial Years, 1943–1944* (Norman: University of Oklahoma Press, 1959).

8. Emerson to Myron Taylor, Aug. 11, 1942, Personal Correspondence, Hull Papers.

9. Halifax to Hull, Jan. 20, 1943, *Foreign Relations of the United States, Diplomatic Papers, 1*:134–37.

10. U.S., *Department of State Bulletins, 8* (Mar. 6, 1943): 202–204.

11. Welles to Campbell, Mar. 4, 1943, State Department Records, 548.G1/63. A more benign explanation that the Hull note was merely a working memorandum and by no means binding on the two countries was offered Canadian Prime Minister W. L. MacKenzie King to relieve him from the pressures of his own Parliament.

12. Morse makes much of the "Stop Hitler Rally" staged by Wise at Madison Square Garden on Mar. 1, 1943. While it is true that such luminaries as Sen. Wagner, Weizmann, La Guardia, Norman Angell, Thomas Dewey, and William Green spoke to the assemblage, the rally did not prompt the Bermuda conference as Morse intimates. Negotiations had already been going on for several weeks (*While Six Million Died*, p. 46).

13. U.S., Congress, House, *Congressional Record*, 78th Cong., 1st Sess., 1943, *89*, pt. 10:A2154.

14. *New York Times*, Apr. 7, 1943, p. 4.

15. U.S., *Department of State Bulletins, 8*, May 1, 1943, p. 201. Welles's immediate, cordial response consisted of a rejection of Murray's evaluation of Evian (Welles conceded that the war had made the work of the IGCR difficult, but not futile), a condemnation of Nazi mass murders, and an invitation to "any organization which desires to present a communication to the conference at Bermuda" to submit its proposals to the State Department, which would then cable them to the delegates (ibid., p. 201).

16. *New York Times*, Apr. 21, 1943, p. 27.

17. Schuster, p. 30.

18. *Long Diary*, p. 307.

NOTES

19. Hayter to Brandt, Apr. 7, 1942, State Department Records, 548.G1/152.

20. Dodds interview.

21. See correspondence between Hull and Beck, Apr. 5, 1943; Apr. 7, 1943; Apr. 8, 1943; Apr. 13, 1943; State Department Records, 548.G1/9, 548.G1/13A, 548.G1/14, 548.G1/19A, and 548.G1/20.

22. *Foreign Relations of the United States, 1*:153.

23. Minutes of Meeting of American Delegates, Apr. 25, 1943, Refugee File, Long Papers, pp. 25, 59, 61, 65. Among other things, Backer was asked what the United States was to do if Hitler suddenly dumped 100,000 Jews into Genoa for the Allies to rescue. "Should we allow American boys to die to save these people?" asked Scott Lucas.

24. *New York Times*, Apr. 14, 1943, p. 19.

25. See *Long Diary*, p. 306, and Roberts and Taylor to Long, Mar. 18, 1943, State Department Records, 548.G1/112.

26. Long to Hull, Mar. 13, 1943, ibid., 548.G1/112.

27. Long to Welles, Mar. 13, 1943, ibid., 548.G1/112.

28. Dickstein did volunteer on Apr. 2, 1943, pointing to his long record of service as chairman of the House Committee on Immigration and Naturalization and also to his close contacts with the Orthodox Jewish community. He was informed that the delegation had already been selected. Dickstein to Long, Apr. 2, 1943, ibid., 548.G1/141.

29. *IJPS Bulletin*, May 21, 1943, p. 2A.

30. Dodds interview.

31. "An Open Letter to a Shabbos Goy," *The Answer*, 2 (Jan. 1944): 12.

32. Confidential memorandum for the chairman, morning conference, Apr. 20, 1943, Refugee File, Bermuda Folder, Long Papers.

33. Memorandum, afternoon conference, Apr. 21, 1943, ibid.

34. Confidential memorandum for the chairman, morning conference, Apr. 20, 1943, ibid.

35. Memorandum, afternoon conference, Apr. 21, 1943, ibid.

36. Long to Hull, Mar. 24, 1943, State Department Records, 548.G1/188.

37. Accompanying Law were George Henry Hall, Parliamentary Under-secretary for the Admiralty; Osbert Peake, Parliamentary Undersecretary for State and the Home Office; Sir Bernard Reilly of the Colonial Office; Sir Frank Newson of the Home Office; A. W. G. Randall of the Refugee Department of the Foreign Office; Mr. Pickett from the Transport Division of the Ministry of War; and Hayter from the embassy in Washington. *Foreign Relations of the United States, 1*, p. 151.

38. For the complete draft, see *Program for the Rescue of Jews from Nazi Europe*, unpublished memorandum of the Joint Emergency Committee for European Jewish Affairs, Apr. 19, 1943, YIVO, 3/48486.

39. Fellowship of Reconciliation to Hull, Apr. 13, 1943, State Department Records, 548.G1/71½; Pickett to Hull, Apr. 15, 1943, ibid., 548.G1/34; Union for Protection of Human Person to Hull, Apr. 15, 1943, ibid., 548.G1/100. The YMCA and Federal Council of Churches of Christ asked that the U.S. and Great Britain provide financial guarantees to neutrals for the care of refugees. They also endorsed the policy of repatriating refugees at the end of the war. YMCA and Federal Council to Hull, Apr. 13, 1943, ibid., 548.G1/27; The National Negro Congress petition appears in "Chronicles," *Contemporary Jew-*

281

ish Record, 6 (June 1943): 277; "Petition of American Scholars to the President Concerning Nazi Persecutions of the Jews," *Newsletter of the YIVO,* #1 (Sept. 1943): 3.

40. Apr. 28, 1943, State Department Records, 548.G1/118.

41. New ZOA to Hull, Apr. 14, 1943, ibid., 548.G1/133.

42. Morse, pp. 26–28.

43. There are several letters in the Bermuda file which suggest this method of treatment of German civilians. See especially the letter of the American representatives of the General Jewish Workers Union of Poland to Hull, Apr. 23, 1943, State Department Records, 548.G1/170.

44. Berle to Long, Apr. 20, 1943, Refugee File, Bermuda Folder, Long Papers.

45. Hull to Dodds, Apr. 20, 1943, State Department Records, 548.G1/30.

46. U.S., Congress, Senate, *Congressional Record,* 78th Cong., 1st Sess., 1943, 89, pt. 3:3434.

47. *New York Times,* Apr. 18, 1943, p. 11.

48. Albert Nirenstein, *A Tower from the Enemy: Contributions to a History of Jewish Resistance in Poland* (New York: Orion Press, 1959), p. 108.

49. U.S., *Department of State Bulletin, 8* (Apr. 19, 1943): 351.

50. *New York Times,* Apr. 20, 1943, p. 11.

51. *Washington Daily News,* Apr. 21, 1943, p. 4.

52. *New York Times,* Apr. 22, 1943, p. 10.

53. At various times "North Africa" meant Cyrenaica, Libya, Algeria, and/or Morocco. All these proposals were reported in the *New York Times,* Apr. 28, 1943, p. 6.

54. *PM,* Apr. 27, 1943, p. 10.

55. *New York Times,* Apr. 19, 1943, p. 18.

56. *New York Post,* Apr. 9, 1943, p. 42.

57. *Washington Post,* Apr. 20, 1943, p. 20.

58. *New York World-Telegram,* Apr. 28, 1943, p. 2.

59. *New York Herald-Tribune,* Apr. 28, 1943, p. 8.

60. Translation of these editorials, printed on Apr. 12 and 14, 1943, respectively, appear in the State Department Records, 548.G1/180.

61. Ibid.

62. See Reams to Hull, Apr. 20, 1943, State Department Records, 548.G1/41.

63. Mimeographed Report on Admission of Hebrew Race, Statistical Section, Division of Research and Education, Department of Immigration and Naturalization, May 14, 1948, p. 1.

64. Emanuel Celler, "The Bermuda Conference: Diplomatic Mockery," *Free World, 6* (July 1943): 19.

65. Roosevelt said, "I feel confident that the Congress is in full agreement that the measures long overdue, should be taken to correct an injustice to our friends." One hundred and five Chinese were to be admitted annually under 57 *Stat.* 600. "Chinese Exclusion Repeal," *Monthly Review of the Department of Immigration and Naturalization, 1* (Oct. 1943): 16. See also Tang Tsou, *American Failure in China, 1941–1950* (Chicago: University of Chicago Press, 1963).

66. 43 *Stat.* 153.

67. Dodds interview.

68. Hull to Roosevelt, May 7, 1943, State Department Records, 548.G1/165A.

69. Roosevelt to Hull, May 14, 1943, ibid., 548.G1/201.

70. Stember et al., *Jews in the Mind of America*, p. 128.

71. "Jewish Question," in Cantril, *Public Opinion*, p. 383.

72. Stember et al., p. 9. For an explanation of this phenomenon, see Gordon Allport's "Bigot in our Midst," *Commonweal*, 40 (Oct. 6, 1944): 582–86. The author blames wartime tensions and frustrations directed at the Jews, who allegedly were responsible for starting the war.

73. U.S., *Department of State Bulletins*, 8 (1943): 352.

74. Memorandum of morning meeting, Apr. 22, 1943, Refugee File, Bermuda Folder, Long Papers.

75. Hull to Dodds, Apr. 21, 1943, State Department Records, 548.4016/22.

76. Williamson to Hull, May 10, 1943, ibid., 822.4016/22.

77. Jacques Vernant, *The Refugee in the Postwar World: Preliminary Report of A Survey* (Geneva, 1961), pp. 330, 387–88.

78. Herbert Emerson, "Postwar Problems of Refugees," *Foreign Affairs*, 21 (Jan. 1943): 216.

79. Taylor to Hull, Aug. 26, 1943, State Department Records, 548.G1/50.

80. Law to Hull, Apr. 19, 1943, and Winant to Hull, May 27, 1943, ibid., 548.G1/37 and 548.G1/142.

81. "Palestine Problem and Proposals for Its Solution," p. 587.

82. *New York Times*, Apr. 24, 1943, p. 2.

83. During the meetings of Apr. 19 and 20 the delegates discussed shipping, but once more the problems of safe conduct, cost, and compatibility with the war effort caused the delegates to dismiss this. Memorandum of afternoon conference, Apr. 20, 1943, Refugee File, Bermuda Folder, Long Papers.

84. Backer talked of rescuing 125,000 persons, most of them children, in this manner. Minutes of meeting of American delegation, Sun., Apr. 25, 1943, Refugee File, Bermuda Folder, Long Papers. The British view was that this was impossible. Beck to Hull, Apr. 21, 1943, State Department Records, 548.G1/46.

85. Malcolm J. Proudfoot, *European Refugees, 1939–1952; A Study in Forced Population Movement* (Evanston: Northwestern University Press, 1956), pp. 76, 77, 142.

86. Harry Fleischman, *Norman Thomas: A Biography* (New York: Norton, 1964), p. 210.

87. For a general view of the Arab contributions to the Allied war effort in the Middle East, see Don Peretz, *The Middle East Today* (New York: Holt, Rinehart, and Winston, 1964), pp. 123–26. Sir John Bagot Glubb Pasha, commander of Jordan's Arab Legion, lamented, "Every Arab force previously organized by us mutinied and refused to fight for us, or faded away in desertion." Quoted in Howard Sachar, *The Course of Modern Jewish History* (Cleveland: World Publishing Co., 1958), p. 461. See also John Bagot Glubb, *A Soldier with the Arabs* (New York: Harper and Bros., 1958).

The Grand Mufti, Haj Amin al-Husseini, was a well known anti-Zionist who had organized the Easter pogrom at Jaffa in 1920, the Wailing Wall riots of 1929, the Arab boycott of 1936, and the Gailani coup in Iraq in 1941. Eluding the British before and during the war, he took up residence in Germany, where he maintained two villas, organized the *Buro des Grosmufti* (which operated schools of sabotage for Arabs in The Hague and Athens), and tried unsuccessfully to raise an Arab Legion for the Wehrmacht. After the war, the Mufti, who according to Abwehr Maj. Gen. Erwin Lahousen was personally responsible for the extermination of several thousand Balkan Jewish children, eluded Allied authorities to lead Palestinian nationalist forces in 1947–1948. Afterward he fled to sanctuary in Farouk's Egypt. See Ismar Elbogen, *A Century of Jewish Life* (Philadelphia: Jewish Publication Society of America, 1944), pp. 597–99, 617, 621, 632, 760; Hay, *Europe and the Jews*, p. 286; Peretz, pp. 258–59, 386; "Palestine Problem and Proposals for Solution," pp. 585–613; Joseph Schechtman, *The Mufti and the Fuhrer: The Rise and Fall of Haj Amin el-Husseini* (New York: Thomas Yoseloff, 1965); and "The Arab Higher Committee: Its Origins, Personnel and Purposes," submitted to the U.N. by the Nation Associates, May 1947.

88. Dodds to Hull, Apr. 20, 1943, State Department Records, 548.G1/40.

89. Memorandum of morning conference, Apr. 21, 1943, Refugee File, Bermuda Folder, Long Papers.

90. Dodds to Hull, Apr. 24, 1943, State Department Records, 548.G1/54.

91. During the first four years of the war the Joint assisted refugees in Stockholm, Tehran, Casablanca, Madrid, and Buenos Aires. JDC soup kitchens functioned in Warsaw to the very end. Seven thousand Jewish children, interned in camps in France, were fed throughout the Nazi occupation. More than 5,000 relief parcels containing shoes, clothing, tea, underwear, medicine, sugar, vegetable fats, and dried fruits were smuggled across the Iranian-Russian border each month, bound for the starving Jews in Eastern Europe. The Joint arranged for some descendants of Sephardic Jews, whose ancestors had been expelled from Iberia 500 years before, to return to Spain and Portugal. Meanwhile, the Joint was spending $100,000 a month in Spain, $150,000 in Switzerland, and $300,000 in Sweden to aid refugees of all faiths. See *JDC in a World at War* (New York: American Joint Distribution Committee, 1944); *Aspects of Jewish Relief*, ed. Norman Bentwich (Jewish Committee for Relief Abroad, 1944), YIVO 8/50130; and Herbert Agar, *The Saving Remnant*.

92. U.S., *Department of State Bulletin, 8* (May 1943): 388.

93. U.S., Congress, Senate, *Congressional Record*, 78th Cong., 1st. Sess., 1943, *89*, pt. 6:8125.

94. *The American Jewish Conference Record, 1* (Sept. 15, 1944): 14.

95. *Baltimore Sun*, Apr. 24, 1943, p. 2.

96. State Department Records, 548.G1/152.

97. *The Autobiography of Sol Bloom* (New York: G. P. Putnam's Sons, 1948), p. 273.

98. Freda Kirchwey, "While the Jews Die," *The Nation, 156* (Mar. 13, 1943): 366.

Chapter 8

1. "Bermuda," by "Sagittarius," *New Statesman and Nation, 25* (Apr. 24, 1943): 271.

2. *New York Times,* May 4, 1943, p. 17.

3. Dodds to Long, Apr. 28, 1943; Hull to Dodds, Apr. 29, 1943; and Dodds to Long, Apr. 29, 1943; State Department Records, 548.G1/85; 548.G1/104H; and 548.G1/88.

4. U.S., Congress, Senate, *Congressional Record*, 78th Cong., 1st Sess., 1943, *89*, pt. 3:4046.

5. Apr. 13, 1943, p. 19.

6. U.S., Congress, Senate, *Congressional Record*, 78th Cong., 1st Sess., 1943, *89*, pt. 3:4046.

7. *IJPS*, May 21, 1943, p. 2A.

8. See *New York Times*, May 2, 1943, p. 17; May 7, 1943, p. 3; May 23, 1943, p. 6; May 24, 1943, p. 13; May 25, 1943, p. 15; and June 21, 1943, p. 2.

9. "Chronicles," *Contemporary Jewish Record*, 5 (Aug. 1943): 394.

10. "Ballad of the Doomed Jews of Europe," *Social Services Review*, 17 (Dec. 1943): 500.

11. "We should be ashamed to array the arguments for rescue," wrote the editors in Jan. 1943:

> If in front of our eyes a Jewish child came running to any of us with a Nazi butcher after him, we would fling open the doors of our homes at any cost and at any risk. Before the test very few of us would fail. Are we simple-minded, if we assume that the United Kingdom, which is merely all of us, with our native humane impulses, embodied as a Power, ought to act in the same way? The only difference is that there is much more it can do, besides opening its doors, and even this it has not done.

See "Our Part in Massacre," *New Statesman and Nation*, 25 (Jan. 9, 1943): 19.

12. "Bermuda," p. 271.

13. The *Times* (London) noted that "the painful and heartbreaking fact is that the saving hand cannot reach the majority of the refugees," May 20, 1943, p. 13. The *News Chronicle, Daily-Herald, Daily Express, Daily-Telegraph,* and *Sunday Observer* all rallied to the defense of the government saying that critics of Bermuda were doing a grave disservice to the war effort. For the *Guardian's* position, see May 20, 1943, p. 6.

14. For the complete debate, led by Eleanor Rathbone, on one side, and Eden, on the other, see Great Britain, *Parliamentary Debates* (Commons) 5th ser. *389* (1943): 1117–1203.

15. U.S., *Department of State Bulletins*, 8 (May 22, 1943): 456.

16. Long to Welles and Hull, June 22, 1943, State Department Records, 548.G1/198.

17. *Long Diary*, June 23, 1943, p. 316.

18. Thomas to Roosevelt, June 17, 1943, State Department Records, 548.G1/165.

19. Fleischman, *Norman Thomas*, p. 209.

20. *New York Times*, Sept. 10, 1943, p. 2.

21. Van Paassen to Roosevelt, Sept. 4, 1943, Church Matters: Jewish, Roosevelt Library. Boxes 19 and 20 are filled with similar remonstrances dated in the fall of 1943.

22. "Chronicles," *Contemporary Jewish Record*, 5 (Aug. 1943): 394.

23. *New York Times*, July 26, 1943, p. 19.

24. *New York Times*, Sept. 11, 1943, p. 8.

25. Dickstein asked, "Are we the people of the United States, going to

NOTES

become the unwitting accomplices of this blood-thirsty guttersnipe, as Winston Churchill so aptly called this modern Hun?" U.S. Congress, House, *Congressional Record*, 78th Cong., 1st Sess., 1943, *89*, pt. 11:A3316. Celler's remarks are in pt. 10:A2154, A2422.

26. U.S., Congress, Senate, *Congressional Record*, 78th Cong., 1st Sess., 1943, *89*, pt. 6:8125. See also pt. 3:4139.

27. U.S. Congress, Senate, *Congressional Record*, 78th Cong., 1st Sess., 1943, *89*, pt. 8:9305, 9371. The bill did not emerge from the Senate Foreign Relations Committee until Dec. 20, 1943.

28. "Aid by the United States to European Refugees: Testimony of Breckinridge Long," *Interpreter Releases, 21* (Jan. 10, 1944): 1–15.

29. U.S., Congress, House, Committee on Foreign Affairs, Hearings, *Resolutions Providing for the Establishment by the Executive of a Commission to Effectuate the Rescue of the Jewish People of Europe*, 78th Cong., 1st Sess., 1943, p. 44. Long's attitude could hardly be distinguished from that of one of the bill's sponsors, Congressman Rogers, who four days earlier rejected a plea from Wise to solve the Jewish question by establishing a homeland in Palestine. Rogers said, "I would doubt the wisdom of injecting this ancient and acrimonious dispute on this resolution." *The Conference Record, 1* (Jan. 15, 1944): 3.

30. *Hearings on a Commission to Rescue Jews*, p. 45.

31. *The Conference Record*, p. 3.

32. Kenen, a former newsman for the Cleveland *News*, served as secretary for the conference during this critical period. Presently he is editor of *Near East Report*, a monthly journal issued in Washington, and is affiliated with the American Israel Public Affairs Committee. He made this statement during an interview, June 5, 1968, with Saul S. Friedman in Washington, D.C.

33. *The Conference Record*, p. 3.

34. Ibid., pp. 3, 43.

35. Transcript of speech by Harrison, Feb. 18, 1944, Chamberlain Collection. Proudfoot's estimates are substantially the same. Of 799,651 "refugees" accepted by this nation during wartime, Proudfoot estimates that only 230,343 were actually persons fleeing for their lives. *European Refugees*, pp. 76–77.

36. Long to Travers, Dec. 29, 1943, Refugee File, Long Papers.

37. Long to Bloom, Dec. 31, 1943, ibid. For memorandums on refugee policies, see Alexander to Long, Feb. 2, 1944, ibid.

38. Emerson to Hull, Aug. 1942, Personal Correspondence, Hull Papers.

39. "The Inter-Governmental Committee on Refugees," *International Labour Review, 49* (Jan. 1944): 96–99.

40. Emerson to Hull, Oct. 14, 1943, Political Refugees File, Roosevelt Library.

41. Jewish Telegraphic Agency, Dec. 21, 1943, in Tartakower and Grossmann, *The Jewish Refugee*, p. 419.

42. In 1945, the IGCR spent less than $300,000 on relief projects in the Balkans. Its 1947 budget for resettlement of displaced persons was more than $10,000,000. As such it naturally collided with UNRRA for allocations of funds. See *Intergovernmental Committee on Refugees: Report of the Director, 30 May 1947* (London, 1947).

43. Report to the governments of the United States and United Kingdom

from Their Delegates to the Conference on the Refugee Problem Held at Bermuda, April 19–29, 1943, Refugee File, Long Papers, Section 1, unpaged.

44. Memorandum of Long for Hull, Sept. 16, 1943, Refugee File, Long Papers.

45. Oct. 8, 1943, ibid.

46. *Jewish Telegraph Agency,* Press Release #91, Apr. 19, 1943, p. 1.

47. Long to Welles, May 15, 1943, Refugee Movement and Nationality Groups File, Long Papers.

48. *Hearings on a Commission to Rescue Jews,* p. 36.

49. Memorandum on the Findings of the Emergency Conference to Save the Jewish People of Europe, YIVO, 3/25195, pp. 11–12.

50. *Report of the International Committee of the Red Cross on Its Activities During the Second World War, September 1, 1939–June 30, 1947: General Activities, 1* (Geneva: 17th International Red Cross Conference, 1948): 643–45.

51. *Hearings on a Commission to Rescue Jews,* p. 22. More recently Dodds supported this view, saying, "Locations were academic. We were constantly up against the problem of shipping. We got some. Visas were issued in excess of available shipping. But no one could have gotten the millions out who should have been taken out." Dodds interview.

52. See Confidential Memorandum for the Chairman, morning conference, Apr. 20, 1943, and afternoon conference, Apr. 20, 1943, Refugee File, Bermuda Folder, Long Papers.

53. The Swedish-American line had two liners with a combined capacity of 10,000 ready to make the Atlantic journey. Both remained idle for eight months in 1943. In like manner, large vessels belonging to the Compañia Trans-Mediterranea were also tied up in Barcelona for the better part of the year, awaiting passengers. See Memorandum on the Findings of the Emergency Conference to Save the Jewish People of Europe, pp. 9–10.

54. U.S., *Department of State Bulletins, 8* (May 22, 1943): 456.

55. Friedrich Ruge, *Sea Warfare 1939–1945: A German Viewpoint* (London: Cassell & Co., Ltd., 1957), pp. 231–38.

56. Churchill is quoted in *Washington Post,* May 20, 1943, p. 1. Naval Fleet Commander-in-Chief Adm. Ernest King later commented, "By the spring of 1943, the war against German submarines in the Atlantic had turned in our favor and we were fully on the offensive in that area." Chester Wardlow, *The Transportation Corps: Responsibilities, Organization, and Operations in the United States Army in World War II: The Technical Services* (Washington: Office of Chief of Military History, U.S. Army, 1951), p. 151.

57. Ruge, p. 238.

58. Chester Wardlow, *The Transportation Corps: Movements, Training, and Supply in the United States Army in World War II: The Technical Services* (Washington: Office of Chief of Military History, U.S. Army, 1956), p. 152.

59. See Program for the Rescue of Jews from Nazi-Occupied Europe, p. 18; U.S. Congress, House, *Congressional Record,* 78th Cong., 1st Sess., 1943, pt. 10:A2154, and Avram Juditch, *Neutral Shipping Facilities* (New York: World Jewish Congress, Mar. 1943).

60. Capt. Struble, ONO, to Berle, Feb. 10, 1943, State Department Records, 548.G1/110.

this country or constructing camps for them. See Strong to Hull, Feb. 10, 1943, State Department Records, 548.G1/110.

9. Harold Flender, *Rescue in Denmark* (New York: Simon and Schuster, 1963), p. 240.

10. Isaac Chomsky, "Among Refugees: Some Medical Observations," *American OSE Review*, 3 (Mar.–Apr. 1942): 170–71; and Celler to Roosevelt, Oct. 10, 1942, Political Refugees File, Roosevelt Library. For evidence that the Vichy government knew these children were going to their deaths see N. Levin, *The Holocaust*, pp. 423–58; Marie Syrkin, *Blessed Is the Match: The Story of Jewish Resistance* (Philadelphia: Jewish Publication Society of America, 1947), pp. 291–307; and Donald Lowrie, *The Hunted Children* (New York: W. W. Norton, 1963), pp. 58–59.

11. Memorandum for the President's Advisory Committee, Sept. 9, 1942, President's Advisory Committee on Political Refugees File, Wise Papers.

12. Report of George Warren, Oct. 16, 1942, ibid.

13. *Long Diary*, p. 282.

14. Personal Memorandum of Breckinridge Long, Oct. 5, 1942, Refugee File, Long Papers.

15. Telephone conversation of Taylor and Long, Sept. 10, 1942, ibid. See also Memorandum of President's Advisory Committee, Sept. 9, 1942, President's Advisory Committee on Political Refugees File, Wise Papers.

16. Minutes of the National Refugee Service, Dec. 9, 1942, Chamberlain Collection, YIVO.

17. "Chronicles," *Contemporary Jewish Record*, 5 (Dec. 1942): 634. Franco-American relations, never good in 1942, deteriorated rapidly in the autumn. Roosevelt had withdrawn the American ambassador when Laval once more became premier and further outraged the collaborationist regime by issuing a congratulatory message to the Free French forces on Bastille Day. In it he expressed the hope that the people of France might soon enjoy the blessings of liberty, equality, and fraternity. The American invasion of North Africa, coming less than twenty-four hours after Laval's precipitate action on the children, was symptomatic of that deterioration.

18. Minutes of the Meeting of American Delegation, Apr. 25, 1943, Refugee File, Bermuda Folder, Long Papers. Some forty-five children were still stranded in Spain at the time of this conference.

19. *While Six Million Died*, p. 70.

20. Roosevelt to Celler, Oct. 21, 1942, Political Refugees File, Roosevelt Library.

21. *Hearings on a Commission to Rescue Jews*, p. 30.

22. Dodds to Long, Apr. 22, 1943, State Department Records, 548.G1/46.

23. Bureau of Budget to Shaw, Apr. 23, 1943, State Department Records, 548. G1/57.

24. Dodds to Hull, Apr. 21, 1943, State Department Records, 548.G1/46.

25. For a detailing of this incident, see Morse, pp. 66–67.

26. More than 15,000 Germans were returned in these operations. American Jews thought that these persons could have been exchanged for concentration camp inmates as well. *Report of the International Committee of the Red Cross*, pp. 378–82.

27. Although Long had made this pledge in Nov. 1943, almost a year later it still had not been honored and the IRC was complaining that its op-

erations had been slowed up for months by the reluctance of the Allied governments to approve concrete relief proposals. *The Conference Record, 1,* #13 (Aug. 4, 1944): 5.

28. "The Morgenthau Diaries," p. 63.

29. Morse, pp. 88–91. Morse includes the complete report, which he maintains was obtained from a private, unnamed source. Reprinted with permission from *While Six Million Died,* Copyright © 1968, Random House, Inc.

30. *UNRRA: The History of the United Nations Relief and Rehabilitation Administration,* prepared by special staff under direction of George Woodbridge (New York: Columbia University Press, 1950) *1:* 4.

31. Allan Nevins, *Herbert H. Lehman and His Era* (New York: Charles Scribner's Sons, 1963), pp. 233–34.

32. Ibid., p. 226.

33. *Public Papers of FDR, 12:* 409–10.

34. Ibid., p. 505.

35. See Taylor's worried memorandum to Roosevelt on the subject of duplication, Mar. 3, 1944, Refugee File, Long Papers.

36. *UNRRA History, 2:* 480.

37. Proudfoot, *European Refugees,* p. 107.

38. *UNRRA History, 1:*28.

39. Hull to Roosevelt, Jan. 15, 1944, Political Refugees File, Roosevelt Library.

40. *UNRRA History, 1:* 113, 216.

41. Ibid., *2:* 81.

42. Nevins, p. 256. Apart from encountering difficulty in Washington in securing supplies for OFRRO and later UNRRA, Lehman was frustrated further by his powerlessness before military authority in North Africa in 1943 and was not pleased by the token relief extended to refugees in that region. Subsequently, he also encountered many difficulties with SHAEF's Refugee and Displaced Persons Section, which extended priorities to twenty million internally displaced Europeans as the Allies pushed across France in 1944. Until the Allies broke the German line at the Rhine in 1945, Lehman had to content himself with anxious tours of inadequate detention camps in France and the Low Countries. Ibid., pp. 230–60, and Proudfoot, pp. 110–15.

43. During the first days of Feb., Supreme Court Justice Frank Murphy announced the formation of the National Committee against Nazi Persecution and Extermination of the Jews. The purpose of this committee, which had been organizing since Dec. 1943, was to rally public opinion to prompt sustained action by the United Nations to rescue those Jews still alive in Europe. Enrolled in what Murphy termed "a test of civilization" were Henry Wallace, Willkie, Gov. Leverett Saltonstall of Mass., Gov. Walter Goodland of Wisc., Gov. Herbert Maw of Utah, Gifford Pinchot, Henry St. George Tucker, presiding bishop of the Protestant Episcopal Church and president of the Federal Council of Churches of Christ in America, Bishop Bernard Shiel of Chicago, Eric Johnston, president of the U.S. Chamber of Commerce, and Henry Sloane Coffin, president of the Union Theological Seminary. See "America Speaks," *Jewish Comment, 11* (Feb. 11, 1944): 1–2.

44. "The Morgenthau Diaries," p. 63.

45. U.S., Congress, Senate, *Congressional Record,* 78th Cong., 2d Sess., 1944, *90,* pt. 1:703–704.

46. For Hirschmann's accomplishments in this position, see Ira Hirschmann, *Life Line to a Promised Land* (New York: Vanguard Press, 1946).

47. Blair Bolles, "Millions to Rescue," *Survey Graphic, 33* (Sept. 1944): 388.

48. Oscar Handlin, *A Continuing Task: The American Jewish Joint Distribution Committee, 1914–1964* (New York: Random House, 1964), pp. 81–85.

49. Morse, pp. 313–85, presents an excellent study of the War Refugee Board. Proudfoot, pp. 64–65, and Wischnitzer, *To Dwell in Safety*, pp. 228–55, also discuss the WRB.

50. Pehle to Morgenthau, Mar. 6, 1944, Refugee Folder, Roosevelt Library.

51. Hirschmann to Lubin, Apr. 20, 1944, Political Refugee File, American Jewish Archives.

52. See Refugee Folder: 1944, Roosevelt Library.

53. Morse (pp. 324–25) reports these incidents.

54. The committee was conducting hearings on the merits of several resolutions calling for "the free entry of Jews into Palestine and the reconstitution of Palestine as "a free and democratic Jewish commonwealth." Frank Manuel, *The Realities of American-Palestine Relations* (Washington: Public Affairs Press, 1949), p. 312.

55. I. F. Stone, "For Jews—Life or Death," *The Nation, 158* (June 10, 1944): 670.

56. Morse, pp. 343–47.

57. Pehle complained to Hull: "Not only has Ambassador Hayes refused to ask the Spanish government to cooperate in implementing the President's policy with respect to refugees; he has even refused to explain the President's policy on the subject to the government, although requested to do so by the Board and the State Department." Celler was even more blunt. He accused Hayes, who worried about German agents slipping into Spain in the guise of refugees, of "cruel recalcitrance" and argued that thousands could have been saved but for his inaction (ibid., pp. 333–34).

58. *The Conference Record, 9* (Apr. 1944): 3.

59. Twelve bills were introduced, but all of them died in committee. See Edward J. Shaughnessy, "Immigration and Naturalization Legislation in the 78th Congress," *Monthly Review of the Department of Immigration and Naturalization, 2* (July 1944): 12.

60. Morse, pp. 340–41.

61. Memorandum of conference of Pehle, Hull, Morgenthau, and Stimson, May 8, 1944, Political Refugees File, Roosevelt Library.

62. Presidential Press Release, June 9, 1944, Political Refugees File, Roosevelt Library.

63. The scheme was enthusiastically endorsed by William Green of the AFL, Vito Marcantonio, Lessing Rosenwald, David Dubinsky and the Jewish Labor Committee of New York, Ben Hecht, Peter Bergson, the Hebrew Committee of National Liberation, the National Council of Jewish Women, the American Jewish Conference, the *New York Times, New York Herald-Tribune, Washington Post,* and *Washington Evening Star.* See Jewish Immigration File, American Jewish Archives. The most curious opposition to the proposal came from the American Federation of Polish Jews, which mimeographed letters to

leading senators outlining its views. Joseph Tenenbaum said his group felt the establishment of such camps would be detrimental to the concept of Palestine as a Jewish national home where Jews could enjoy complete freedom. Internment of Jews in camps where their personal freedom was restricted would not only be a violation of traditional American principles, he argued, but also would be "a serious violation of the Jewish national conception." See letter of American Federation of Polish Jews to Sen. Robert Wagner, Sept. 1, 1944, Palestine File, Wagner Papers. A year later the federation had changed its position somewhat, continuing to affirm that Palestine was the chief hope for European Jewry, but demanding that the U.S. open its doors to more displaced persons. See Joseph Tenenbaum, *Let My People In* (New York: American Federation of Polish Jews, 1946), p. 9.

64. New York State Canners to Roosevelt, June 10, 1944, Political Refugees File, Roosevelt Library.

65. June 22, 1944, ibid.

66. J. A. Krug, *Token Shipment: The Story of America's War Refugee Shelter* (Washington: U.S. Dept. of Interior, War Relocation Authority, 1946).

67. Roosevelt to Biddle, Jan. 17, 1945, Political Refugees File, Roosevelt Library.

68. Allen Freehling, "The American Jewish Community's Reaction to the Fluctuating Immigration Policy of the U.S. Congress," unpublished rabbinical thesis, Hebrew Union College, Cincinnati, 1967, p. 68. Ultimately the 984 were permitted to stay in the U.S. and to apply for citizenship under a special directive issued by Harry Truman in Dec. 1945. A legal fiction was applied whereby the group voluntarily departed for Canada and then reentered the U.S. with full immigration status. HIAS was the organization chiefly responsible for sparing these few fortunates. See "Current and Postwar Immigration Problems," *Social Service Review* 19 (Sept. 1945): 417.

69. Roosevelt to Mary Hun, Aug. 14, 1944, Political Refugee File, Roosevelt Library.

70. *The Conference Record*, 1 (Sept. 1944): 32–37.

71. Ibid., 1 (Aug. 1944): 1.

72. July 24 and Aug. 3, 1944, Jewish Immigration File, American Jewish Archives.

73. *The Conference Record*, 1 (Sept. 1944): 33.

74. Originally Eichmann offered Brand 100,000 Jews in exchange for trucks and other war materials. Subsequently, he altered the demand, asking for soap, coffee, cocoa, tea, and money. Brand was released to seek the approval of the Allies. Unfortunately, his travels took him to British lines and the frustrated intermediary was detained by officials who would not countenance another wave of Jewish immigration in the Middle East. See Alex Weissberg, *Desperate Mission: Joel Brand's Story* (New York: Grove Press, 1958).

75. Ibid., p. 266.

76. Morse, pp. 353–58.

77. Roosevelt to Wise, Oct. 25, 1944, Roosevelt File, Wise Papers. Wise again demonstrated his timidity when he wrote David Niles about the struggle to save the Jews of Hungary. "I haven't troubled you with the details of the fight, which has been as nasty as it can be." Jan. 8, 1945, Presidential Advisers File, ibid.

78. "The Morgenthau Diaries," p. 63.

79. There is some dispute as to whether the WRB was responsible for the rescue of 22,000 concentration camp inmates, including Danes, Norwegians, Belgians, Poles, Frenchmen, and Jews, between Feb. 19 and May 5, 1945. Proudfoot (pp. 308–309) believes the credit should go to Count Folke Bernadotte of the Swedish Red Cross, who had four special meetings with Himmler during this period and who secured the release of prisoners from Ravensbruck, Dachau, Matthausen, and Theresienstadt. This was more a token gesture on Himmler's part to defray war criminal proceedings against him than anything else.

80. *Final Summary Report of the U.S. War Refugee Board* (Washington, 1945), p. 10.

81. The Allies welcomed 180,000 ethnic Germans, Balts, and Ukrainians who refused repatriation to their Bolshevik-dominated homelands by 1946. Proudfoot, p. 277.

82. *The Plight of the Displaced Jew in Europe,* a report to President Truman, Sept. 29, 1945, pp. 4–5.

83. Proudfoot, p. 344.

84. *Manchester Guardian,* Oct. 16, 1945, p. 18.

85. Proudfoot, p. 355.

86. U.S., *Department of State Bulletins, 10* (Dec. 23, 1945): 983.

87. *UNRRA History, 2*: 510.

88. Proudfoot, p. 336.

89. For "humanitarian reasons," 8,000 Ukrainians and 15,000 German POWs were permitted to remain in the British Isles rather than return to Russian-dominated regions at the end of the war. For similar reasons, 54,000 Volksdeutsch Germans, the source of Hitler's provocations against Poland in 1939, were ultimately admitted to the United States under amended immigration laws between 1950 and 1952. Richard Robbins, "The Refugee Status: Challenge and Response," *Law and Contemporary Problems, 21* (1956): 318.

90. *UNRRA History, 2*: 498.

91. Celler, *You Never Leave Brooklyn,* p. 98.

Chapter 10

1. Interview with Benjamin Cohen, June 5, 1968.

2. Bloom to Hull, Mar. 19, 1938, Personal Correspondence, Hull Papers.

3. "The Morgenthau Diaries," p. 63.

4. Ibid., p. 63. The friction between Hull and Welles was open talk in Washington during the war and ultimately led to Welles's forced resignation in 1944, as Hull claimed Welles had more influence with the president than he did.

5. At the time of Kristallnacht, the secretary was planning for the Eighth International Conference of American States at Lima. When the Nazis launched their extermination of the Jews in 1942, the U.S. was still reeling from a series of defeats sustained at the hands of the Japanese. When Long defended erratic government policies emanating from Bermuda before Congress in Nov. 1943, Hull had just returned from Moscow where he, Eden, and Molotov had laid the groundwork for the Teheran Conference later that month. And by

1944 Hull was preoccupied with his vision of making the United Nations a viable instrument of world peace.

6. *Long Diary,* July 4, 1940, p. 118.

7. Church Matters: Jewish File, Roosevelt Library.

8. Ringelblum, *Notes from the Warsaw Ghetto,* pp. 291–92.

9. Bohlen to Early, Mar. 24, 1944, and Berle to Hasset, Aug. 4, 1944, Church Matters: Jewish File, Roosevelt Library.

10. Memorandum for FDR, Mar. 6, 1944, Refugee Folder, Roosevelt Library.

11. Ibid.

12. Memorandum for FDR, undated, Refugee Folder, Roosevelt Library.

13. Burns has commented on the president's "astonishing usurpation of power" during the war, when the situation was sufficiently imperative. *Roosevelt: The Lion and the Fox,* p. 463.

14. "Hitlerism Comes to America," pp. 66–70.

15. Personal interview with Maj. John F. Briggs, U.S. Air Force, May 5, 1967.

16. See Syrkin, *Blessed Is the Match.*

17. Louis Tursky, "Could the Death Camps Have Been Bombed?" *Jewish Frontier, 31* (Sept. 1964): 2.

18. Morse (pp. 359–61) argues that the Russians vetoed any such maneuver. It is difficult to imagine how they could have profited by such a stance, unless the traditional anti-Jewish bias of the Russian government was making its force known. Even more difficult to imagine is Anglo-American acquiescence in such inaction after the issuance of so many condemnations of German atrocities.

19. They were not always successful in this endeavor. See Robert Sherwood, *Roosevelt and Hopkins* (New York: Harper and Bros., 1948), p. 760, for the charge that Harry Hopkins, together with Frankfurter, Rosenman, and Niles, were planning to turn the War Department into "a global political organization."

20. Celler to Roosevelt, Jan. 25, 1944, Personal Correspondence File, Roosevelt Library.

21. This uneasiness is typical of first generation hyphenates who feel compelled to prove their integration into society by legitimizing any action that furthers "nation interests" as contrasted with special action on behalf of their particular racial or ethnic stock. See Nathan Glazer, "The Integration of American Immigrants," *Law and Contemporary Problems, 21* (Spring 1956): 256–69.

22. Roy and Alice Eckardt, "Again, Silence in Churches," in *Israel and American Jewry, 1967 and Beyond* (New York: Union of American Hebrew Congregations, 1967), pp. 27–28.

23. "The Refugee Puzzle," *New Republic,* p. 87.

24. *New York Times,* Apr. 20, 1968, p. 41.

25. Joseph P. Schechtman, *The Refugee in the World: Displacement and Integration* (New York: A. S. Barnes and Co., 1963).

26. See "Historic Homage," *Time, 86* (Oct. 1, 1965): 27–28, and "With Change in Immigration Law—Who New Americans Will Be," *U.S. News and World Report, 65* (July 15, 1968): 10.

27. Arthur Miller, *Incident at Vichy* (New York: Viking, 1965), p. 105.

Index

297

Saul S. Friedman is assistant professor of Jewish and Near Eastern History at Youngstown (Ohio) State University. He has taught previously at Ohio Dominican College and Otterbein College. He received his B.A. degree (1959) from Kent State University and his M.A. (1962) and Ph.D. (1969) degrees from Ohio State University.

The manuscript was edited by Linda Grant. The book was designed by Richard Kinney. The typeface for the text is Linotype Caledonia designed by W. A. Dwiggins in 1938; and the display face is Bookman originally cut as a bold face for Miller and Richard's Old Style.

The text is printed on Nashoba text paper and the book is bound in Columbia Mills' Llamique cloth over binders' boards. Manufactured in the United States of America.